AARON BETSKY

MAKING IT MODERN

THE HISTORY OF MODERNISM IN ARCHITECTURE AND DESIGN

AARON BETSKY

MAKING IT MODERN

THE HISTORY
OF MODERNISM
IN ARCHITECTURE
AND DESIGN

Acknowledgements

I want to make clear that this is an opinionated survey. It leaves out more than it covers, but then it was never my intention to create the kind of narrative listing of works produced in the last few centuries that already exists in many different versions. I wanted to explain what I thought was important, wonderful, and troubling about modernism.

As much as possible, I have concentrated on those artifacts I have actually experienced, which itself gives the book an unstated focus. It also means that I have not included a full listing of every piece of documentation or every monograph, preferring instead to give you a selection of books and articles that might be useful for more study and reference.

This work is the result of four decades of looking at, analyzing, studying, discussing, and teaching the buildings, objects, and images I discuss in this book. It has been shaped by many lectures, conversations, and arguments. It began with the first teachers to expose me, respectively, to modernism in architecture and theory: Vincent Scully and Fredric Jameson. My education continued under many other teachers, some of whom became colleagues. Kurt Forster, Tony Vidler, Mike Davis, and Ann Bergren were especially influential during my years as a young teacher and designer, as were my mentors Cesar Pelli, Frank Gehry, and Frank Israel. Lorraine Wild and Timo de Rijk educated me in design beyond architecture.

In developing this project, which was commissioned by Karen Stein, I had wonderful conversations with Cor Wagenaar, who helped focus my research and argument.

I am also thankful for the hard work of Giedion Fink Shapiro, who acted both as a valuable research assistant and an initial editor of great acumen. Paula Woolley's editing helped make this work clear and presentable, and I am beholden to Ramon Prat and Ricardo Devesa of Actar for finally bringing this book to fruition.

This project was made possible through a grant from the Graham Foundation for Advanced Studies in the Fine Arts, and I am deeply grateful to them and their director, Sarah Herda, for their support.

Finally, I was initiated into a love of modernism by two professors of English literature who just happened to be my parents, Seymour Betsky and Sarah Betsky-Zweig; my sister, Celia McGee, educated me in nineteenth- and twentieth-century American culture; and my husband, Peter Christian Haberkorn, supported me with a passion for modernism he learned from his architect father. I could not have completed this project without them.

Aaron Betsky

Contents	
9	**WHAT MODERN IS** Introduction
31	**SPACE OPENS UP**
61	**STAGING MODERNITY** The aesthetics of the future
95	**A NEW STYLE OF LIFE** Artifacts of modernity
123	**AT HOME IN THE BRAVE NEW WORLD**
155	**BUILDINGS LIKE CRYSTALS, FORMS AS COLD ICE** The styling of modernity
185	**TOWARD TOTALITY** Planning for perfection
217	**THE HUMAN FORM ENDURES** Contingent modernism
245	**WOODEN SHIPS** The modernism of complexity and contradiction
277	**AFTER MODERNISM** Experimental design
307	**RE-MODERNISM** Design for sprawl
335	Selected readings
346	Index of names
351	Illustrations credits

WHAT MODERN IS

I went to architecture school at a time when the periodic debates about the uses and the ethical qualities of modernism flared up. Our younger teachers taught us that modernism had failed. It had produced dysfunctional housing blocks in which the lower class was imprisoned. It had led to the creation of soulless office blocks. It had wiped out the beauty and mystery of the natural world. It was producing ugly objects and indecipherable messages. What was needed was a return to forms that were recognizable, scaled to the human body, and made out of natural materials. Though we accepted what our teachers wanted us to believe, we soon found that it was impossible to design things as they had been before industrialization. We could not give large-scale projects a human scale; we could not afford to use natural materials; and we could not ignore the technology and the landscape human beings had made in the last century, as it was all around us. We lived in a modern world, and had to act within it.

As a result, many of us began looking back at what not our teachers but their teachers, and their teachers' teachers, had done to try to give shape to the modern world. Was there a point at which modernism had gone wrong? Was there something about modernism that had led to inhuman constructions, or was it merely the direction modernism had taken in the latter half of the twentieth century that was at fault? As we were casting around for suitable images and forms, something strange happened: many young designers began to mine modernism. They self-consciously adapted the shapes, spaces, and images of early modernism to create a collage of possibilities for shaping the contemporary world. Today, many of these designers, who were considered avant-garde in the 1970s and 1980s, are successful practitioners who have reshaped modernism into a self-reflexive way of working, and are producing buildings, objects, and images across the globe.

What is even more astonishing is that this neo-modernism is everywhere. You see it in everything from Apple products to W Hotels, from haute couture to Zara, and from Shanghai to Santiago. This knowing use of abstraction, clean lines, forms without decoration, and open, fluid spaces has by now become the new normal, the little black dress of architecture and the default mode of design. Is modernism, after a brief defeat, finally triumphant? Are we seeing a celebration of the brave new world that modernity has opened up for us, without guilt but with a critical consciousness? Or are we just living through the disappearance of modernism into a way of working and appearing that cannot be avoided, because it is embedded in how we build, how we work and play, and how things are made? Might that mass production of forms, spaces, and images without human affect be as destructive of humanity as our modern world has in many ways always been?

This book is a part of my attempt to figure out what modernism is and whether it is still viable or meaningful. It comes out of my engagement with architecture and design and my belief that we can and must act in a modern world, with a full realization of all the horrible mistakes that have been made in the very attempt to do so. I am still a convinced modernist, and this book attempts to show why.

The very terms I use to ask the questions above raise the question of what modernism is. I believe that question is easy to answer: modernism is the representation of modernity. Any attempt to give shape to, represent, express, or otherwise allow us to experience our modern world—or, more precisely, that which makes our world modern—I would call "modernism."

This definition instantly begs the question, What is modernity? That is an altogether more difficult question. The earliest uses of the term "modern" date back to the twelfth century, when arguments first arose about whether you could invent something new, and whether that new poem (in this case) could be representative of the world the poet was living in, or whether his task was merely to copy and interpret the wisdom handed down over the ages. This long-simmering debate did not erupt in full force until the seventeenth century in the French "quarrel between the ancients and the moderns," led by Nicolas Boileau on one side and Charles Perrault on the other (cited in Nelson, "1687"). By then, anything French, innovative, and reflecting contemporary language—especially in theater—was "modern," whereas the "ancient" was the dramatic tradition imported from Italy. An invisible boundary had been crossed, as the Italian tradition was itself a fairly recent import. That the making of a cultural artifact was a conscious choice between various modes of representation which in themselves stood for a host of political as well as aesthetic structures (native or foreign, different parts of the ruling class) meant that the "moderns" had won the argument: making a play was something a free individual did as a deliberate act, not as an automatic transcription of some unquestionable truth. Modernism had been born, and the modern world was the one both the writer and the viewer inhabited. It was the here and now.

Yet, modernism is not just a matter of what style you choose and in what manner you thus ally yourself with a particular movement. Nor is modernity merely the consciousness of being alive at a certain time and space. At its root, modernism is a question of having something to represent that is of the moment. In the most radical interpretation of the term, modernism always comes too late. The modern is that which is always new, which is to say, always changing and already old by the time it has appeared. Modernism is always a retrospective act, one of documenting or trying to catch what has already appeared—an attempt to fix life as it is being lived. Modernity is just the very fact that we as human beings are continually remaking the world around us through our actions, and are doing so consciously. Modernism is a monument to or memory of that act, which in its own making tries to remake the world it is pretending to represent.

These philosophical definitions, however, ignore an evident truth: something changed in our world at the end of the eighteenth century, accelerated in the nineteenth century, and completely altered all reality as we know it by the twentieth century. That thing was a combination of the so-called Industrial Revolution, real revolutions in France and the United States, discoveries in science, and large social movements that led to an explosion not only in the sheer size of the world's population but also in its mobility. That movement of people and peoples, paralleled by the increasingly frenetic movement of goods and ideas, meant that our reality was increasingly in flux. You can—and many people continue to—argue about which of these phenomena came first, what was the underlying root cause, or what caused all others to appear. I will leave it to others to try to answer those questions. I will instead attempt to engage in a modernist act: to describe the particular reality of that phenomenon of modernization—exactly what kind of world, physical and around us every day, those forces produced. That leads to other questions. What exactly are the contours and what is the character of modernity as we can experience it all around us, as fact? How has it been made, by whom, and for what reason? How does it function?

You can ask these questions in an abstract manner, through numbers and statistics, or through narratives. For instance, economic developments and political actions certainly caused cities to appear, changed the nature of the spaces we inhabit, and led to the refashioning of vast territories. But I want to approach that apparent reality in another way: by looking at it as a continually evolving reality. I want to examine the images, forms, and spaces modernity has produced, and analyze the ways in which we have tried to give shape to them. I believe that this approach will allow us to begin to understand that modernity is what we make of it, how we find our way through it, and how we make ourselves at home in it. Modernism is a way of consciously making the modern world; a way of figuring it out in form, space, and image; and a way of transforming it into a container in which we feel we belong. Modernism thus can act in parallel to analytic, data-driven, and data-expressed attempts at understanding and working within our modern world while at the same time constructing or reconstructing that world. It is that which is always present at the same time that it represents.

The task of this book is to describe the phenomenon of modernism in the field of architecture and design, where conscious makers have tried to answer exactly those three questions of how we can find our way through, figure out, and be at home in the modern world. I would argue that they have chosen to work out these questions in this particular field because of the impetus of something strange, a derived phenomenon that is difficult to define. Something new appeared to them, something called space, and the forming and representation of that space stood at the core of modernism in this field. Space was not place but its derivative, its forming, its representation. It was, like such other engines of modernization as the zero (which allowed for advanced mathematics as well as interest calculations), invisible, but crucial in making the world operative, productive, and usable. Like modernism itself, space had very old roots, but in the nineteenth century it suddenly took on a scale and presence that was startling to many observers. Its definition became the justification at the core of most modernist design.

This space was the natural habitat of the modern human being, a being that we would in economic terms call a middle-class individual. It was the middle class who stood at the core of the changes that made the world thoroughly modern, and modernism made that class at home in modernity. Further, I would argue that the tools for the production of the modern world—namely, technological artifacts—became the second arena in which modernist designers acted, as they worked to utilize, house, contain, and represent that technology. Finally, the methods they used to understand, shape, and represent space and technology tended toward abstraction, the use of geometry, a tension between revealing and framing technology and space, and an attempt to extend that modern world through this abstraction, geometricization, revelation, and framing toward something postulated as perfect. In all these ways, modernism is plastic—it molds and melds everything continually toward an unknowable purpose.

The Industrial Revolution and the political movements that paralleled it, as well as the developments in science and general thought, were led, or produced, by a particular class of people. These were men and women who were not dependent for their survival on agriculture, nor did they support themselves by controlling the work of those who did. They generally lived in cities, which were in themselves places made by humans and set apart from nature. You could argue that this class of humans inhabiting an artificial world and surviving by the manipulation of derived value (the finishing of goods, the trading of those goods) had existed since time immemorial. By the eighteenth century, at least, their numbers and the sophistication of their activities had reached a stage such that this class had a significant impact on the world around them. There is no one moment or occurrence that marks the emergence of the middle class, and you can find middle-class spaces far back in history. But there are moments when the middle class developed the power to control their environment at such a scale that urban places changed in a radical manner. The extension of Amsterdam through its semi-hexagonal rings of canals starting in 1613, at the same time that the first stock exchange appeared there, is certainly an early version of such a new kind of space. The space of the trading ship, an artificial community floating freely around the globe and moving people as well as goods and ideas, is another early prototype. The marketplace, an open square with temporary stalls made out of more or less mass-produced wooden elements that had a modular character, might be a third prototype.

All of these spaces shared characteristics. First, they had been made by human beings and had few, if any, traces of the nature they replaced or on which they floated. Second, many different technologies came together in their production, and they were constructed of elements that were modular and usually mass-produced. Third, they appeared as figures of abstract geometries that ordered and organized their various components. Fourth, there was something at their core that was difficult to define, but around which they existed: space. It was merely an empty place, one that allowed for trading, communication, and movement (such as the canals of Amsterdam), and that was free. It was what had always defined cities: the free space in which you were not bound by the rules of the land and its lords, a space that consisted of the streets, alleyways, and squares between the dwellings and churches, but also of the property in which you dwelled—or, more exactly, in the fact of property (one's "proper" place) itself.

This space was the place of the middle class. If peasants lived on and were of the land in hovels that were of the earth, and princes lived off of and above the land in castles and palaces, the middle class lived exactly there—in the middle. They were on the ground, in the stores below the piano nobile (noble floor) where the aristocracy lived, crowded together below the castle, and yet outside of and separate from the land itself. They were in a space that they had made and continually remade to suit their lives. The middle class appeared in a space they could use, but where they could also appear as themselves.

The attempt to shape that space in a conscious manner began in most cases not through the agency of the middle class, but through the needs and the desires of the aristocracy. The first consciously designed open spaces that were kept free of objects or people, organized and paved, or ordered with surrounding gateways and facades so that they could be used and would have a clear frame, were made not by the middle class but by princes as parade grounds and by the church as places for ritual gathering. Streets that were straight and efficient were usually made for marching, not merchandise. Space was opened up by the aristocrats, who cleared out the messy vitality of middle-class life.

The story of modernism starts with the appropriation of this space. When the open parade grounds and church squares were turned into avenues for circulation and empty spaces where the middle class could appear, a new kind of world opened up. It was a place organized according to the needs of the middle class, and where they could show themselves, or show off. Building on some of the earlier prototypes where the middle class had controlled space, as in the Netherlands, these new middle-class places began to take over more and more of the city. Appearing first on what was the edge of the city, they gradually became or took over the city's center. Along the way, places were produced in which the middle class could literally be at home: storehouses for human beings called apartment buildings. These were efficient grids for living that still cloaked themselves with a thin veneer that made them resemble the palaces of the rich, but which dissolved on the inside into modular spaces inhabited by different families at different times.

Nor was this public space the only one to appear as the place of the middle class. At the edges of daily life, new kinds of spaces made possible by technology rose up. Their basic elements were glass windows and their frames; their basic space was that of the grid. Their prototypes were not only the factory or workshop, with its rational and empty space, flooded with light that allowed for the most efficient production of goods, but also spaces for commerce and social mixing that opened up starting in the eighteenth century in the city itself. The gallery and the arcade, the rows of shop windows with their glass facades set in a gridded frame, and the temporary framework of the stall or fair all set the stage for a new kind of space. It developed after new technologies appeared that enabled the production of large plates of glass at an affordable price, as well as the thin frames made out of metal that could contain them. First used in exotic locales such as greenhouses, this technology of construction showed itself off in exhibition halls and other temporary celebrations before becoming part of the city's fabric. Designers used methods of abstract thinking to plot rational and logical organizations of space, first for military and ritual uses, and then for production, consumption, and eventually living. New technologies made construction of these places of consumption and production affordable to the middle class and easy enough to adapt to meet their continually changing needs.

When these spaces revealed the gridded reality out of which they were made, they also revealed new materials. At first, designers treated metal and the grid of wood, or later steel or concrete, as something to be hidden, but soon they flaunted those materials, and their expression became the way to instantly tell that a building was new and belonged to the world controlled by the middle class. These spaces were at their grandest when they contained the engines of the transformation of reality. The train stations and the exhibition halls at the edge of town, as well as the department stores that appeared in the heart of the city, replaced the churches as the largest structures around, and developed their own cults of objects and rites of adoration and consumption. Over time, these objects became smaller and were integrated into the life of the middle class. They became the implements of daily life, from sewing machines to toasters to, eventually, cars and televisions.

A third phenomenon appeared along the way: embedded technologies. A hidden space began to appear in the city, one inhabited by and connecting machines. Tunnels were dug for underground railroad systems and for the sewage lines that made the inhabitation of public space possible. Gas lines and later electrical lines coursed through the city, transforming space from something you experienced only during the day to a completely artificial place liberated from nature by human-made light. Eventually, even more invisible rays and emanations turned almost the entire world into a place of middle-class habitation, allowing you to be wired to information or trade goods even in a cabin in the deepest woods. These hidden systems, snaking out into the area beyond the city and eventually across the globe, spread middle-class space and made it ever more abstract.

Giving shape to space and technology was a challenge that designers confronted in the middle of the nineteenth century when they became clear and evident realities. At the same time, design turned from the hobby of aristocrats or a collective activity performed in workshops, on site, or in guilds, into a profession. Spurred on by the rationalization of all cultural activities initiated by Louis XIV and his ministers at the end of the seventeenth century, schools began producing trained designers, and the state began regulating their activities. The teachers at these schools used the same tools that had produced space and technology to discipline activities. Geometry, invention, rational thought, and the fact that you could make your living by trading in such abstractions all led to the formalization of architecture and design into viable trades. In architecture especially, however, there was always a nagging problem with this newfound definition of design. The schools used ancient models, and designers had to build what had been made in the past. They had to work in cities that were never quite modern, using existing building trades and materials, as well as artistic and legal conventions, that lagged far behind the ideas and technologies they knew to be available.

This uneasy position was not particular only to the design fields, though it was especially evident there. The middle class had few models on which to base their space and their appearance, other than those established by the aristocrats. The history of the nineteenth-century representation of space and technology is, like that of painting, sculpture, literature, and music, one of the acceptance, deformation, and finally stripping of these inherited modes. That has become the canonical tale of modernism: how the past was abstracted, rejected, or deformed to such an extent that something appeared that the new class of people, whether they were artists or the bourgeoisie, could call their own.

As a result, modernism took on the quality of representing not what was, but what should be. It became a prospective movement, digging down through reality with the tools of abstraction and geometry to discover some form that it could posit as a rational truth which it could then reveal and extrapolate over all of reality. Modernism became a "movement"—itself a telling phrase, implying that this was a process that was never quite finished, as there was an ever-purer truth to be found somewhere in or beyond modernity. The search was one for pure space, pure technology, and the pure representation of those phenomena. A completely open space made possible by technology became the goal.

Modernism articulated these goals in contradictory and halting ways in the second half of the nineteenth and first half of the twentieth centuries, producing experiments along the way that produced startlingly new objects, images, and spaces within the city. This period was the most self-conscious moment of modernism: a time of fervent debates, manifestos, and a millenary belief in the ability to make a perfectly modern world. As it became evident that a new world was literally rising all around the makers of that world, designers threw off whatever they had inherited with exuberance and even violence, reveling in the destruction of place and the human form as well as in the construction of space, machines, and their representations.

After the First World War, at a time of tremendous scientific and social upheaval, this modernism applied itself to producing the results of its experiments at an ever-larger scale. As modernist space was meted out in apartment blocks and whole neighborhoods, a kind of consensus style, though with many variations, developed across the globe. Modernism in architecture and design relied on glass and steel, concrete, and soon plastic. These were human-made and fluid materials that allowed shapes unknown in nature and unrelated to the human body to appear. Designers now either used grids with pride or, paradoxically, covered their edges, producing forms that were streamlined to encourage the movements of modernity as well as expressing them. At the same time, these modernist designers claimed to base their work on both nature and the human body, abstracting them into geometry and pure white. They rationalized space into gridded environments and condensed machinery into compact elements. Representing the modern world as nothing but emptiness, modernist designers tended toward the love and production of pure nothingness.

At its most extreme, modernist architecture and design wished for its own disappearance. It wanted to be the nothing that underlay modernity—which is to say, the zero that allowed modern science and modern capitalism, the vanishing point of the perspective that allowed for the organization of space, or the point in the future toward which a society based on progress, the ever increasing profits and the ever more rational organization of reality, tended. It wanted humans and nature to fuse through the agent of technology into pure space.

Unfortunately, this desire for nothingness turned into the destructive forces that killed millions of people during the Second World War, by becoming the forces that sought to wipe out nature to turn it to productive use—forces that imploded due to the weight of their own internal contradictions, first in the Great Depression and then in that war. Architects and designers found themselves complicit with this wholesale destruction of humanity, helping to create environments that were so vast and so abstract, so defined by technology and so radically new that they became the very emblems of the alien world humans were creating for themselves. At the moment of its greatest triumph, modernism turned from a millenary project meant to produce perfect space through technology, which would be a home for whatever humans might become in that new world, into a force that seemed to be destroying nature, the human body, and the past. It also threatened to do away with all that remained by which humans knew that they were not just elements, nodes, or cogs in modernization, but something else, namely that which remained, that which was always outside of those processes, even if humans caused them. When modernism turned from a movement into a lived totality, it became an alien thing, and many began to seek alternatives to it.

Of course, not all designers were part of modernism's movement toward a kind of productive nihilism. And many designers who did find themselves in this movement tried to turn that progressive drive toward nothing into something more conducive to human habitation, intelligence, and control. Some of the most beautiful moments in modernism occurred at the edges of the movement, where designers tried to engage forms, places, and images beyond the making of a middle-class emptiness and technological future. Some designers tried to join a social and political revolution that they believed would cause the middle class, as well as the rules of nature, to disappear. Others tried to integrate technology and nature or turn the shaping of space into the making of places with definable and recognizable boundaries. In doing so, these designers had to give up some aspects of modernism, eschewing geometry or reason, emptiness or technology, or the combination thereof. They became interested in that which remained even as modernization scoured everything that was not efficient and productive.

At the core of many of their activities was a way of working that was itself premodern and yet had become a central part of modernism: collage. Design became the gathering together of the fragments the modern world had created, assembled as if by chance, and organized in a way that was not rational and that carried the associations of all the objects contained in the finished product along with them. The result was an artifact that, like the modern world, appeared never to be finished. Collage and assemblage became the alternatives to the perfect nothing of modernism.

Yet, in a society and economy still defined by the cycles of production and consumption, it did not seem possible to make many things using collage. One of the great unfinished projects of the second half of the twentieth century became the transformation of the whole world not into nothing, but into a collage of disparate, already existing pieces that were open enough to allow for continuous change, adaptation, adoption, and interpretation.

Eventually, however, many designers rejected modernism altogether, attempting to resurrect a world that had existed before the modern world became an inescapable fact. By the end of the twentieth century, many designers were looking backward, not forward, and most had come to realize that modernism would not and could not lead to a perfect and pure nothing, at least not in any way that a human being could experience. The rejection of modernism could never be total, though, both because it proved impossible to reject all technology and all rational ways of building, and because the middle class continued to be both the group commissioning most design and the class to which most designers belonged. The past was resurrected to become once again a cloak thrown over this reality, and thus a thoroughly modern thing: a freely taken choice of a way of appearing. It was not by coincidence that the debate between the ancients and the moderns was revived at this time.

A few designers speculated that the answer to the question of how to survive in a modern world and how to represent that act of remaining was to reject the very notion of the human being altogether. Many more put their faith in the latest technology, that of the computer, to produce something that would be truly modern. In the computer, space and technology would finally fuse to create something that would dissolve human action into the continuum of a completely smooth artificial landscape (in the act of design, for instance, which was to become the mere interpretation or guiding of the computer program, if that).

At the beginning of the twenty-first century, modernism has dissolved into a variety of different ways of making things. They range from a self-conscious continuation of the methods developed over a century ago to represent modernization to the collages and assemblages that reuse what modernity offers up into objects, spaces, or images and that are themselves only temporary. Though these directions appear disparate, they are connected; they share common roots and common working methods. Most importantly, there is no goal to these modes of modernism other than the one that started the search for the utopia of nothingness in the first place: how to represent, figure out, and make ourselves at home in a modern world.

These modes operate within a modern world that has become almost total. Today there is almost no place in the world that exists outside of modernity, which is to say, that is not made by humans, infused by technology, or accessible to our experience only through modern modes of thinking and behaving. We live in a global space, one that is completely fluid and abstract. Place and time dissolve as we speed along in cars or airplanes or, even more, on the Internet. Capitalism appears completely triumphant over all remaining ideologies. Even those people who would seek to resist modernity have to do so on its own terms, claiming science for the creation of humans by a deity or attempting to destroy spaces of reason through violent technologies. Ironically, the most extreme forms of modernism and its most adamant rejection have come together, as they have over the last two centuries, in the postulation of nothingness, whether positive or negative. The other modes of modernism can only reject this rejection and try to produce a modernism we can use, understand, and inhabit.

This book attempts to trace the development of these very attempts, from the first appearance of the empty space that was the physical manifestation of the modern world, all the way to the dissolution of that space into the ether of the Internet. Certainly, modernity and modernism both began long before the first designs described in this book and will continue long after this book is published; and certainly, modernism occurs in modes that are far beyond the purview of architecture and design. In this book I will trace only the astonishing opening up of a brave new world of open empty space, the arrival of the beauty and terror of the machine into daily life, and the attempts to represent them in the construction of a modernist world. I believe modernism is a beautiful construction, one that I wish to both inhabit and show to you.

1. SPACE OPENS UP

The bourgeoisie cannot exist without constantly revolutionizing the instruments of production, and thereby the relations of production, and with them the whole relations of society… All fixed, fast frozen relations, with their train of ancient and venerable prejudices and opinions, are swept away, all new-formed ones become antiquated before they can ossify. All that is solid melts into air, all that is holy is profaned, and man is at last compelled to face with sober senses his real condition of life and his relations with his kind.

- Karl Marx and Friedrich Engels, The Communist Manifesto, 1848.

This book is about the air that emerged when all had melted, about the profane forms that emerged after the holy had disappeared, and about how the new broke open the ossified remains of the past. It is also about how we have experienced that new space.

It is no coincidence, I think, that the signal moment of uprising that preceded and inspired Marx and Engels's dream, the French Revolution, was the Oath in the Tennis Court: the political moment that wiped away inherited constraints took place in a space that was empty, open, and almost without ornament. It was a place designed for play, not a place for power; in its liberty from monumental constraints and its nature as a place of free play, it allowed a new kind of space to appear—that of the nascent middle class, who fought with tennis racquets and ideas, not swords and certainties.

The middle class needed space, for they did not have a place that was historically and naturally their own. They did not belong to the land, nor did the land belong to them; they were neither peasants whose existence was bound up with the land in which and on which they toiled, nor

001. Jacques-Louis David, *Oath in the Tennis Court*, 1791.

002. Étienne-Louis Boullée, Cenotaph for Newton, 1784.

were they aristocrats living off the ownership of that land. They did not inhabit sheltering hovels or protective castles; they did not define their appearance through ritual frames, whether ecclesiastical or political. Instead, they made their own space: they made cities, where they were free; they made their own homes and their own workshops, their own stores, and their own places to create social networks for both profit and self-definition. The middle class needed a space of their own and, little by little, they created more and more of it. They conquered large parts of the landscape for their apartments and dwellings. From the interior of home and shop, they moved on to the café and the clubhouse, the large-scale emporium and the factory, the public park, and even the housing project, where they could live with others like them. They began to postulate theories on how the city and the landscape could be made more productive and efficient, envisioning perfect and utopian environments, colonies, and other places of rationality and perfection.

The late eighteenth and early nineteenth centuries saw a proliferation of such plans and visions, such as those of architects Étienne-Louis Boullée, Claude Nicolas Ledoux, and Jean Jacques Lequeu, who posited perfect worlds beyond the messiness of their reality. These utopian worlds consisted of forms reduced to their most basic geometric shapes, and often of a vast scale. They took to their logical extremes the essence of classicism, but also the logic of a universal and open space where new libraries, factories, or tombs could be housed. They proposed monuments for the Enlightenment, such as Boullée's Cenotaph for Newton, and proposed whole cities where only free men would live, as Ledoux did both before and after the French Revolution.

Utopian thinkers such as Jean Baptiste, Joseph Fourier, and Owen Jones designed colonies out in the land, places that were meant to be the building blocks of a better, more

rational world. These were fortresses that enclosed a free space with its own rules–more rational ones, according to their founders. They were palaces for free people. There were no central monuments or grand palaces, but only the building blocks for a new community.

Something new was appearing, if only in theory, if only on paper, in radical outposts, in the anonymous workshops and interiors of the middle class, or as a dream of free space sung by romantic poets.

What resisted was reality. The city everywhere remained the result of centuries of construction and constraints, and was hemmed in literally by the power of the sovereigns. Walls contained it, ramparts surveyed it, and palaces dominated its major avenues. It was not planned but had grown, and in that growth reflected a lack of rationality, functionality, and equality. It was only during the period of social revolutions that culminated with the widespread outbreaks of 1848 that this new space began to make headway, a room for itself, in the city. After 1848, a modern, free, and flexible space appeared.

Nowhere was this process more evident than in the city of Vienna. In 1848—the year that revolts and revolutions broke out all over Europe, deposing the king in France and costing minor princes and noblemen their lives throughout Germany and eastern Europe—a coalition of workers and middle-class agitators led by the students' Academic Legion drove both the imperial army of the Austro-Hungarian realm and the city's bishop from Vienna. For a while, it seemed as if a republic would rise on the shores of the Danube as it had fifty years earlier along the Seine. In the end, the Emperor Ferdinand dismissed his government, assimilated some of his critics into the power structure, and agreed to a series of reforms that gave the middle class the ability to vote. By allowing them a voice in the administration of the realm, Ferdinand acknowledged the economic power the middle class had amassed in recent decades.

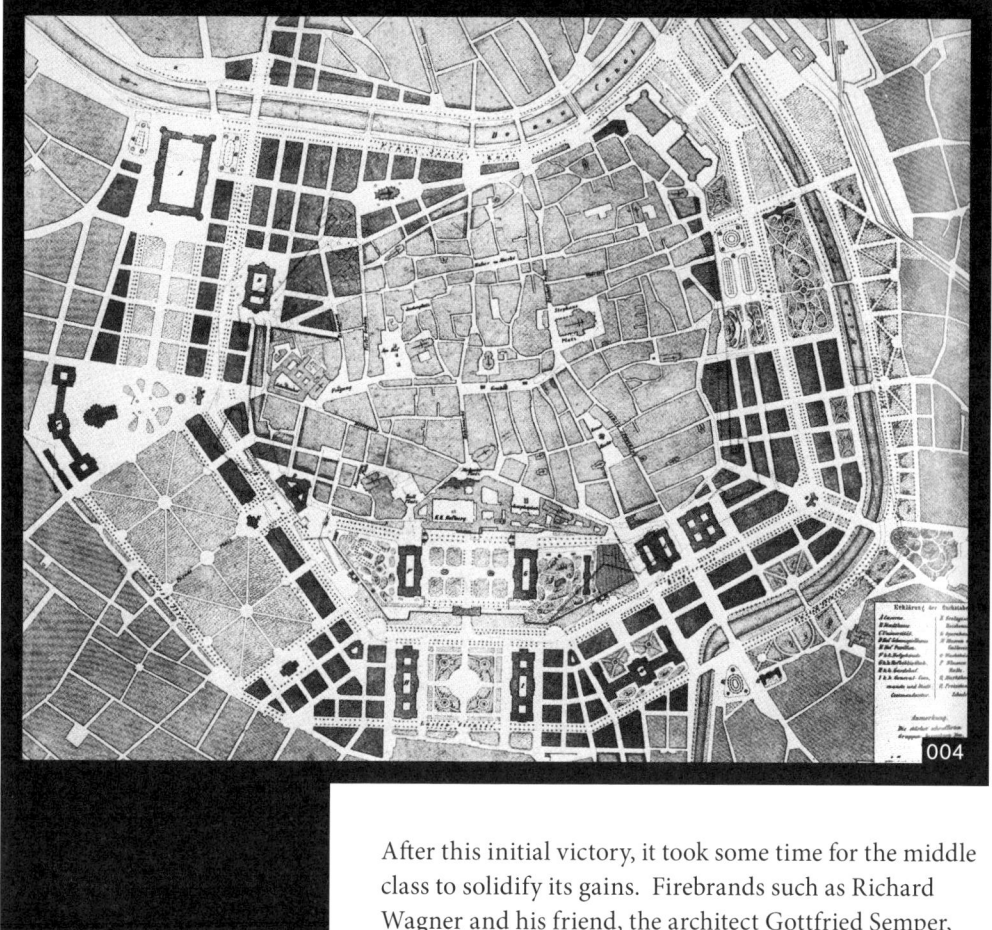

003. City of Vienna, 1683.
004. City of Vienna, 1859.

After this initial victory, it took some time for the middle class to solidify its gains. Firebrands such as Richard Wagner and his friend, the architect Gottfried Semper, had fled. The army and church reasserted their power. Though the previous Emperor, Joseph II, had already torn down the city walls, the army demanded a halt to any further plans for this newly available land. Then, in 1857, Ferdinand finally decreed that the semi-octagonal swath of land that enclosed the old city would be opened up for non-military functions. A new state agency sold off lots to developers, using the monies to pay for a large new boulevard, the Ringstrasse or "Ring Boulevard." The development also paid for a series of new monumental buildings

along that street: first, army barracks and a large new church, to appease these still powerful forces; then a parliament, a university, a theater, an opera house, a new school of design, and museums. The flows of the new city would move on its daily rounds along the boulevard between these new monuments for the middle class.

The most astonishing aspect of the new Vienna was the preeminence of the space of flows. The street, which remains intact today, came first and dominated everything else. It is extraordinarily broad, eighty-two feet in most areas, and it expands with such regularity into the forecourts of the monumental buildings that it is difficult to find its continual edges. To most Viennese, this was a wholly new kind of environment. Though the popes had long ago opened up great axes through Rome and the Prussians had just been cleaning up Berlin to make a combination boulevard and park of Unter den Linden, all of these were lines that went from one point to another and were hemmed in by buildings of a more or less uniform height. But the Ringstrasse goes from nowhere to nowhere.

If this boulevard had any model, it would be the canal rings with which that prototypical middle-class city, Amsterdam, had surrounded its historic core starting in 1609. There, as well, the land had been sold off to allow the new middle class to build their homes and businesses, but the space between was filled with water and there were no monuments. In contrast, the Ringstrasse was a huge swath of purely open space. It was open for business, for movement, for seeing and being seen. It functioned as a space for a new class of people who had not inherited land on which to base their wealth, or a place after which they were named (the mark of an aristocratic name in German is still the addition of the "von," which means "of" a certain place). They were also a class that was not bound to place by fealty or servitude. They were making their own world through commerce and manufacturing, and were defining themselves in that making by creating homes and places for themselves wherever they chose. They

005, 006. Theophil Hansen, Austrian Parliament, Vienna, 1874–1883.

were a class on the move, and they needed to go around town to do their business, for they no longer worked where they lived and their goods also needed to move. They made the Ringstrasse their own.

What opened up along the Ringstrasse was thus above all empty, open, and undefined space. It had few edges, it was horizontal, and it had no beginning and no end. The imposing buildings that began to appear along it were, on the whole, unremarkable as individual designs. They exhibit a variety of styles: a neo-baroque Votifkirche, designed by Heinrich Ferstel, went up starting in 1856 in a gesture to the old powers that had built their baroque monuments. Ferstel also designed the massive new university to appear like an expanded version of a Renaissance Italian palazzo. In contrast, Friedrich Schmidt designed the city hall in 1872 as a vaguely neo-Gothic assembly of turrets and a tower, as if he were trying to evoke a community of monks that might give a sense of purpose to this quickly changing city. The Viennese imported a talented Dane, Theophil Hansen, to design their new parliament. It is the most powerful building of the Ring monuments because it is the simplest: it attempts to resemble Hansen's vision of a Greek temple—white, plain, and unadorned. A statue of Athena stands guard in front, calling the citizens back to the roots of democracy. The parliament is the most modern building because it was modeled on something so ancient and outside of the recent styles used by either the church or the state that it could appear both startlingly new and absolutely true in its recall of ancient beginnings. Even the most celebrated building on the Ringstrasse, the Hofburgtheater designed by Gottfried Semper in 1874 after he returned from his exile, could not match the clarity of that gesture.

The Ring thus represented the triumph of the middle class: symbolically, monumentally, and spatially. The buildings along it might have been large, but they were not as big as the Ring itself, and the function of the Ring was not to serve as their forecourt or to be the axis on which you traveled to get to the parliament or the theater. The Ring was the real monument. It was also a place of use, along which you could circulate; it was the continual potential of connection made real. It was the space the middle class had made within the city. The Ring also defined how and where they inhabited that city, because they had to move through the city to work, live, and sell. They had no center, only operative urban elements of which they availed themselves.

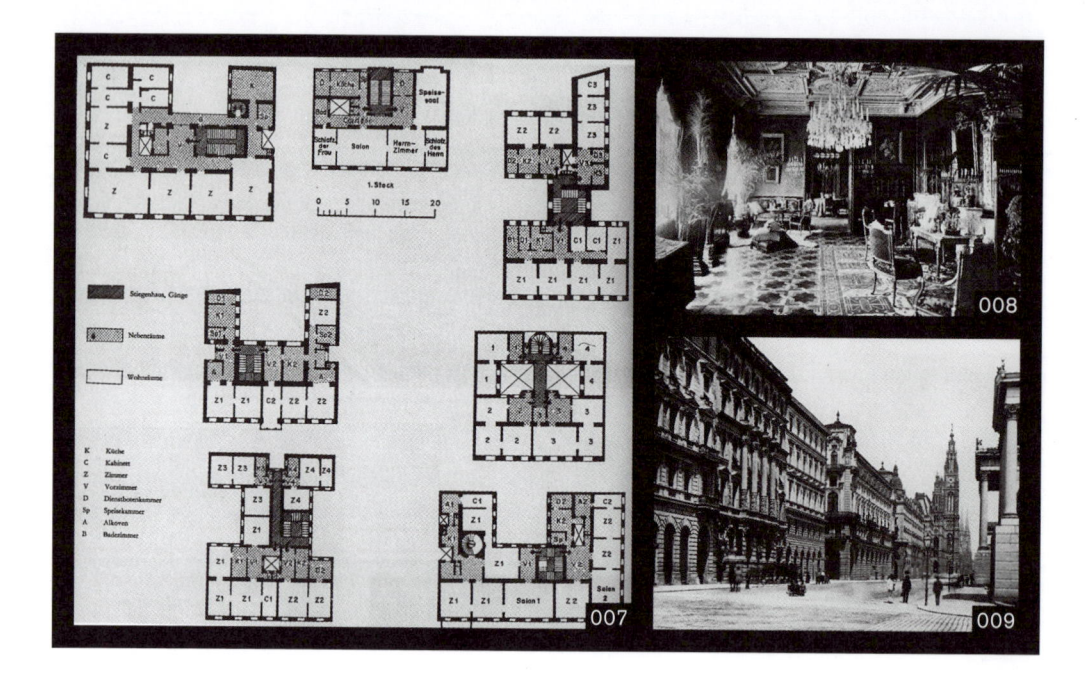

The Ring was for them a place to appear, but not on horseback in a regiment, or in a procession. Rather, it was a place where you could see and be seen, appraising others according to their clothes—in other words, according to their wealth and taste, not their family—while they did the same to you. You became a commodity in this space as well, in some cases literally so, as the Ring was also a place for prostitution. There had been spaces for this before, but they had been on the edges of the city, in parks, or inside cafés and theaters. Now you could appear in public as the person you had made yourself to be, performing the character you constructed for yourself.

But the Ring was also another kind of new space: a real estate development. Like the Amsterdam canal district and the massive interventions that had begun to appear in Paris, the construction of the Ring opened up whole new districts for working and especially living. Here the middle class could create its own community.

For their own homes, the middle class built apartment buildings both along the Ringstrasse and in the streets around it. These are essentially the palaces of the aristocracy turned into multifamily dwellings. They look like single homes, but you enter into an elaborate staircase—the open and communal space of the Ringstrasse brought inside and turned vertical. You then circulate around and up to fourteen separate homes. The press called them *mietpalasten* (rental palaces) or, even more succinctly, *zinspalasten* (palaces that bear interest), as they were built as speculative ventures. As such they are something in between the real palace and the *mietkasernen* (rental barracks), in which the former peasants were stored when they moved to Vienna to work for the inhabitants of the mietpalasten.

This new kind of environment has particular spatial qualities, though it took quite a few decades until they became evident. The designer who, more than any other, brought them into conscious appearance was Adolf Loos. In 1911 he designed a department store for Goldman and Salatsch with apartments above, not on the Ring itself, but right across the square from the imperial palace. Loos worked with irony and indirection, rather than trying to create a completely new alternative. For this purveyor of the most up-to-date fashions, he designed a building that at first seems like a tasteful, if rather sparse, version of similar structures all around Vienna. Its base, however, is clad in a particularly lurid marble that pushes and pulls around columns scaled more to a palace than to the framing of a relatively small store. Loos' model for all things elegant was English fashion, which he at one point described as the most perfect

010

007. Elisabeth Lichtenberger, Plan of Vienna Apartment, Vienna, 1978.

008. Apartment on Reichstrasse, Designer Unknown.

009. Vienna Apartment, view Reichsratsrasse.

010. Apartment Building at Franz Josephsquai 49, Vienna, Architect Unknown.

emblem of human achievement. Its well-cut clothes of the most luxurious material would allow a gentleman to stand out not because of who he was intrinsically, or because of where he came from, but because of the way he had transformed his money and taste into a perfect assembly of elements that accentuated his figure.

In the case of architecture, as in fashion, that also meant employing a bit of wit. Loos used completely logical and correct materials and forms for the Goldman and Salatsch structure, but made them more abstract, larger, and slightly off. The windows of the apartments are at times above the columns below, so that a careful viewer realizes that either there is something off-kilter about the building or, thanks to modern technology, the forces of gravity do not have to be brought straight down past the windows to the elements of vertical support below. Steel beams and careful engineering calculations enable a new space of commerce to open up according to its own rules, designed to allow for a flow a shoppers and their seduction.

What appeared, in other words, on the Ring and elsewhere, was not just an empty space of flows but also the profound uncertainty that comes from the lack of inheritance that fixed one in place. Flats and suburban homes were inherently disconnected from the land, as were the shops and the whole city the middle class was making. You had to make it, and if you failed, the space would remain empty. You had to define yourself in and through these new spaces.

If that was something that created anxiety in Vienna, the same appearance of a new and empty space enabled a realization of possibilities in the United States. It also created another model for the middle-class city. In some senses, the whole country was a modern invention: a utopian vision—a "City on the Hill" in secular imitation of Jerusalem—that had wrested its own space from its colonial overlords and had, under Thomas Jefferson in 1803, bought most of its future domain as if it were just another piece of real estate. Jefferson and his successors

011. Adolf Loos, Goldman & Salatch Department Store, Vienna, 1910.

as president then proceeded to lay out the land west of the Alleghenies as if it were such a speculative terrain, gridding it into sections that every free man could develop. It was a completely rational perspective waiting to be filled in to become a modern nation. It was also, despite Jefferson's agrarian focus, a place for the middle class: his ideal gentleman farmers were enlightened, cooperative, and engaged in craft and trade, rather than being tenants or owners of vast estates.

The Jeffersonian grid was Enlightenment mathematics and science made real. It was a completely abstract invention, disconnected from any reality of the landscape. To implement it, Jefferson employed scientific teams of explorers, mapmakers, and surveyors to etch the squares into a landscape that might go uphill and down, be forested or open, but was always subject to the ordering device. In the

012

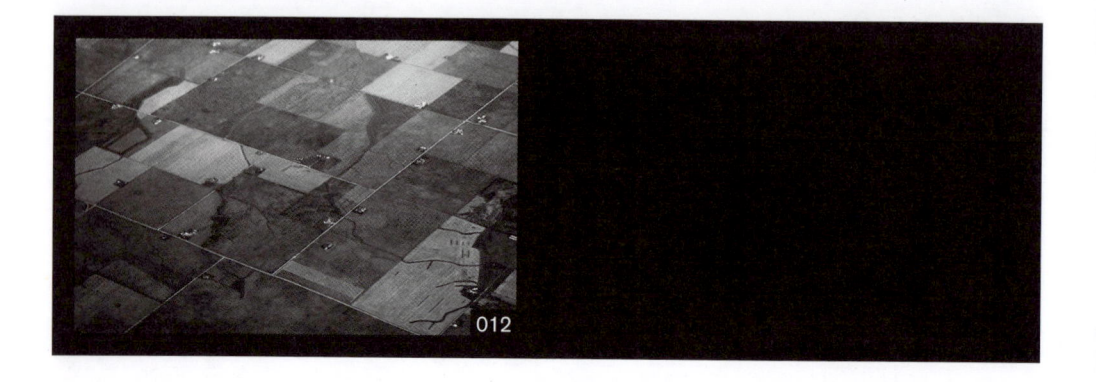

United States beyond the Alleghenies, none of the historic patterns of lease and fiefdoms applied (or they were wiped away by the new arrivals), leaving the whole country a tabula rasa.

Like the Ringstrasse, the Jeffersonian grid above all else allowed for movement, change, and systematic development—progress. It facilitated the colonization of what Americans saw as an empty terrain. The land was open for occupation, and the roads into and through it often followed the grid. Within that grid, the space could become anything, even if Jefferson himself envisioned a continuous network of small, independently owned farms. What was forest could become field, then forest again when the population moved on (as happened in much of the eastern part of the grid), and eventually space for industrial development or suburbs. There was little intrinsic constraint to define this space as a specific place, and whatever constraints there were could be remedied through technology: drainage, fertilizer, water supplies, and later, electricity grids.

To this day, you can drive through or fly over the expanses of Ohio, Indiana, or Illinois and follow the grid, watch it intensify into towns and peter back out into empty land. You can find its centers of development around courthouses or see where it opened itself up to the wider world where railroad lines or, later, highways cut through, spawning first silos to store and load the grain or ore, then shopping malls and distribution centers. At the core of that development was the small town, a place of commerce and trade whose spaces were rational and fluid, allowing it to grow (and contract, turning into the holey reality of sprawl) according to economic ebbs and flows. The grid made America as a unified and progressive country real.

At the same time as the Ringstrasse was developing in Vienna, the United States was creating its own spaces out of that grid. In some places, it was filling it as cities whose scale rivaled the largest in Europe but without their legacy of historically accrued streets and buildings. Instead,

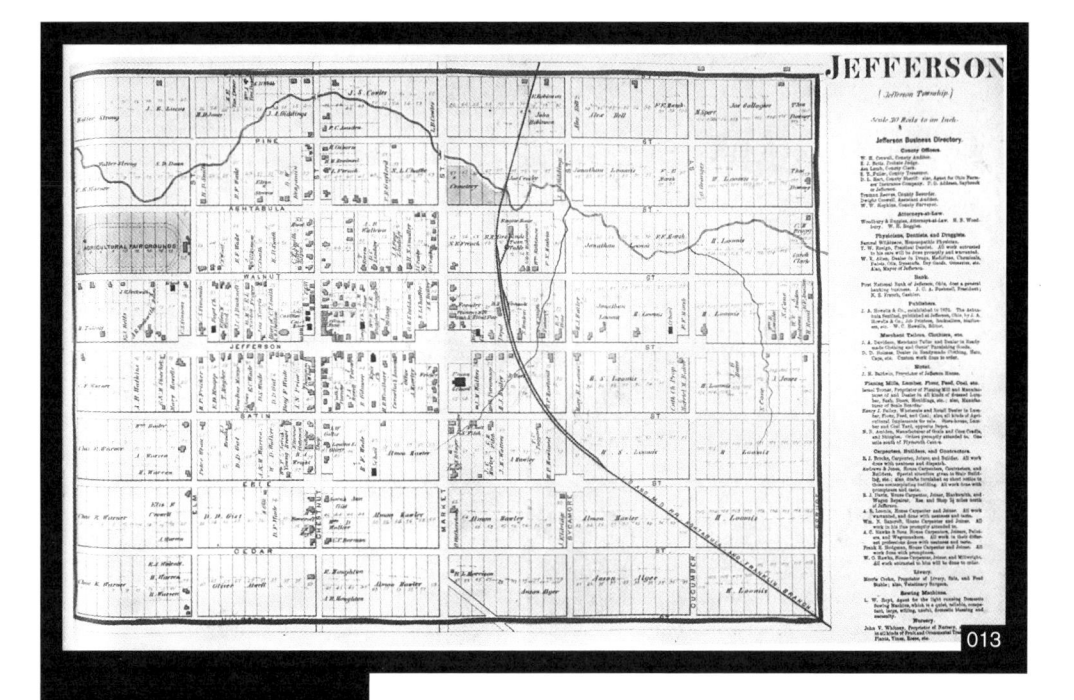

012. Aerial View, American Landscape, Author Unknown.

013. Plan of Jefferson, Ohio, 1874.

these were three-dimensional translations of the grid into space, covered with only the lightest cloak of neo-classical references. That filling in, and the manner in which the buildings were cloaked, was, however, haphazard. American cities and landscapes were uneven in their development, driven by speculation and without the kinds of constraints that a city such as Vienna still presented. America simply sprawled out and up, leaving as much land undeveloped or underdeveloped as it built up. Moreover, most structures did not last very long, as development and redevelopment were the norm. Here modern space appeared as chaos, and the Marxist prediction of relentless change and instability seemed truer the further west one traveled into a kind of new, lawless utopia or dystopia.

Out of and within that grid, though sometimes in contradiction to it, dense moments of urbanity appeared.

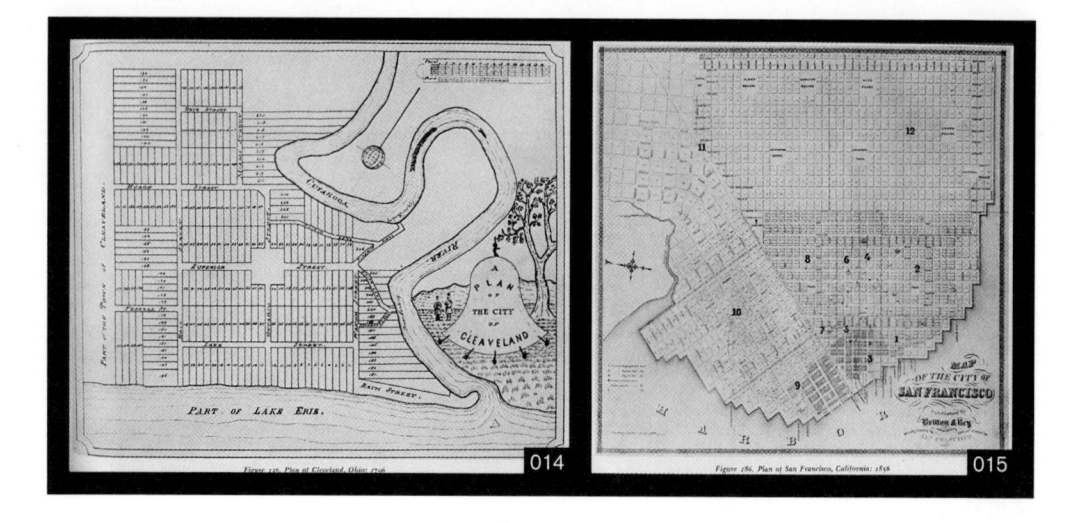

Figure 135. Plan of Cleveland, Ohio; 1796. Figure 286. Plan of San Francisco, California; 1846.

This was where the middle-class nature of the United States developed. The dense moments of urbanity that appeared in this grid were not defined by city walls and did not focus on central squares or churches; nor were they a packed mass riven with cuts that became roads. They were intensifications of the grid, sometimes oriented differently because of local conditions, but always a grid. Within that grid, anything and everything was again possible: a square area could be the site for a house, an office building, or an empty space awaiting development. Only the density of occupation and sometimes the size of the grid made the American city of the west different from the overall spatial continuum of the whole human-controlled landscape.

The space of the American city was on the whole orthogonal. Its streets and avenues, crossing at right angles and often numbered, contained developable lots that subdivided those blocks even further. Both theoreticians and developers experimented with the optimal sizes and proportions of those blocks, as it turned out that a perfect square did not maximize frontage the way a rectangle did. Services could be hidden within the block, and buildings could form a continuous facade; their grid of windows could be lightly decorated with any sort of pediment or column to designate identity and achievement or wealth within the grid's democratic constraints.

Over time, the city became more and more dense, and the land thus more and more valuable. Though buildings were covered in ornament that made them adhere to styles or fashions, they were still grids of rooms, often constructed with a mass-produced system, the balloon frame. The grid could and eventually did extrude up ever higher, and nowhere did it do so with more bravura than in Chicago. What had been a minor trading post at the beginning of the nineteenth century quickly became one of history's great boomtowns, doubling, quadrupling, and eventually turning into the country's second-largest city by the end of the century. It was a place of continual construction and reconstruction as it grew ever denser and sprawled out into the countryside. At its core was a central business district where the pressures on the grid had caused it to explode upward.

The Chicago architect Louis Sullivan, one of the prime authors of such elongations, described the result beautifully: floors "piled one upon another" led to an increase in height and "[t]hus has come about that form of lofty construction called the 'modern office building.' It has come in answer to a call, for in it a new grouping of social conditions has found a habitation and a name." Now, continued Sullivan, it needed a form:

> Problem: How shall we impart to this sterile pile, this crude, harsh, brutal agglomeration, this stark, staring exclamation of eternal strife, the graciousness of those higher forms of sensibility and culture that rest on the lower and fiercer passions? How shall we proclaim from the dizzy heights of this strange, weird, modern housetop the peaceful evangel of sentiment, of beauty, the cult of higher life?

The steel or concrete grid, which resolved complex physical forces into simple, orthogonal forms, was what allowed this multiplication of space into the sky. As technology advanced around the hidden core of the "safety elevator" invented by Elisha Otis in 1853, the grid shed its clothes, emerging as a "curtain wall" or scrim that kept the weather out while revealing, through its glass panes and later floor-to-ceiling expanse, the grid's reality. Later still, the cubicles of the open office only further specified the flexible grid, allowing for change and mobility even at work.

014. Plan of Cleveland, Ohio, 1796.

015. Plan of San Francisco, California, 1856.

The grid was turning into tall, dense, and extensive structures. As these new open structures were rising up, they necessitated another kind of grid. The very logic of the emerging city was shaping structures in which much of the grid was invisible—hidden underground, in electricity, water, and sewage systems that followed the grid while also connecting its pieces. The sheer scale of the city was such that you could not comprehend it. Open spaces were increasingly more difficult to find, as everything could be turned into developable space and thus into buildings. The grid was becoming a machine that swallowed up space and people, turning them into the constituent parts of a new reality. The urban machine was arising.

Frank Lloyd Wright, a young architect who had worked for Louis Sullivan, saw the nature of that reality. In a 1904 text, "The Art and Craft of the Machine," he described a kind of fever dream in which city, machine, and man—or perhaps even city, machine, man, and some unknown beast—had all become fused into a strange new entity to which he wanted to give shape:

> Be gently lifted at nightfall to the top of a great down-town office building, and you may see how in the image of material man, at once his glory and menace, is this thing we call a city. There beneath, grown up in a night, is the monster leviathan, stretching acre upon acre into the far distance. High overhead hangs the stagnant pall of its fetid breath, reddened with the light from its myriad eyes endlessly everywhere blinking. Ten thousand acres of cellular tissue, layer upon layer, the city's flesh, outspreads enmeshed by intricate networks of veins and arteries, radiating into the gloom, and there with muffled, persistent roar, pulses and circulates as the blood in your veins, the ceaseless beat of the activity to whose necessities it all conforms…
>
> Its nerve ganglia! The peerless Corliss tandems whirling their hundred ton fly-wheels, fed by gigantic rows of water boilers burning oil, a solitary man slowly

016. View of Chicago, 1892.

pacing backward and forward, regulating here and there the little feed valves controlling the deafening roar and the flaming gas, while beyond, the incessant clicking, dropping, waiting—lifting, waiting, shifting, of the governor gears controlling these modern Goliaths seems a visible brain in intelligent action, registered infallibly in the enormous magnets, purring in the giant embrace of great induction coils, generating the vital current meeting with instant response in the rolling cars on elevated tracks ten miles away, where the glare of the Bessemer steel converter makes a conflagration at night...

> If the pulse of activity in this great city, to which the tremor of the mammoth skeleton beneath our feet is but an awe-inspiring response, is thrilling, what of this prolific, silent obedience?
>
> And the texture of the tissue of this great thing, this Forerunner of Democracy, the Machine, has been deposited particle by particle, in blind obedience to organic law, the law to which the great solar universe is but an obedient machine.
>
> Thus is the thing into which the forces of Art are to breathe the thrill of ideality! A SOUL! (Wright, "The Art and Craft of the Machine")

This, then, was the new space of the American city. Its space had turned into a giant, interconnected machine and had become the embodiment of the soul of industrialization, or, if you will, of democracy–but certainly the manifestation of how the middle class was remaking the world. It was not so much the city as the essence of modernity in urban form.

Within the space that modernization was opening up, something new was appearing. One of the other great spaces it invented stood in contrast to the open grid and the Ringstrasse—this was the dark space of the cinema, where Wright's image could become a reality. The cinema presented a direct challenge to the physical world. It showed a convincing reality, but one that was completely without form or definite place. It was a space that was as abstract and unstable as the one of the Ringstrasse, the Paris boulevards, and the Jeffersonian grid, but even more fragmented and given to continual change.

The first publicly screened film simply documented the arrival of a train, and yet it had terrified people when it was first shown in 1895 in Paris. Film went on to develop not only more elaborate narratives and settings, but also a set of techniques that made sense of the visible world in a truly new and modern way: the edit, the cut, the pan, and the close-up all reconstructed reality in a radical manner. Film made visible what scientists were already discovering with microscopes, giant telescopes, X-ray machines, and other instruments of research: there were other worlds out there, and you could construct sense from them in entirely new constellations. At the same time, new technologies allowed physical space to be manipulated more malleably, as if it were part of a film set. Plastics were joining concrete and steel as material available for shaping the real world, letting manufacturers not only mimic existing shapes more cheaply, but also letting them create altogether more fluid and pliable forms.

It took a while, however, before people realized what film was doing to their world. It was not until 1936 that the German critic Walter Benjamin summed up the explosion of new worlds in his essay "The Work of Art in the Age of Technological Reproducibility." For Benjamin, the greatest machine of the twentieth century was the camera:

> Our taverns and our metropolitan streets, our offices and furnished rooms, our railroad stations and our factories appeared to have us locked up hopelessly. Then came the film and burst this prison-world asunder by the dynamite of the tenth of the second, so that now, in the midst of its far-flung ruins, we calmly and adventurously go traveling. With the close-up, space expands; with slow motion, movement is extended. The enlargement of a snapshot does not simply render more precise what in any case was visible, though unclear: it reveals entirely new structural formations of the subject. ... Evidently a different nature opens itself to the camera than opens to the naked eye–if only because

an unconsciously penetrated space is substituted for a space consciously explored by man. ... The camera introduces us to unconscious optics as does psychoanalysis to unconscious impulses. (Benjamin, "The Work of Art")

If the camera could do all of that, could you translate this freedom into built form? Could you inhabit such an explosive reality outside of the movie theater? You could create a home that came close, if you were rich enough, but even there most of the spaces and objects remained rather static. Many designers felt that their task had to be the translation of that explosion into the objects, images, and spaces of everyday life.

The explosion of film found a parallel in the reality of war, which swept away not only millions of lives and countless structures, but many of the social barriers and distinctions already eroded by modernization. The First World War ruptured space with a large-scale horrific violence, mechanized and irrespective of traditional boundaries, that shocked the middle class and all of Europe. Out of it, immense upheavals arose, not the least of which was the Russian Revolution of 1917. The world was being made new, whether by design or by conflict. The uncertain space of flows had found its radical, violent counterpart.

For at least a few years after the First World War, there was no better producer of new worlds than Russia. Instead of building the place of the middle classes, it sought to go further, creating the place beyond the point where all that was solid had dissolved. It would be the place of the worker, liberated and in control of a new land. Ironically, Russia produced the images and forms the middle class was able to use for the development of their own spaces: it became the producer of avant-garde spaces that helped invigorate middle-class culture.

In 1919, the Russian artist El Lissitzky created a propaganda poster entitled *Beat the Whites with the Red Wedge*. In the poster, a red triangle breaks through a white plane, sending a shattering of fragments floating out into space. It was meant to represent the Red Army breaking through the encircling forces of the reactionary "white" armies. The image gave a complex political statement a simple, graphic reality, one that could be easily understood, but that also represented the idea that all forces could be reduced to abstract elements that humans could manipulate: politics, science, and art would together make a new world.

El Lissitzky did not leave it with graphic images and paintings. In 1924, he proposed a "Cloud Prop": an immense forest of columns reaching high up above the city and supporting a few floors of what could be either office space or apartments. His compatriot Kazimir Malevich reduced painting to nothing more than a few red, black, and white squares and circles. Malevich also taught that even gravity could be defeated by the science and social logic of the new Soviet. Then architects such as Konstantin Melnikov and Ivan Leonidov tried to put these ideas into practice.

Melnikov designed a series of Workers' Clubs that shredded the conventional coherence of buildings. In his design for the Rusakov Workers' Club of 1927, he broke the auditorium apart into a series of balconies that could each be their own theater and that protruded over the sidewalk. In his Russian Pavilion for the 1925 Paris Exhibition of Decorative Arts, Melnikov created an intersection of lines at acute angles, dividing the building into two parts. Inside this space and similar exposition spaces meant to show off the radical art of the new Russia, artists further dissolved space by hanging works of art not just on the walls, but also around corners and on ceilings. Leonidov dreamed of constructing buildings that would consist of giant globes and towers connected by nothing more than wires (as in his proposal for the Lenin Institute of 1927), and of buildings that would rise up into the clouds as perennially unfinished constructions, such as his Heavy Industries Ministry design of 1934.

017. El Lissitzky, *Beat the Whites with the Red Wedge*, 1919.

018. Konstantin Melnikov, Russian Pavilion, Paris, 1925.

019. Ivan Leonidov, Lenin Institute, Moscow, 1927.

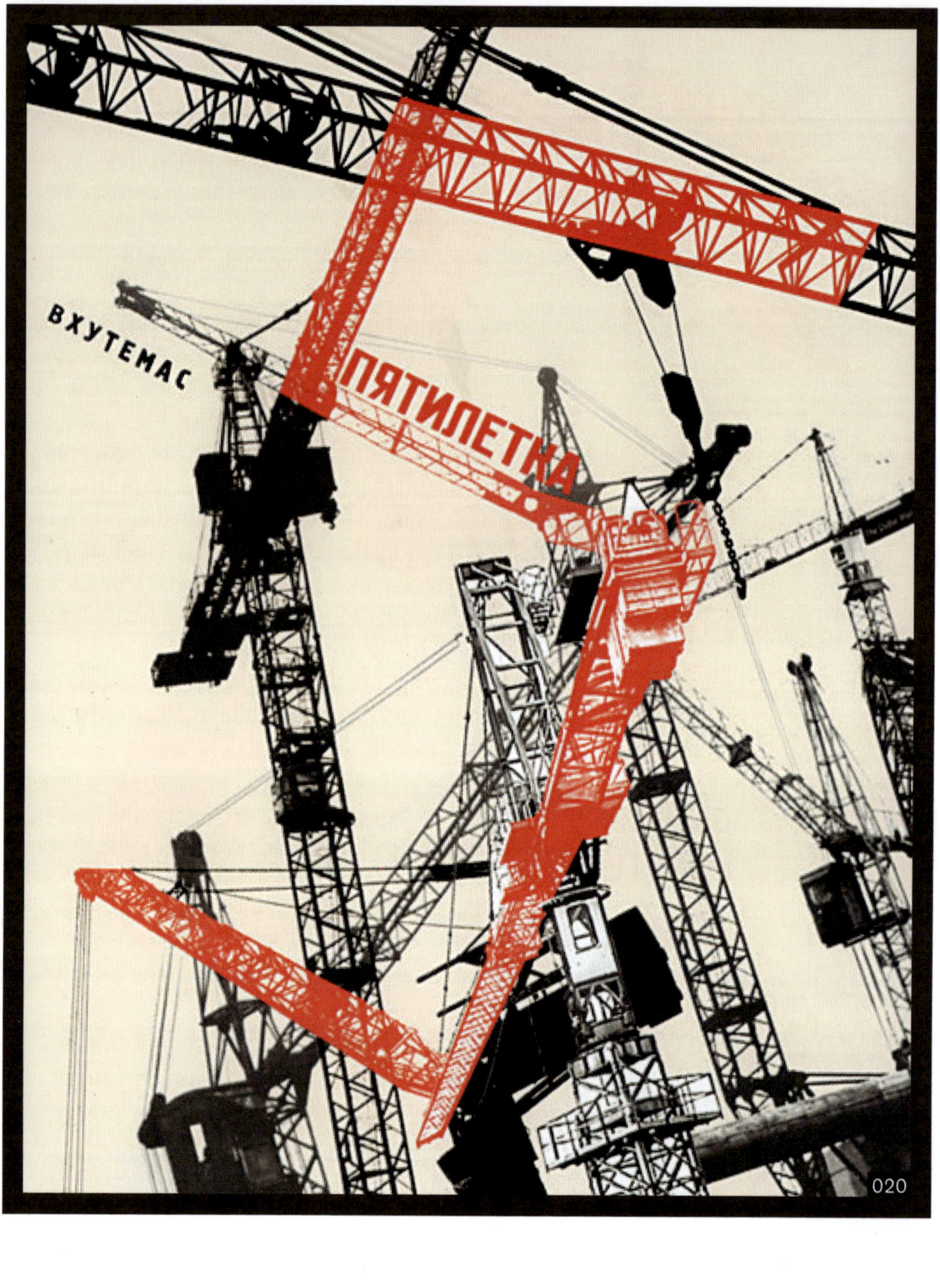
ВХУТЕМАС
ПЯТИЛЕТКА
020

In addition to their collaboration on the production of buildings, all of these designers and artists also worked together to design stage sets, uniforms, and propaganda material. For they were literally helping to build a new world: their efforts became part of a state plan to conquer more space and build a new reality. The engine for this project was the Vkhutemas, a combination school and workshop. Its teachers and students engaged in spatial experiments not just in the abstract, but also in the form of uniforms for sanitation workers, cups and saucers, posters and stage sets. The most integrated efforts were the various stage sets and traveling road shows ("agitprop") they produced. In them, metal scaffolding, moveable parts, and primal forms painted in primary colors came together to enact a different reality than the one the spectators inhabited. The aesthetics of film turned into three dimensions as the prototypes for new construction that would move beyond performance.

Though the revolution did not spread as these Russian idealists hoped, artists, designers, and architects all over Europe and America began active discussions and collaborative experiments with each other on how to build a new world out of the ashes of the First World War and on top of what they saw as outmoded physical, economic, and social structures. At the heart of that discussion was a place called the Bauhaus, or "House of Building." It was founded in Weimar right after the war with the goal of providing integrated training in all of the arts. In its introductory course, it forced all students to start with the most elemental of forms and shape, giving them a foundation that went beyond the representation of reality or the traditions of arrangement. In a somewhat mystical manner, students were meant to come to a unified understanding of their reality that they could then elaborate scientifically with tools once they specialized in painting, sculpture, graphics, ceramics,

020. Soviet Poster, Designer and Date Unknown.

021. Aleksandr Rodchenko, Soviet Poster, 1924.

022. Walter Gropius, Director's Office, Bauhaus, Dessau, 1927.

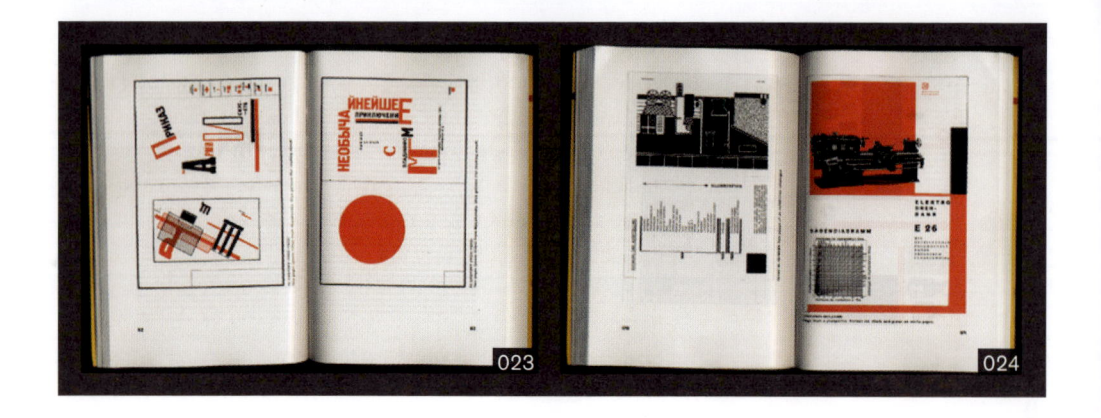

weaving, or architecture. They could then apply their inventions to the mass production of new images, objects, and spaces. In this manner, the Bauhaus could become the R&D center for consumer objects, as well as for the spaces and images in which such objects would have a rational, if always unstable, place.

In 1926 the Bauhaus, by then headed by architect Walter Gropius, moved to Dessau, just south of Berlin, where the director designed a new building for the institution, as well as homes for some of the faculty and several structures for the municipal government. The Bauhaus attracted the best designers from all around the world. It taught all of its students to experiment with new materials, to make things that could be reproduced or mass-produced, to reduce forms down to their most basic colors and shapes, and to compose in a manner that dissolved preconceptions, hierarchies, and expectations. You can see this aesthetic in graphic work that rearranged text into blocks of type, running headlines at angles or breaking them apart into fragments. You can see it in carpets made up of colored blocks moving by each other. You can see it in the bent aluminum chairs on which the students sat. You can see it above all else in the Bauhaus building itself.

Rather than being a single building, the Bauhaus consists of a series of separate blocks connected by lower elements. The facades are white-painted stucco over a concrete frame, filled in with glass set in metal grids. There is no angle at which you can take in the whole composition; it unfolds in space and over time. The building is filled with large, open spaces whose corners don't quite meet, that skip from glass walls to solids, and that are devoid of ornament. Bauhaus faculty and students designed all the storage elements, furniture, and other furnishings. There were Marcel Breuer's chairs, Marianne Brandt's lamps, and fixtures made of metal and plastic. Gropius's office itself was the kind of space the Russian graduates of the Vkhutemas wanted to make, with all industrial materials, pure geometries, and lines intersecting in space.

Gropius had hoped that the Bauhaus would work directly for industry, helping to mass-produce housing and furnishing as well as the implements of everyday life. It turned out that most of the Bauhaus designs were too radical. But from Dessau, students spread out throughout the world, designing white villas and posters, chairs and lamps, and experimenting with ever more radical spatial arrangements. They linked up with designers in other countries who were also experimenting along the same lines, and building by building, interior by interior, catalog by catalog, the new world began to take shape.

The graphic design of these pieces played an especially important part in their message. It dissolved the space of the page. Often created by some of the artists teaching at the Russian schools or at the Bauhaus, such as El Lissitzky, Malevich, or László Moholy-Nagy, these pieces combined photography with strong lines and blocks. In Georgii and Vladimir Stenberg's undated, mid-1920s poster, a dancing woman comes apart into her various appendages while skyscrapers jut up around her. In the other posters they designed during this period, as well as in those of Gustav Klutsis, human figures are jumping, somersaulting, dancing or otherwise proclaiming a vigorous life, while the text and graphic underlining emphasize the energy of the new world.

Outside of the Soviet Union, graphic experimentation not only presented new forms within the context of the old format of the book or magazine, but sought to reorganize the white space of the page as much as architects sought to create a new urban environment or home. In 1928, the Czech designer Jan Tschichold published *The New Typography*, which he followed up in 1930 with *The New Form*

023, 024. Jan Tschichold, The New Typography, 1928.

025. Piet Zwart, Trio-Reclameboek, 1931.

026. Lucian Bernhard, Pelikan, 1914.

in Typography. In words and especially in the design of the pages itself, he argued for using the arrangement of text and images to break through the frame implied by the page's edge. In a pin-wheeling composition, he opened up the book's center and let the eye wander freely.

While the Dutch designers Paul Schuitema and Piet Zwart, along with some of their Russian counterparts, emphasized the use of diagonals to liberate space and express the dynamic quality of the new world, German designers such as Willi Baumeister and Max Burchartz tended to punch up their imagery with the use of bold typefaces and a strong contrast in the size and shape of blocks of text. As these designers began to influence the more mainstream companies, designers such as Lucian Bernhard, especially in his work for the Pelikan pen company, combined some of these aggressive geometries and streamlined forms with a soft-edged monumentality to create a sense of solid but dynamic elegance.

In 1927, the Rotterdam firm of Brinkman and van der Vugt designed a new factory complex for the Van Nelle Tea and Tobacco Company. Situated slightly outside of Rotterdam along a canal, it consists of a single concrete block eight stories tall connected with diagonal bridges to a lower warehouse structure. The buildings, which also include an office block, various warehouses, and a boiler room, look almost transparent: you can see the columns on the inside, as well as (once) all the workers at their assembly lines. The bridges give the factory the impression of being a giant machine with levers and pistons. The architects set up a curved approach past the office block, and then released the visitor into a space between the buildings where all that transparency and complexity are overwhelming.

That view was photographed over and over again, and it was through the mechanism of the camera and mass-produced magazines that the Van Nelle Factory, along with several other buildings of the period, became icons of modernism. The photographs were usually taken

027. Johannes Brinkman & Leendert van der Vlug, Van Nelle factory, Rotterdam, 1926-1931.

at acute angles, emphasizing the visual layering of the structures. Heavy retouching brought out the edges of the volumes to make their geometric properties clear. Once published in one of the many magazines devoted to modernism, ranging from *De Stijl* in the Netherlands to the *Esprit Nouveau* in France to many more short-lived and specialized publications, the photographs joined texts and typographic layouts that emphasized the radical nature of the proposed buildings. This was more than a factory: it was also producing the relationship of production and consumption as a built reality.

The Swiss-born French architect Le Corbusier made a trip from Paris to see the Van Nelle Factory shortly after it was finished. He saw it as a prime example of an international movement to make modernist architecture, of which he was the leader. The Van Nelle factory inspired him, but he was also developing his own building blocks of modernism. The grandest of these was the new Parisian home of the Salvation Army, the Cité de Refuge (Refuge City), completed in 1932. It consists of a central slab against which a set of smaller elements, each shaped into a geometric solid, played off and to which they connected with ramps. Instead of articulating functions or creating loft-like expanses of space, Le Corbusier showed the main building as essentially a stack of individual cells for the indigent, hovering over the ground on massive concrete columns. The dining hall, auditorium, offices, and reception areas are all partially tucked under or next to the main block, forming a plinth that resembles a collage of different concrete fragments. Inside, the collage of concrete structures, which Le Corbusier emphasized with light coming in from the top or through narrow slot windows and by using bright colors, continues. The Cité de Refuge is a social condenser, a machine for processing, housing, and making a community out of people. It is both a larger version of the private home and a miniature of the whole city. Its architecture worked to establish the kind of social structure of which modernists such as Le Corbusier dreamed, and did so in a way that made that structure concrete. You could move around and through this structure, and it would surround you with clarified and monumental elements that together made up the mechanized reality of a rationalized social fabric.

While the Cité de Refuge was only a single building, Le Corbusier dreamed of creating a more effective way of building up the new world. In 1927, he won the international competition to design the headquarters for the League of Nations in Geneva. His design, which bore many similarities to the work of the Russian constructivists, was like a giant Swiss watch. It consisted of a splayed auditorium, a giant arch to hold up this vast space, office slabs for the League's bureaucracy, ceremonial buildings that were shapes displaying simple geometries, and ramps, stairs, walkways, and other circulation or ceremonial elements connecting all of these pieces. Le Corbusier saw the building as the model for how any institution of power should work, a kind of governing gear for world democracy. Unfortunately, the jury, which had originally picked this scheme as the competition winner, lost its nerve and reversed itself, rejecting his design. The plan lived on, however, in the same publications that were pushing modernism all over the world. Perhaps there was still hope that the modern world could be tamed and designed.

In less than a century, modern space had appeared, opened up, and corroded much of the world around it. It promised a revolution—the revolution the French had foreseen, now made real. The mechanisms by which it achieved its aims were not military or ideological, but the products of human beings and the structures that housed them.

028. Le Corbusier, Cité de Refuge, Paris, 1929-1933.

2. STAGING MODERNITY
the aesthetics of the future

While space appeared in the boulevards and grids of the middle-class city and new spaces were devised by designers pushing the boundaries of abstraction and coherence, modernity was also appearing in another group of places and structures. One such place was the world's fair, which both created and collected examples of modernism in space, structures, and objects. In cities, places such as train stations, entertainment centers, and department stores also continued that work within the rhythms of everyday urban life. Certain architects and designers, meanwhile, self-consciously created stage sets for a modernist world, in which the breaking of boundaries, the pursuit of radical rationality, the abstraction of form and image, and the fluidity of space presented themselves as a model for all future construction. In the end, however, it took an event as cataclysmic as the First World War to fix the reality of a modern world in people's minds.

For at a least a century, between roughly 1850 and the New York World's Fair of 1964, a peculiar event, occurring once every few years in different cities around the world, summed up an emerging modernity. World's fairs, or expositions, brought together new technological marvels and showed how designers and manufacturers were trying to shape these new things and spaces. These fairs were the staging ground for modernism. At these events and in the structures that housed them, modernist space began to take on a character all its own. The structures that contained the fair made them emblematic, and the myriad objects within them set the scene for the artificial, middle-class environment. The world's fairs were the laboratories for modern life.

The 1851 exposition was England's coming-of-age party. It celebrated the achievements of the Industrial Revolution that that country had spearheaded, and that had by then transformed every aspect of daily life of the country's fast-growing urban areas. The fair was a chance for manufacturers to show off and the public to see what was new. But the most startling aspect of the 1851 exposition was the building that housed it. The so-called Crystal Palace was a greenhouse of immense dimensions. Five parallel naves stretched for almost 2,000 feet through

029, 030. Jules Charles, Greenhouses, 1600.

031. Sir Joseph Paxton, Crystal Palace, London, 1851.

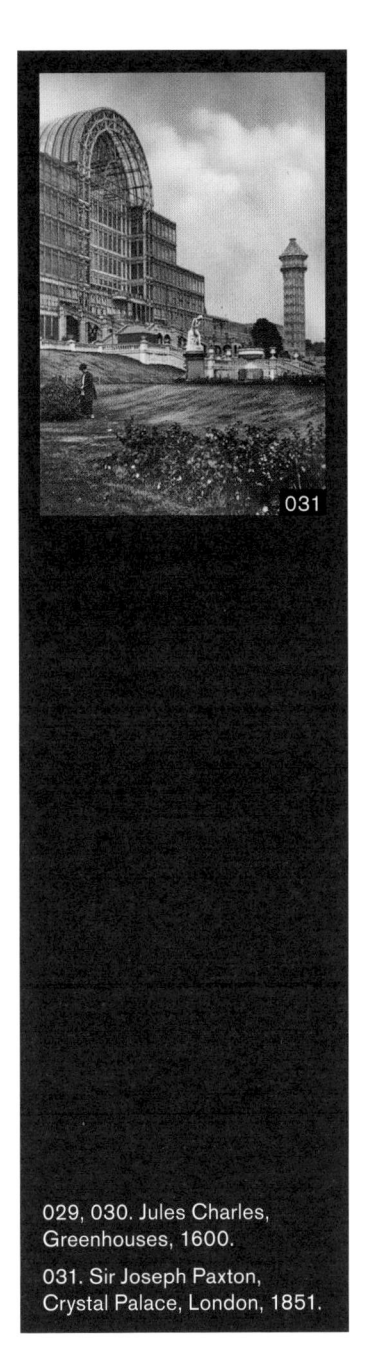

the bucolic countryside on the outskirts of London. The behemoth structure, clad entirely in glass and steel, even swallowed up nature: it encompassed a group of elm trees that stood under the 186-foot-high central nave.

The type, however, was very familiar. The greenhouse containing the 1851 Exposition was created by a young specialist in the field, Joseph Paxton, who had never designed anything but such structures until then. Greenhouses were a peculiar English invention (though the French claimed otherwise) that enclosed a piece of nature and thus transformed it into an artificial and exotic version of itself. In the greenhouse, natural things such as flowers, trees, and shrubs could grow in a region where they did not belong. Through the greenhouse, humans tricked nature and imploded space by making England contain the tropics, the desert, or the savannah. They were making a modern place using technology that could make any place anywhere.

The greenhouse used the most advanced technology then available. New factories could make glass easily available in large quantities, although only a short time before it had been so precious only the very rich could use it, and then only in small amounts. Social and political developments also affected the technology with the 1840 repeal of the "glass tax," which had confirmed the place of glass as a rich person's building element. Glass could now be contained in a frame made out of metal. Again, human beings had known for a long time how to draw ore out of rocks, melt it, and form it into implements. Only recently, however, had they figured out ways of creating repetitive elements that could be assembled to create a frame for enclosing space. The desire to use this technology to build greenhouses and shopping arcades arose from the impetus to create an artificial environment, whether to grow exotic plants or to show off exotic goods and people in shopping environments. The artifice that allowed that desire to be

032

fulfilled thus came from the peculiar accumulation and interaction of capital, knowledge, labor processes, social conditions, and tastes that we have come to call the Industrial Revolution.

The Crystal Palace was the Industrial Revolution's great temple. In it, the nations of the world (or at least Europe and its colonies) exhibited their latest inventions and products. The jacquard loom was exhibited to show how clothes could be mass-produced. The Americans brought machines with which crops could be reaped mechanically. Small gadgets to facilitate everyday life, from hand-cranked cleaning devices to affordable pottery, proliferated under the glass arches. Carriages of every sort vied for visitors' attention alongside precious inlaid swords from India. Leading Englishmen who were proud of their technical skills, including Prince Consort Albert, were impressed by the decorative means by which the French and others could make their household goods look attractive. The public came in huge numbers just to see the amount of things the world was now producing. Though the building was meant to be temporary, it was so popular that it was recreated in Sydenham, where it stood until it burned down in 1936.

The Crystal Palace made clear to its more than six million visitors that a new world was emerging—one that would focus not just on palaces and churches, but also on temples of production and consumption. Factories, warehouses, department stores, railroad stations, and apartment buildings were the building blocks for this new world, and the Crystal Palace was their ethereal, idealized image. Here the modern world in all its grand abstraction and machine-based reality stood before people, and what they saw was not their ability to have "true relations with [their] kind," as Karl Marx and Friedrich Engels had imagined in their *Communist Manifesto* of three years earlier, but rather the material possibility of making a new place for themselves. They saw objects they could buy and use, things that would make them wealthier and would let them show their wealth. They saw intangible things that they could believe in as a matter of faith embodied in concrete objects and presented in a transparent, open environment that did not constrict them but was open to change. The ability to build an almost utopian image of the modern world and to contain within it the elements of that world proved to be a powerful antidote to those who believed that modernity should be built into social and economic conditions, and not just bought and sold. As the architect Le Corbusier wrote almost a century later in his *Towards a New Architecture* (1924) : "Architecture or revolution. Revolution can be avoided."

The "official" world fairs were held every few years in one major city or the other. In 1876, it was the turn of Philadelphia. The Centennial Exposition there marked the century of freedom the United States thought it had won for itself. Its main building, though almost as large as the Crystal Palace and also made of glass and metal (though steel here replaced iron), was not nearly as transparent and thus exciting as the original. There were so many exhibits, however, that the fair spawned auxiliary buildings for machinery, agriculture, horticulture, and art. States and other countries also had their own buildings, which they constructed with an architecture that the commissioners thought appropriate to the place or activity represented: glass and steel for machinery, an octagonal stone pavilion for the Spanish.

What was inside this architecture was even more astonishing: gadgets such as the sewing machine, the telephone, and the typewriter made their debut. With each of these machines, the world could and would be changed drastically. Each had the tendency to implode space and time, making goods and information available almost instantaneously.

But as objects, they did not look like much. How things worked and how they appeared were becoming completely disconnected. The telephone was a collection of black-painted metal forms that somehow worked its

032. Henry Pettit & Joseph Wilson, Centennial Exhibition, Philadelphia Fair, 1876.

033. Telephone, 1896.

034

magic. The typewriter displayed keys that the fingers could touch, but that translated the human being's motions to a flat paper through levers that could not quite be seen. The housing for these objects was usually cobbled together from previous types, in the manner that the automobile was later based on the horse-drawn buggy.

Over fifteen years later, America put on another great fair. One observer in particular saw its importance. In the spring of 1893, Henry Adams, the descendant of two U.S. presidents but with a rather uncertain profession, was traveling in Europe on a train with some fellow Americans. Suddenly, he was called back by telegraph to his native Boston because he and his family faced financial ruin due to a stock market crash. Though this situation might not seem so strange to us today, every aspect of this experience would have been unforeseeable when Adams was born. That one could be traveling in a metal conveyance on rails, that communications could be conveyed by electric signals crossing in a cable under the Atlantic, and that one's fortune would be subject to the machinations of an unknowable accumulation of capital known as a stock exchange—it was all very new and very modern. It was all part of a world of interconnected communication, the incessant movement of goods, peoples, and ideas, and financial structures and industry that had arisen, as if out of nothing, in just a few decades.

Adams wasn't quite sure what to think of that modern world. That it existed, of that he had no doubt. He was fascinated by its machinery, its culture of instant connections and interpretations, and the vast new wealth—both in a literal sense and in the sense of possibilities—that it enabled for people like him. He felt, however, that it needed an order and a meaning; there had to be a reason why all these new things existed and why the world was changing so rapidly. As he wrote in his autobiography, *The Education of Henry Adams* (1918), the alternative was not something he cherished: "The instability was greater than he calculated; the speed of acceleration passed bounds. Among other general rules he laid down the paradox that, in the social disequilibrium between capital and labor, the logical outcome was not collectivism, but anar-

034. Hubert Howe Bancroft, World Columbian Exposition, Chicago, 1893.

chism." Modernity needed to have a meaning, Adams was pointing out—an appearance and relation to the past—so that people like him could understand it and gain not just monetary but also spiritual value from it and its products.

So Adams, his personal fortune secured once he was back in Boston through a mechanism he declined to explain in the *Education*, set out for Chicago to see the World Columbian Exposition, the world's fair of 1893. Here Adams thought he would be able to take stock of the modern world, for here modernity was on display. He took a train across the Alleghenies and the Midwest, arrived in a metropolis that had been a village when he was a child, and went to the fairgrounds at the edge of the city. He entered under the immense, white columns of the portico, where guards made sure to keep non-whites and the shabbily dressed out, in case the architecture did not intimidate them enough. He entered into what had been, until a year earlier, sand dunes and marshes. Now there rose a new city, a shining white apparition on the shore of Lake Michigan. Around an oval pool in which a barque representing the United States sailed toward the future in all her allegorical glory under the watchful eye of a statue of Columbia, he found a group of buildings that represented the arts and industry. They housed all those creations of the human mind that were helping this brand-new city of Chicago to transform the geography and resources of the Midwest into finished and consumable goods. Here was a collection of machines, tools, and art objects that represented how human beings could take natural ingredients and make something truly new out of them.

The buildings themselves surrounded these inventions with a paper-thin shell that was meant to give them a sense of belonging together in a particular culture. Each was stylistically a variation on a theme taught at the École des Beaux-Arts in faraway Paris. That the neo-classical temples were built out of "staff," a form of plaster of Paris, and harmonized together, meant that a way of making things perfected in one place could be exported to what was then the wild frontier and result in the appearance of a coherent universe. This instant classical world put up for a year represented a way of doing things that had nothing to do with the materials or the character of that patch of prairie that had become Chicago. It was an imported culture, part of a complex of ways of speaking, dressing, eating, and even thinking that a group of immigrants had imposed on this land. The architecture as well as the exhibits of the Columbian Exposition celebrated this new, alien world, showed it in all its beauty and inventiveness, and asked viewers to marvel at its achievements.

Henry Adams did. He was in awe of what his country was producing, but he was also a bit scared by the speed of change he saw all around him. He had come to Chicago after his last crisis to make sense of it all. Once arrived, he remembered in his characteristically anonymous way of relating his observations.

> One sat down to ponder on the steps beneath Richard Hunt's dome. ... Here was a breach of continuity–a rupture in historical sequence! Was it real, or only apparent? One's personal universe hung on the answer, for, if the rupture was real and the

new American world could take this sharp and conscious twist towards ideals, one's personal friends would come in, at last, as winners in the great American chariot-race for fame. (Adams, *The Education of Henry Adams*)

Adams's friends were the ones who argued for finding moral and aesthetic principles that could be defined as fixed and true, while accepting the rush of changes the modern world was bringing about. They believed that ordering principles could and must be found within change. They also believed that you might find something you could think of as truth or beauty in that new world, as long as you stood far enough away from the objects, images, and spaces it was throwing up every day to make sense of them. Those principles might be abstract, but they would by that very token be fundamental. Some thinkers sought such anchors in things themselves, others in basic tenets so abstract they were almost mystical. Adams found his principles eventually in Catholic traditions. For him, the modern world revolved around "The Virgin and the Dynamo," as he called one of the later chapters in his *Education*. The dynamo made his world hum, while the Virgin Mary gave it meaning. He had come to the exposition to see the dynamo and to try to find the Virgin.

The dynamo was housed in the virginally white Electricity Building. Designed by Henry Van Brunt, then the president of the American Institute of Architects, this pavilion sported a façade of semi-detached columns, grand porticos, and a dome rising over the central crossing of two orthogonal axes. It was an imposing, rhythmic, and academically correct structure—until you entered. Then suddenly the certainties and good graces of classicism gave way to a riot of steel and glass that supported a transparent roof over a hall big enough to house the giant machinery out of which electricity emerged. The

035. World Columbian Exposition, Chicago, 1893.

logic of engineering and of the Crystal Palace took over. To Henry Adams, such places were quite literally inexplicable. Looking at the dynamos, he wrote, "He expected answers and was astonished to get none." Dynamos worked invisibly, in ways the eyes could not see or the nose smell or the ears hear. They produced a force that you could sense, but through impulses you could not. The way things worked had become unknowable in the strictest and most basic sense that you could experience it, though you could explain it through science and its diagrammatic representations.

The builders of these dynamos tried to make them resemble something familiar by covering them with columns and other elements of classical architecture. They celebrated what moving parts there were by accentuating their lines through a carving into the steel of grooves and extra, nonfunctional ridges. In Chicago, they even garlanded some of the machines with flowers for the duration of the exposition. But these mechanical beasts remained alien, the product of abstract thinking that worked in an unknowable manner to produce something immensely tangible and valuable: power, whether to heat a building or to move another machine to produce something. They were the engines of the modern world.

What was important to Henry Adams was that they were contained. The new world existed, was accessible, and was hard at work, but a sheen of order made sure that it had its place. His friends—the self-created elite of politicians, writers, painters, and architects, many of whom had worked on the Chicago exposition—had produced a coherent method of housing all the elements of a modern world and were hard at work trying to come up with a meaning for this dynamic environment. In Chicago, local architect Daniel Burnham would soon develop a comprehensive plan for the city's development. It contained everything from a plan to extend the street grid—regularizing the radial boulevards that led from the business core to the wheat fields, pastures, and mines that fed the great city-machine—to proposals to improve the city's infrastructure and provide parks in which the fast-growing population could find some respite from the pressures of modernization.

Adams, having toured the exposition, sat back down again under the central, empty dome that his friend, New York architect Richard Hunt, had designed as the ceremonial core of the whole ensemble—leaving it empty except for murals depicting both the history and the future of the United States—and thought he had found an answer to his question of what all this modernity meant:

> Chicago asked in 1893 for the first time the question whether the American people knew where they were driving. Adams answered, for one, that he did not know, but would try to find out. On reflecting sufficiently deeply, under the shadow of Richard Hunt's architecture, he decided that the American people probably knew no more than he did; but that they might still be driving or drifting unconsciously to some point in thought, as their solar system was said to be drifting towards some point in space; and that, possibly, if relations enough could be observed, this point might be fixed. Chicago was the first expression of American thought as unity; one must start there. (Adams, *Education*)

036. Henry Van Brunt & Frank Maynard Howe, Electricity Building, Chicago, 1893.

If you see America as an emblem of modernity, as Adams to a large extent did, then the "Chicago" to which

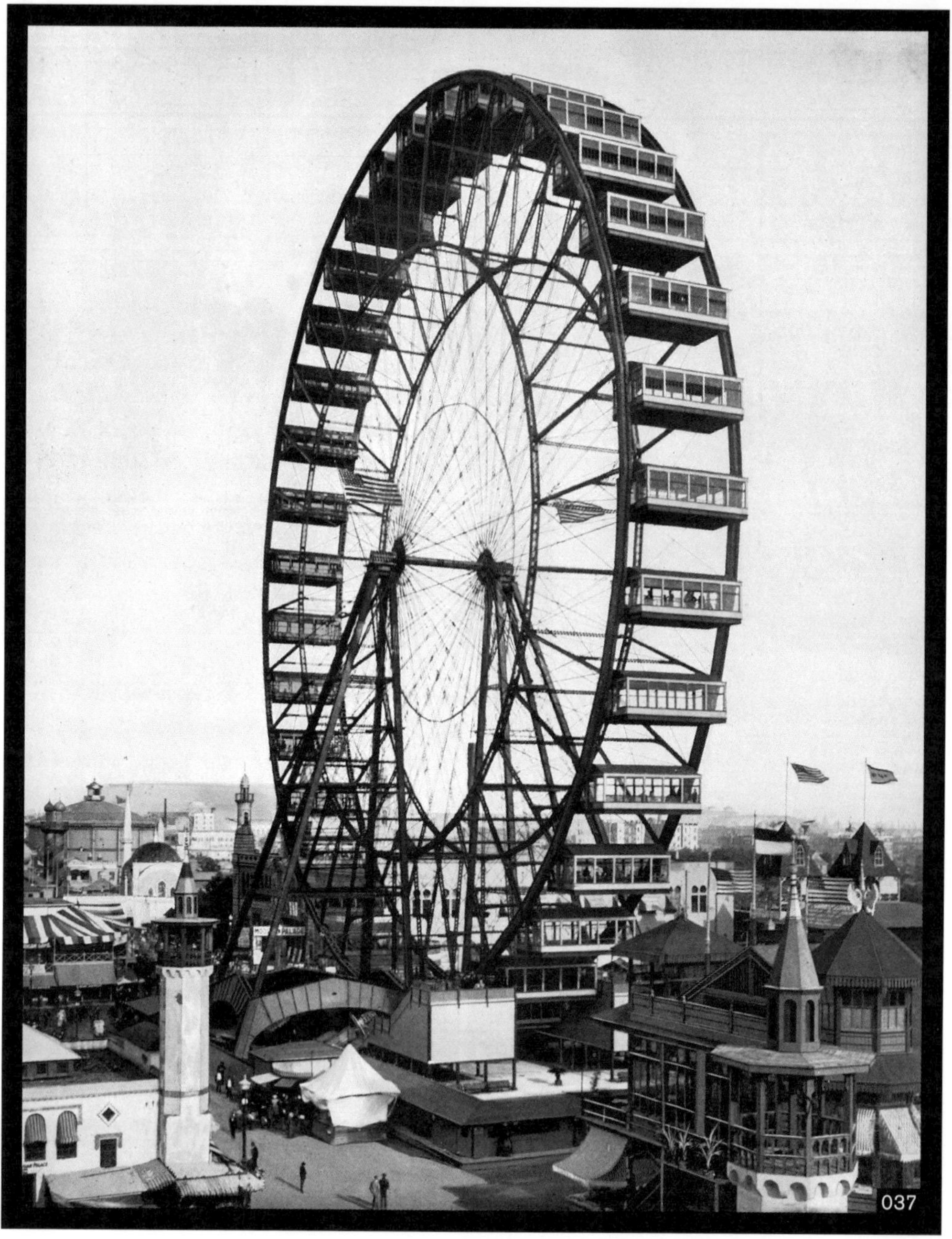
037

he refers represents the modern world coming together in some form by which you could see and, through the medium of architecture and design, understand it. The designers of the fair were able to bring together all those elements that would let one derive meaning and sense from the machines of change they celebrated in their buildings and objects. You could indeed dream of a coherent modern world there.

Until you noticed, out of the corner of your eye, something looming over even the soaring dome of Hunt's central pavilion. It was a metal circle with very little adornment. It was a giant wheel onto which, in an almost surreal collage, carriages that looked as if they had been lifted from train cars were attached. In those carriages people were perched, looking out over the fair and the city from a perspective that was radically new. They sat, if only for the moment the slow revolution of the giant wheel allowed them, where they imagined God to be, overlooking all and everyone. This new device, the Ferris wheel, made all the architecture below look small. It trumped the artifice Adams believed would contain modernity.

Nor was the Ferris wheel alone. It stood in the middle of a riotous addition to the official exposition that came to be called the midway. Here were the truly amazing elements of the modern world: the freaks of nature and science alike, mutations of people and animals, along with gadgets that one could play with. Carnival rides, expositions of two-headed goats, shooting galleries, and exotic people from all around the world jostled with each other for attention. Here it did not matter how you were dressed, or how you behaved. Here chaos seemed to be near, but was controlled by one simple device: you had to pay to play. The exhibitors had to pay rent, the fairgoers had to pay to see the

037. George Ferris, Ferris wheel, Chicago, 1893.

marvels on display. Capitalism, the logic of modernity, controlled this world as architecture controlled the White City.

In 1889, Paris built the next great icon of the new age as part of their exposition: the Eiffel Tower. Designed for the Exposition Universelle of 1889, Gustave Eiffel's functionless spire was nothing more or less than a vertical symbol of the industrial and artistic achievements housed in exhibition pavilions that had been largely standardized into huge, flexible blocks. Below this icon, the Parisian designers, under Eiffel's supervision, had stripped away much of the additions and ornamentation, but also the hierarchical relation of building parts, that had distinguished the exposition buildings not only in London and Philadelphia, but also in Melbourne, Antwerp, and Amsterdam. Smoke stacks stood naked and unadorned next to the halls. Inside the Machinery Building, giant trusses came down to the floor and rested on tiny feet, expressing the logical distribution of forces in their sweeping forms, while breaking aesthetic rules that objects should look heavier at the bottom than at the top.

The Industrial Revolution showed itself in all its power in Paris and reached toward the skies in the Eiffel Tower. Its architecture was a perfection of and prototype for the new infrastructure that was transforming western Europe into a new, interconnected, and artificial terrain grouped around factory complexes. The bridges and spans the engineers were devising became in the tower the components of a new kind of obelisk, an expression of the power of the ruler to control peoples and landscapes. It was, however, an open and accessible obelisk in which space and object had a new relationship: that of the web or network. Instead of a world in which solid objects stand in space with closed walls containing functions, the Eiffel Tower promised a world in which everything would be interconnected and all that was solid would indeed melt into air, leaving material and social relations to stand out clearly.
What appeared in the world's fairs, in other words, was not just a new kind of space, but a new kind of spatial relationship between things. Instead of a heavy frame defining rooms that were,

038. Ferdinand Dutert, Gallery of Machines, Exposition Universelle, Paris, 1889.

039. Gustave Eiffel, Eiffel Tower, Paris, 1889.

in turn, decorated to fill in the architecture, and then the placement of furniture within this frame, the fairs' buildings were almost invisible structures in which the objects had to develop their own relationship to each other, to that frame, and to human users. The artifacts also had to develop their own design, one that would respond to the new uses out of which they arose and to which they were being put.

The fairs were prototypes for the domestication of industrial processes, products, and structures for everyday use by the middle class. They helped inspire the form or technology of department stores, office buildings, and even homes. However, the fairs were temporary, and often existed in isolated places such as parks. While they served to show what was possible, it took another class of buildings—the railroad station—to install those possibilities in the heart of the city and at the center of people's lives. Such structures served movement itself, but also the presentation of consumer goods and even the kind of spectacle the world's fairs had hosted, now in a specific and more or less permanent place.

The railroad stations of Paris and London, celebrated by writers and painters alike, were the most concrete embodiments of the new world they helped make possible. The Gare du Nord, designed by architect Jacques-Ignace Hittorff, opened in 1863, while Kings Cross in London was constructed eight years before that. Both were typical of how the new world entered into the old one. The buildings' fronts, neo-classical in the case of the Gare du Nord and more abstract in the case of Kings Cross, were relatively solid in appearance, symmetrical, and carefully composed. The whole facade of Hittorff's building was like a section of a Gothic cathedral, as it sported a central arch and two flanking naves. Groups of pilasters tied the building down to the ground. In the Kings Cross station, two massive piers contained the large arch. Both buildings became more conventional at ground level, providing openings at a human scale into dark and contained spaces.

Then space exploded into the vastness of the actual train hall. Even to this day, as the stations have become filled with kiosks and information boards, the effect in either the English or the French cathedrals to speed is exhilarating. A thin filigree of metal trusses holds up the barest excuse of a roof that is itself shot through with skylights. At the far end of the hall, the building just ends, letting a flood of light in to cut off any sense of what is beyond this cavern. Within this space, in the time of the steam engine, the trains drew the eye with their wheels, pistons, and gears at eye level, their smokestacks, plumes, and boilers reaching up to the roof, and the endless line of cars, each an abstracted and elongated version of a carriage, stretching out to the vanishing point in that wash of light. These powerful engines had escaped from the world of mines and factories, and were the only pieces of large-scale machinery most of the middle-class would encounter. The carriages were mass-produced and simplified versions of the overstuffed home interior familiar to the middle class, with more pared-down versions for the lower classes.

The stations were the staging grounds for the conquest of first the city, and then the country, by the modern world and its aesthetics. Within them, a new scale and a new materiality found its home and became familiar to countless travelers. Though the church-like design of most stations arose from the practical fact that the church was the only model most architects had for a very large public building, its effect was to make travelers feel as if they were transcending the world they knew and moving out into a new space. That is also how the painters of the time, especially the French impressionists, depicted these stations.
Beyond the railroad station, the trains moved out through the city, the massive cuts for their lines slicing open the urban field from the edge of the old town, where most nineteenth-century train stations were located, all the way out to the newly developing sub-

040. Lewis Cubitt, Kings Cross, London, 1851-1852.

urbs. Buildings and streets were cut off to make way for the tracks, leaving behind discontinuity and breaks in the metropolitan fabric. The vast new space of the train hall moved out to become an interruption, a realization of something at a different scale and speed moving continuously through the patterns of the modern city. Here the new space opened up by the middle class began to reveal its more disturbing side. Former inhabitants of the cuts saw their homes destroyed, while those living nearby experienced the corrosive effects of the cut, the noise, and the coal fumes. For the travelers in the train, that disconcerting space was the result of a speeding up of time. As the train gathered momentum and moved out into the countryside, the world became a blur.

Contemporary observers noted a profound change in the way the world is experienced from a speeding train. You could no longer understand the elements that had been so familiar to you in relationship to each other. There was no fixed horizon, vanishing point, or hierarchy of near and far. Everything started to bleed together. A space had opened up that was not so much empty as incomprehensible.

This space appeared not just in the fairs or because of the advent of the trains. In 1852, the ruler later known as Napoleon III put Baron Haussmann in charge of a renovation not of his palace or his parade grounds, but of the very city from which he derived his power. The result was the most extensive urban surgery ever attempted. Haussmann had no city walls to tear down and reclaim, no new suburban location for the middle class. Instead, he slashed the new right through the heart of the old Paris, cutting straight lines out from the old centers of power, such as the Louvre, through working-class neighborhoods and estates alike. He connected the lines with monuments that ranged from the abstract—such as the relics of previous civilizations either imported directly (the obelisk Napoleon had brought from Egypt) or copied (the Arc de Triomphe)—to the institutional elements of a new middle-class culture, such as the opera.

A new geography appeared as if out of nothing. Through the open streets, troops could march and, what was more important, the continual movement of goods and people so central to the world of production and consumption could flow. In Paris, the endless circulation found in Vienna had a less clearly shaped, but still continuous counterpoint. Instead of one geometric figure, the Haussmann plan consisted of a constellation of lines, with two "ring" boulevards created, as in Vienna, upon the sites of previously demolished city walls, but also new avenues crossing the city, each leading into or intersecting the other. Paris received a palimpsest of itself, in which its traditional "hôtels," or private homes, and rows of more modest dwellings were cleared away or cleaned up, turning into the apartment buildings that, as in Vienna, became the domain of the new middle class. The streetscape of the new Paris was again the result of real estate speculation that helped pay for the civic improvements, but here middle-class space took over the whole city, reducing what was left in between to a confusing and almost invisible residue.

Once the new boulevards had been completed, they became great canyons, their scale unlike anything people had seen in a street before. They were linear versions of the square, often with different zones that allowed for everything from high-speed movement in the center to deliveries on the side and roaming or resting in the zone between. In this new public space, you were always surrounded by movement.

The facades of the apartment buildings and stores that arose to form these urban canyons were even more anonymous and repetitive than the ones in Vienna. The buildings followed more or less the same division between expensive apartments on the piano nobile, or first floor, lesser floors above that, and servants' quarters (later the famous artists' garrets) in the attic. They usually left less space available for ceremonial purposes, and they were less easily distinguishable from each other than were the "rental palaces" that arose in the Hapsburg empire.

One of the most remarkable additions to the urban scene was an interior version of the boulevard—an everyday version of the world's fair. It was the space of the galleria or shopping arcade, which actually predated the appearance of the train station and world's fairs. Developers took leftover lots in streets, or sometimes tore down buildings, to create a linear, covered environment. These arcades were glassed-in alternatives to the boulevard, but they were also miniatures of the train station sheds. Covered with glass set in a grid of iron or later steel, the

041. Railroads cutting through Paris due to the Haussmann plan, 1852, Period Lithograph, Author Unknown.

042. Samuel Ware, Burlington Arcade, London, 1819.

043. Arcade Passage du Grand Cerf, Paris, 1825, Architect Unknown.

044

045

arcades usually did not have any defined place of their own (the Galleria of Milan, built in 1873 with a grand octagonal center, was a notable exception), but led from one street to another. Nor did they have a central focus or facade. Instead, they were voids leading past rows of shops that themselves opened onto the arcade with shop fronts defined by plate glass. The frames that had in the past so carefully and necessarily separated the inside from the outside, the private from the public, and the open from the closed, disappeared. What shone forth in this new ambiguous in-between space were the myriad goods the Industrial Revolution was making available.

In Paris, the fluid landscape continued underground, first of all in the new sewage system implemented starting in 1850, whose complexity and impact rivaled those of the boulevards above. Then, between 1899 and 1905, Hector Guimard designed the stations for the system of underground railroads that Paris, in imitation of London, had started to build. This other hidden space that made the city above it work so much more efficiently was now filled with tile, stucco, and especially metalwork that moved down the long lines of the underground tubes and surged up the walls, reaching up into the glass-and-metal entrance canopy which announced the system to the aboveground city. There, the entrances became emblems of the new style emerging from the domestic interior and private parks into the public scene.

Once this space of flows had opened the city, not just places but also objects were more available. Shopping could become integrated and concentrated, drawing consumers from far away. Soon the logic of the arcade extended to a new kind of building altogether: the department store. Starting with stores such as the Samaritaine in Paris, which opened in 1869, these palaces of consumption began appearing in cities all over the Western world. They took the logic of the small store, where you could find yourself surrounded with a variety of goods, and made its scale monumental. That scale astonished people in the way that the world's fair buildings

044, 045. Frantz Jourdain & Henri Sauvage, Samaritaine Store, Paris, 1883-1933.

and train stations had. The availability of goods did as well. The department store was open to anybody, as long as you followed proper codes of behavior and were properly dressed: as long as you acted, in other words, like a member of the middle class. The store was also your entree into that class, where you could acquire the elements from which you could construct a middle-class life.

As a space, the department store was essentially an open grid where the structure disappeared into metal lines. There were few focal points and little hierarchy; there was only a grid of cases. For its furnishings, the department store took the cabinets and armoires of the middle-class interior and gave them a much larger scale, while making them simpler and more open, so that you could clearly see the merchandise inside. The only interruptions in the rhythm of the various stalls and stations dedicated to different kinds of goods were the grand staircases that transformed the means of movement into altars of marble and turned wood. At the heart of the department store, light flooded down from skylights, but there was no escape here from the new world, as there was in the railroad stations with their one open end. The department store was all about the interior and its furnishings. But because it was not a domestic interior, it was a strange hybrid, both public and private, both open and democratic and yet reserved only for those who could afford to shop there. With its grid and its furnishings, its inward turn and its status somewhere between a private and an open, but always a middle-class, environment, the department store was the harbinger of the modernist spaces in which the middle class was to live, work, and play in the following century. Such open environments appeared more and more within even normal structures. The flood of middle-class institutions, such as opera houses, museums, and universities, brought with them interior public spaces focused on movement, of a vast new scale, and where entry depended

046

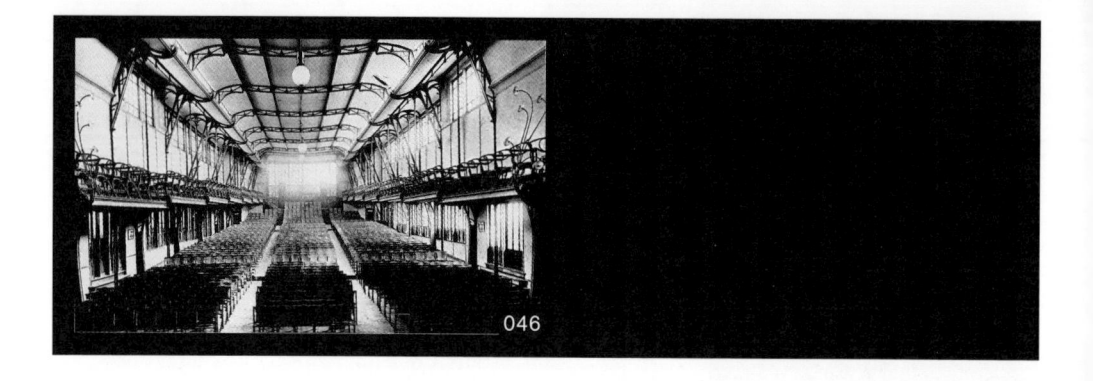

on your comportment and appearance, more than anything else. (The working classes were also kept out of the museums because they were not open on Sundays, the one day they had free.) Often these structures had glass-enclosed atria.

The most famous of all these structures was the Paris Opera, which sat at the point where several of Haussmann's axes intersected. The building therefore had not just one but three main facades, each completely dominated by different entry pavilions for those arriving by different modes of transportation. Circulation took up a third of the actual building's space. There were entry halls, stairs, foyers, hallways, bars, lounges, more stairs, corridors, more lounges, more stairs, and, only at the very interior, the actual auditorium. The Opera's main space was an interior version of the boulevard's meeting point, a riot of intersecting levels and overlooks. The point was as much to be seen as to see, and the middle class made a grand spectacle of itself here.

What disappeared from sight were both the actual building itself and the rooms it contained. Because all of its elements had to get out of the way of movement, there were fewer columns, pilasters, pedestals, or other elements to define and translate structure. It is difficult to understand how the Opera is made or what its parts are, either on the inside or the exterior. What matters more is the interconnectedness of all the parts and the way they put you and others on display.

Such structures proliferated around Europe as operas, theaters, meeting halls, and other places for bourgeois culture. They slowly shed more and more of their stone, stucco, or brick containment and became ever more free in composition. However, they still remained boxes that tried to contain the gathering of the middle classes as they came to appear, to learn, to decide, to shop, or just to move. History and a sense of proper place clung to them. Then, in certain provincial capitals, the containers began to melt away.

In Brussels, architect Victor Horta designed a series of houses and public buildings whose surfaces are so asymmetrical, so elongated in their curves, and so eccentric in their composition that they seem to be willful challenges to established taste. In his own house, of 1900, and in the Socialist Party's Maison du Peuple, of 1899, Horta went a step further: he dissolved the buildings' central spaces into greenhouses. Glass—some of it stained and leaded—ironwork, and plaster all fused to create a truly other world, suffused with light, but without any view to the outside world. The facade seemed about to melt, its stone remnants taking on the quality of glass and giving way to the expanses of that material. Inside the Maison du Peuple, you found yourself under a canopy of glass that was tethered more than held up by columns and arches that bled into each other and that seemed to flow down and around you. The whole building appeared to be coming apart. This was an almost dangerous building, a dream or a nightmare space where the working classes, not the middle classes, were rising.

Horta filled his buildings with references to plants, trees, and rocks, so that you felt as if you had entered an artificial nature in which the hothouse and its contents were becoming one. This was an architecture that was tending toward a new logic, one that moved beyond the industrial imagery and mathematical principles that had allowed new forms to appear and tried to reveal deeper truths in which all that was solid would indeed melt into air.

Yet, such grand structures stood outside of many people's daily lives. In the United States, however, designers began to open up the house and the neighborhood where people lived, as well as the places where they worked, giving these structures some of the qualities developed in exhibitions and in stores or cultural monuments. The architect who most clearly realized the potential and the

046, 047. Victor Horta, Maison du People, Brussels, 1899.

underlying logic of the space of movement and dissipation was Frank Lloyd Wright. Working in a suburb of Chicago called Oak Park, he began to develop prototypes for exploiting a place's spatial implications. In 1904, he designed two structures that provided an entirely new model for spatiality. The first of these was Unity Temple, a cubic volume surmounted by a flat roof extending far beyond what would be necessary for eaves. At its corners, what look to be massive piers rise up, but fall short of the ceiling, ending at the middle of a line of clerestory windows. Only from a distance can you see that the actual interior volume is higher, and that the piers and walls where the windows are located form a second layer around the building. There is no door visible here. Instead, you have to walk past a long wall, into the heart of the suburban block, face a subsidiary volume, turn sharply to the left, and then enter into an extremely dark and low area. Here you are surrounded by smaller versions of the shifting, layered planes, implying both volume and the lack thereof, that you had encountered on the building's exterior. A few more turns, and you suddenly find yourself in the main sanctuary. It is filled with light but is not a glass-and-metal greenhouse. Instead, the building's structural grid frames the skylights. Piers at the corner appear to be holding up the roof, but balconies float between them. Everywhere planes shift, slide, and stack up in front of you, frustrating your ability to understand the building's logic, but creating a sense of a space that has no boundaries. Wright was dissolving the building into its parts and setting them free. He was, as he said in a 1904 essay, "breaking the box."

At the Larkin Building, an office structure Wright designed for a soap manufacturer in Buffalo, New York, around the same time, the box was even more enigmatic and the sense of spatial freedom it released must have been even more exhilarating (the building was torn down in 1950). Here the corner piers became everything—they were massive and completely blank, containing only stair towers. It was as if the columns that marked important buildings had turned into functional masses at a grand scale. Between these flanking rectangles, a facade

049

050

048. Frank Lloyd Wright, Midway Gardens, Chicago, 1914.

049. Frank Lloyd Wright, Unity Temple, Oak Park, Illinois, 1908.

050. Frank Lloyd Wright, Larkin Building, Buffalo, 1904.

consisting of a grid of windows hid behind two smaller piers that held up globes. As with the Unity Temple, you did not enter into the front, but slipped around to the side, where the structure came apart into more massive piers, between which you moved to again arrive, after several turns, into one vast hall, eight stories tall. At the bottom of the hall, a grid of desks were surrounded by balconies where the clerks and company officials sat in serried rows of identical desks and chairs also designed by Wright. Here you could finally inhabit the urban grid as a vast new void.

Wright filled the Larkin Building with technical innovations, including cantilevered chairs attached to desks so that the cleaning crew could sweep underneath them. What made the building most remarkable was its naked revelation of the order inherent in the modern city. The architecture began to peel away from the structure, letting space flow freely around the columns and cantilevered

85

051 052

planes while you also moved through, along, past, and into spaces that seemed to have no beginning and no end.

In 1913, Frank Lloyd Wright designed the freest expression of his architecture. Midway Gardens in Chicago was really no more than a collection of open pavilions devoted to eating, drinking, and dancing. The architecture consisted essentially of towers: brick and concrete spires that contained small spaces or that were grouped together to define other spaces. Roofs, shelves, and eaves cantilevered off these vertical elements in a horizontal direction, and ornamental metalwork shot up in the other direction, emphasizing their verticality. Between these towers were endless steps, planes, balconies, terraces, and other places for people to gather or move around. Midway Gardens was really just an overblown café turned into a landscape. Where he could, Wright avoided giving you any sense of being in a defined space by allowing walls to overlap and open up as the floor level changed. Midway Gardens was a place built for the pure pleasure of being in a place, and it celebrated the completely undefined qualities of that space.

Places of entertainment and spectacle took the fluidity of space as far as it could go. As the Industrial Revolution progressed, bringing an ever larger scale of spectacle to more and more people, the potential to create spectacular spaces became even greater. Of these spaces, the most remarkable was the Jahrhunderthalle in Breslau (today Wroclaw), Poland. Designed by City Architect Max Berg and completed in less than two years in 1913, it is a giant cupola—the largest in the world at the time it was built. Constructed out of reinforced concrete, the Jahrhunderthalle resembles a group of nested circles stacked on top of each other, leaving only strips of clerestory lighting to separate them from each other. Though the entrances are traditional temple fronts (albeit stripped down to their simplest forms), the Jahrhunderthalle's main space gives you a sense of pure geometry. Bare concrete is all you see: this building does not hide how it was built. It sits in its own new park, dedicated to pure civic enjoyment and created as part of the infrastructure by which the city was trying to answer its growth, while on the inside the hall can accommodate any kind of activity. The Jahrhunderthalle made the temporary structures of the nineteenth-century expositions permanent.

Thus, everywhere in Europe and America, and increasingly on other continents as well, monuments to the new were appearing. The rationalization of urban design was leading to copies of the plans used in Paris, Chicago, and Vienna. The department stores and galleries, the exposition spaces and the theaters, the railroad stations and their railroad lines, were corroding traditional space. Movement appeared, and with it freedom and the importance of appearance itself. Fixed forms began to melt away. Architects slowly began to realize that they not only were faced with creating variations of new types or finding a proper form for boulevards, stores, or stations, but that they had to invent a new approach to the definition, enclosure, and representation of space.

The German architect Bruno Taut, while convalescing from the First World War, dreamed of such an architecture as a form of salvation. In his Alpine Architecture notebooks of 1919, Taut sketched a new city that would arise out of the mountains. This new structure would not mimic the pistons of engines, the stretch of roads, or the reach of skyscrapers melded into a unity, but would replace all those with a single form: a giant glass dome that would encompass the whole city. In the artificial Eden created by this greenhouse, finally liberated from the hidden heart of buildings or exile on fairgrounds to shine forth as an emblem of the new, a new democracy would come together. He was inspired by the architectural visionary Paul Scheerbart, who in 1914 wrote:

051, 052. Max Berg, Jahrhunderthalle, Wrocław, 1911-1913.

053. Bruno Taut, *Alpine Architecture Notebooks*, 1919.

87

054

> The surface of the Earth would change greatly if brick architecture were everywhere displaced by glass architecture. It would be as though the Earth clad itself in jewelry of brilliants and enamel. The splendor is absolutely unimaginable. And we should then have on the Earth more exquisite things than the gardens of the Arabian Nights. Then we would have a paradise on Earth and would not need to gaze lovingly at the paradise in the sky. (Scheerbart, *Glass Architecture*)

Taut felt that his architecture would create new and better social conditions, translating the discoveries of technology through form, figure, and space into a lived reality.

Taut was never able to build his dream, but right before the First World War he had produced a small emblem of that utopian ideal. The Glass Pavilion he designed for the 1914 Werkbund Exhibition in Cologne was a colored glass dome meant to celebrate the achievements of that industry. Rather than being a pure, classical dome, it had an elongated shape that looked somewhat like a large bullet. Taut placed it not only on a plinth, but also on a row of slender, concrete panels. You had to walk up to the podium underneath the enigmatic objects and along curved stairs before you entered into the exhibition area, where an eerie light and what seemed like the fragments of an endless geometry surrounded you.

But the pavilion was still recognizable as a building. In Europe, a new challenge arose. On February 20, 1909, the good citizens of Paris opened their morning newspaper and received quite a shock. The complete front page of Le Figaro was taken over not by news of war or famine or political upheaval, but by a strange hybrid of an autobio-

054. Bruno Taut, Glass Pavilion, Cologne, 1914.

graphical essay and a manifesto. "We have been up all night, my friends and I," it began, evoking a dream state in the eclectic middle-class interior:

> beneath mosque lamps whose brass cupolas are bright as our souls, because like them they were illuminated by the internal glow of electric hearts. And trampling underfoot our native sloth on opulent Persian carpets, we have been discussing right up to the limits of logic and scrawling the paper with demented writing…
>
> "Come, my friends!" I said. "Let us go! At last Mythology and the mystic cult of the ideal have been left behind. We are going to be present at the birth of the centaur and we shall soon see the first angels fly! We must break down the gates of life to test the bolts and the padlocks! Let us go! Here is the very first sunrise on earth! Nothing equals the splendor of its red sword which strikes for the first time in our millennial darkness."
>
> We went up to the three snorting machines to caress their breasts. I lay along mine like a corpse on its bier, but I suddenly revived again beneath the steering wheel—a guillotine knife—which threatened my stomach. A great sweep of madness brought us sharply back to ourselves and drove us through the streets, steep and deep, like dried up torrents…
>
> We drove on, crushing beneath our burning wheels, like shirt-collars under the iron, the watchdogs on the steps of the houses.
>
> Death, tamed, went in front of me at each corner offering me his hand nicely, and sometimes lay on the ground with a noise of creaking jaws giving me velvet glances from the bottom of puddles.

"Let us leave good sense behind like a hideous husk and let us hurl ourselves, like fruit spiced with pride, into the immense mouth and breast of the world! Let us feed the unknown, not from despair, but simply to enrich the unfathomable reservoirs of the Absurd!" (Marinetti, "Manifeste du Futurisme")

And so it went on, ending with a car crash that left the author in a muddy ditch that, strangely, reminded him of the arms of his Abyssinian wet-nurse. What followed was the actual manifesto, itself a strange grab bag of machine imagery, the glorification of war and speed and great masses and every other aspect of the modern world, and a desire to translate that love into highly aestheticized objects. "Standing on the world's summit we launch once again our insolent challenge to the stars!" was its conclusion.

The manifesto's author was the writer and polemicist F. T. Marinetti, who used the essay as the launching pad for his very own movement, Futurism. He and the group of artists, architects, and writers he collected around him believed that a new world was being born, and that it was up to them not only to describe it and sing its praises, but also to help let the new explode through the old by the very power of their imagery.

The architect who became most associated with the movement was the young Antonio Sant'Elia. He wrote his own manifesto on Futurist architecture, in which he proclaimed:

> We must invent and rebuild the Futurist city: it must be like an immense, tumultuous, lively, noble work site, dynamic in all its parts; and the Futurist house must be like an enormous machine. ... That Futurist architecture is the architecture of calculation, of audacity and sim-

055. Antonio Sant'Elia, Città Nuova, 1914.

plicity; the architecture of reinforced concrete, of iron, of glass, of pasteboard, of textile fiber, and of all those substitutes for wood, stone, and brick which make possible maximum elasticity and lightness. (Sant'Elia, "Manifesto of Futurist Architecture")

Sant'Elia also tried to design structures that illustrated how the new world should appear. It would rise, much as Marinetti and his friends did after their car crash, out of the earth itself. There would be no single buildings standing in a grid. Instead, the "New City," as Sant'Elia dubbed it, would rise like a mountain range into peaks that could be—as far as one could tell from the evocative, but not always very specific pen and ink drawings—apartment buildings, office towers, or some other component of the urban fabric. Some of the structures Sant'Elia designated as "power plants" or "monuments," but mainly they were just masses rising up from splayed bases, past grids of windows and pylons to crenellated crowns. It was as if the architect was trying to build Frank Lloyd Wright's vision of the city as beast, robot, and machine all at the same time.

The New City was an amalgamation not just of buildings, but of all the infrastructure that fed the places to work, live, and play: giant elevated highways or train tracks and even airplane landing fields were part and parcel of the urban geography Sant'Elia depicted. Here the new was rising as a single force, sketched in the most abstract outlines.

Sant'Elia never managed to translate his vision into built form. He was killed in the First World War for which the Futurists had so fervently hoped and which to some was the logical outcome of the Industrial Revolution itself. Though the war did not lead to the creation of a utopia, it did create a kind of tabula rasa on which some dreams of new worlds were realized. The Futurists, all members of the middle class, wanted to destroy the world which that class had made and which they themselves inhabited. If this seems like a contradiction, it is also the fulfillment of Marx and Engels's prediction that the middle class and their world would dissolve as social forces did away with more of the very conditions that had created them. Whether or not that was the reason for the dissolution of middle-class space, it is amazing how what began as a rational place of movement abstracted and corroded more and more buildings, created more and more space, and then became an emblem and a force in the dissolution of society itself.

The First World War was to many the trauma that ended the first era of the invention and development of a middle-class society. The war can certainly be seen as a turning point that marked the emergence of a total kind of space, one that had finally moved beyond the logic of the forces that had created it. The conflict brought total war into the heart of Europe, killed millions either directly or indirectly, leveled cities and landscapes as well as social distinctions, and bred social revolutions.

If you step back from the historical conditions that created the possibility for modernism to finally enter the mass-production of homes, cities, products, images, and spaces, however, you might say that the stage was set in the decade before the final bombs cleared out the fields of Flanders and caused the fall of so many old governments. That possibility for modernism started in 1908, when Henry Ford produced the first Model T and set the city on its way to becoming the setting for automation. Or perhaps it started in 1909, when Sigmund Freud proclaimed the division between the ego, the id, and the superego. Or it may have been in 1908, when Niels Bohr published his atomic theory. Or it may have been a more gradual process that arose from the accumulation of such events and the sheer build-up in scale and speed that turned our experience of everyday life into something that was no longer in our control and was even beyond our knowledge of what we saw. Modernism was the moment when the world as we could understand it became radically divorced from the world as we experienced it.

3. A NEW STYLE OF LIFE
artifacts of modernity

While the Industrial Revolution astonished with the sweep and abstraction of its great structures, people experienced its reality every day. For the millions at the lower end of the economic pyramid, it was a dark place—quite literally so: the pollution of cities such as London was suffocating. Modernity here presented a new kind of abstraction, one of blackness, dearth, and poverty.

The landscape through which most people moved was grim, featureless, and continually changing. There was little that did not change. Though already vast, the city was ever increasing in scale. Even the highly designed cores of some of the old cities, with their grand new cultural and political institutions, their parks, and their allées and boulevards, were places for movement and appearance, not sites that made you comfortable or at home. The new urban landscape was not one of belonging, but one of acting—trading, moving, and appearing. What those who controlled this new environment needed was an anchor, a place to call home.

The apartment or the house had to become that place. As much as modernism realized its ambitions in new public spaces and grand structures, its reality as most people experienced it consisted of smaller rooms filled with things. It was up to designers, whether amateur inhabitants or professionals, to make sense out of these places, and to make them inhabitable. They had to rely on the pieces they inherited or could assemble, placed within structures that were designed for them. They had to make a home within modernity.

Thus, the nineteenth century was the period when the middle-class interior came into its own. It became a space for the conscious collection, arrangement, and tuning of prefabricated elements into a whole that would provide an artifactural mirror to those who were making a place for themselves in the modern world. The middle-class interior was essentially eclectic, a three-dimensional collage of pieces and images in a space whose contours disappeared progressively as the interior composition came into being. As that space filled, it became strangely unified, turning into an amalgamation and abstraction of both times and places and the things that came from them (from furniture based on seventeenth-century French models to Chinese ceramics, for instance) that established an idealized version of how the middle class saw themselves. As it developed, this three-dimensional mirror moved out from the interior, becoming a style that marked buildings as being middle class.

Early in the nineteenth century, many different styles intersected in middle-class space, ranging from a sparse evocation of an invented classical civilization, to the lavish layering of neo-baroque salons, to the wooden capsules of neo-Gothic libraries. Perhaps the most effective name for such interiors was the French term, "Style Rothschild," after the elaborate and distinctly eclectic interiors that rich family assembled at their homes in France and England. In general, though, several themes ran through the cornucopia of furniture, carpets, wall hangings, curtains, and accoutrements that made up the middle-class interior.

The first was the free appropriation of historical styles in and of itself. For the first time in history, the interior could be anything you wanted or desired. Whereas in the past a family had been limited by what they had inherited, or by very traditional styles of furnishings that changed only very slowly over time, now you could choose, for instance, any of the "styles Louis": the grand, heavy baroque popular under Louis XIV, the frivolous and asymmetrical rococo of Louis XV, or the more disciplined and elongated forms popular under Louis XVI. Or you could go "exotic" and choose to import either motifs or whole objects from China, such as made-for-export Ming vases. There were no set rules, and all of these elements were available at the same time—if you had enough money to pay for them. When Queen Victoria traveled to Coburg, Germany, in 1860 to visit her husband's ancestral homes,

056. Chateau de Ferrieres, William Paxton , Eugene Lami et.al., Interior, Ferrieres-en-Brie, 1855 - 1859, Artist Unknown.

057

for instance, she brought back paintings of a variety of interiors that contained rococo chandeliers vying with heavy, baroque armchairs and carpets with both neo-classical and oriental motifs. But, based on the evidence of the images she collected, she apparently also encountered sober spaces with wood floors and simple chairs with lyre backs.

In such interiors, the middle-class family could create a microcosm of the whole world. They could make a physical mirror of the way in which, through knowledge and economic power, they could control more and more of the known universe. By collecting and arranging artifacts, they showed their ability to acquire bits and pieces from far-off places and times, and the knowledge to know which ones to choose and what to do with them. That knowledge, in turn, showed they had taste, which is to say that they had converted their economic power into a cultural one that distinguished them by those very choices from the lower classes, but also from the upper classes who might not have such connoisseurship. They could also create an arrangement that was logical, comfortable, and continually changing. This was their world, and it was modern in the sense that it gave them the freedom to create the personages they were making themselves to be.

Not only did the styles of furnishings increase, but the nature of their elements did as well. In the previous century, the courts of Europe (and especially the one at Versailles) had taken the use of chairs, for instance, as a means of establishing status to new heights. There were separate chairs not only for men and women, but for men and women of different status and age. Where you sat signaled who you were. The middle class of the nineteenth century took these distinctions even further, demanding chairs not only for the eldest, the middle, and the youngest son, but also for the different kinds of rooms where you might find the chair or uses to which you might put it. There was a particular chair designed to be used in the salon and the drawing room, one for the library, and one for the dining room. There were also summer chairs and winter chairs.

This specialization reached its highest degree in cutlery. There were implements for every imaginable sort of dish, as well as for every festive occasion, and sometimes even for every day of the week. The dishes of the nineteenth century also display an amazing variety of designs in a limited terrain, as well as all the variations on a basic round form you can imagine. Decorations could refer to the kind of fish or vegetable you might encounter on the plate as well as to the family's past.

This variety was a major engine of the cycle of production and consumption. With the availability of more plates for more occasions came a demand for an even greater choice. Factories and distributors as well as stores helped make these objects available, and magazines and books helped spread knowledge about them. Together, these furnishings and their images became a system that fed further demand for goods, encouraging innovation—or, if you look at it with a more cynical eye, an absurd degree of redundant objects. Hence the overstuffed look of the nineteenth-century domestic interior, but also the depth of the Industrial Revolution. For, the manufacturers and often even the craftspeople who fed the demand were themselves middle class. The production of goods was one of the reasons the Industrial Revolution occurred. We often concentrate on the factories and the great civic works, such as bridges and train stations, that marked this era, but the era's real home within these technological upheavals was the domestic interior.

What made the middle-class interior so comfortable was the increased availability of cloth in a larger variety of patterns. The availability of mass-produced wallpaper starting in the 1840s had been preceded by the ability of new looms to create large amounts of patterned carpet several decades before that. In England, lush Axminster carpets and more austere Kidderminster carpets sup-

057. English Axminster Carpet at The Blue Drawing Room in Buckingham Palace, London.

planted French Beauvais products. A middle-class interior could now banish any hint of its construction or of the outside world, and with it any sense of reality, in favor of the sylvan scenes, intertwined vines, or baroque fantasies that could cover floors and walls. Only the ceiling, hiding in semi-darkness beyond opulent chandeliers, remained relatively plain.

The middle-class interior, in other words, was padded and stuffed. Every part of the interior that could contain some form of cloth, usually as thick or filled with stuffing as possible, did. Not only the surfaces were covered, but so were the chairs, the tables, and every other bit of furniture. Doilies and throw rugs competed in their colors and patterning with the carpets and curtains. This wealth of pattern, color, and texture was a visible sign of wealth, but it also created comfort. It screened out the noise from the outside world, which was becoming increasingly cacophonous, and it cushioned the body from the harshness of mass-produced goods. A middle-class person could bask in the patterns and comforts of the interior, forgetting the reality just beyond the windows.

058. John Nash, The Great Banqueting Hall at Royal Pavilion, Brighton, 1826.

The "grand styles" or the "style Rothschild" and the mass-produced variations on furnishings whose basic forms had been set by the eighteenth-century French court, or by the Hanoverian kings in England a little later, lost their popularity as the century went on, first in the major style centers, such as London, Paris, and Vienna, and then in provincial capitals. Instead, interiors began to evoke other traditions and places. The medieval was the most popular choice, and the taste for "the Gothic" (which in reality meant anything made of carved wood, with arches and floriated decoration, including furniture that resembled Romanesque and even Italian Renaissance models) merged with the so-called Arts and Crafts traditions to represent the longing for a more organic community tied to the land and faith. Soon, however, the incredible profusion of goods coming from Europe's colonies began to enter the middle-class interior. First came Chinese and Japanese porcelain and some furniture, then screens and more elaborate pieces; finally, designers began copying what they assumed were the interiors for which the Asian pieces had originally been destined. Chinoiserie also had eighteenth-century aristocratic roots, but it soon became a sign for exotic retreat in dens, withdrawing rooms, and other more private spaces in apartments and townhouses all over the Western world. Then Moorish and other North African motifs entered the middle-class home, bringing a profusion of carpets and carvings with intricate geometric designs.

The models for these interiors remained royal. In England, exotic interiors that mixed Arabic, Gothic, and Asian motifs became popular after John Nash completed the Royal Pavilion in Brighton for the Prince Consort, later George IV, in 1823. The building celebrated the wealth of India, the country's greatest colony, and transformed that bounty both literally and figuratively into the ordered spaces of the English ruling order. In Germany,

102

the model for domestic places of retreat was the type of fantasy castle "Mad King Ludwig" the Second had built around Bavaria (especially Neuschwanstein, designed by Peter Herwegen and completed in 1869, which became the model for Disneyland's Magic Castle). Ludwig had started by commissioning a miniature version of Versailles for himself, but over the years he retreated further away not only from the city of Munich and its intrigues, but also from canonical trappings of grand style. He reached the deepest recesses of retreat in a grotto he had constructed under the palace at Herrenchiemsee, a place where architecture dissolved into a truly organic, womblike space.

Perhaps the greatest monument of middle-class interior design was Fonthill Abbey, designed by James Wyatt between 1796 and 1807 for William Beckford, then the richest man in England. The building reached a scale and complexity that made it a complete alternative to the outside world. Beckford was the ultimate parvenu, the son of the owner of sugar plantations who had bought himself into the English aristocracy; he thus represented the validation of the newly wealthy middle class in England. He was also homosexual and a romantic. After his liaison with a distant cousin was discovered, he exiled himself to the abbey, which was then considered to be at the furthest reaches of civilization, and devoted himself to writing novels as well as to collecting. At the latter, he was voracious: his library helped found the British Library, while his artifacts became one of the core components of the British Museum. The abbey he had designed to house his life resembled a hybrid of an Elizabethan country estate with medieval remnants and the kind of grand abbey Henry VIII had destroyed. Its interiors ranged from a sedate library to a den completely covered with a spider's web of Gothic fan vaults and a central hallway that soared up to a purely ornamental tower that was so high and so light that it collapsed soon after construction.

059. John Nash, Royal Pavilion, Brighton, 1826.

060. Christian Jank Franz Seitz, Georg von Dollmann, Germany, 1878-1885.

061. George Cattermole, Fonthill Abbey, Interior, 1823.

062

063

By the middle of the nineteenth century, the neo-Gothic and other, more exotic forms of primitivism were accepted ways of housing the new institutions of the middle class. The style allowed the middle class to build alternatives to the palaces of the lords and to refine the medieval mass out of which they were molding a new city. Its articulated, spindly forms and large spaces also proved to go well with the new technology of iron and glass and the demands for large new spaces, as in train stations with their Gothic fronts and glass shed exteriors. Deane and Woodward's 1860 Oxford Museum, with its Gothic facade and sky-lit courtyard, became the model for many similar structures.

Yet, the Gothic style was only a way station in the middle class's search for its own space. They adopted and adapted other medieval variants, Asian styles, and Arab motifs, as well as even more exotic elements, such as bits and pieces from the Americas. Soon all these elements became mixed together, often with little regard for what would seem to be their mutually exclusive forms and textures, through the Arts and Crafts movement. Arts and Crafts designers saw in all these exotic products a single aspect that interested them the most: a more "primitive," honest, and organic approach to furnishings that stood in opposition to the finish and elaboration of industrially manufactured goods. Wood was used in such a way that you could understand how it had been sawn, cut, and carved; carpet designs mimicked flowers and bushes; and walls could be made to look as if they were windows into what appeared to be the gardens of paradise regained. James McNeill Whistler's 1877 Peacock Room, now in the Freer Gallery of Art in Washington, D.C., showed how a generally Japanese set of elements could be combined with some Gothic lines and modern fixtures to create a sense that you were in a garden pavilion in some faraway place—even though you were in the middle of the industrialized city.

062. Thomas Newenham Deane, Benjamin Woodward, Oxford University Museum of Natural History, Oxford, 1861.

063. James McNeill Whistler, Peacock Room, Washington, D.C 1877.

Behind the movement from eclecticism, through neo-Gothicism, to the fluid forms of the turn of the century, a wealth of theory arose. Gottfried Semper, the young rebel who had fled Vienna in 1848, claimed in his 1851 treatise *The Four Elements of Architecture* that, rather than being based on a primal form of shelter—the primitive hut—the roots of architecture lay in the more elemental act of weaving together of twigs into a covering or wall. This enclosure was an intensified version of nature that established a realm apart, around the hearth, where humans gathered. Architecture should represent this history in its very forms, Semper argued. Though wood and stone columns and beams had later come to provide a structural framework, the majority of the building's surfaces were still no more or less than a form of covering. The true model for the house was not the classical temple, Semper wrote, but the nomadic tent. The French theorist Viollet-le-Duc made a parallel argument about the centrality of nature in design, positing that the truly great traditions in architecture came out of the imitation of nature in their structure: both the Gothic cathedrals and the bourgeois salon should have an organic logic.

In 1862, John Ruskin published *The Two Paths*, a series of lectures he had given about the role of art in the age of Industrial Revolution, which gave these theories a social dimension. Not only should the architect and the maker of furniture and furnishings imitate nature, Ruskin argued, but human beings should also recall a long tradition of making with natural materials as a reaction against the spread of homogenous, mass-produced objects. Ruskin hated the factories that were then spreading across England and revolted against the metropolitan sprawl they brought with them. He had a vision of a nation made up of small villages where people would engage in handicraft in order to create a community. Ruskin also believed in an organic architecture, eschewing the abstract forms of the classical tradition in favor of what he thought were the more natural forms that had been developed between the fall of the Roman Empire and the advent of the Renaissance. In this he agreed with the likes of Semper and Viollet-le-Duc, but he took his ideas even further. What the world needed, Ruskin thought, was a complete system of production and consumption, and the environments that went with it, that would bring human beings back to an honest relation to each other and their environment.

In essence, Ruskin dreamed of a completely middle-class world without the Industrial Revolution. It would be a community dedicated to craft and producing artful beauty in everything it made. Hence the name that Ruskin's followers gave to the movement he helped spawn and they developed: Arts and Crafts. Though there were other roots to this movement, this particular modernist style developed mainly through Ruskin's followers, who turned *The Two Paths* into the most popular book on design and art of the whole century. Arts and Crafts furniture took all of the historical styles available to designers and simplified them. It took off as much ornament as possible, concentrating on only those incisions and additions that would emphasize the essential lines of each piece. The dominant influence on furniture design became a kind of generalized vision of medieval design, though influences as disparate as Japanese art and neo-classicism crept in over time. The best artists, such as William Morris and C. R. Ashbee, fused all these influences and melded them into something that was truly new. Arts and Crafts homes such as the so-called Red House, designed by Philip Webb in 1860, presented the domestic interior as a place where all furnishings and architecture not only were crafted with care, but were woven together into a seamless alternative to the grand styles and the giddy piling-up of elements that marked the emergence of the middle-class interior.

The Arts and Crafts interior did not announce a particular status or use, but instead presented itself as another place, rooted in an ancient, unassailable past. It had to be judged not by one's knowledge of the history of its artifacts and antiques, nor by the exact profession or wealth of its inhabitants, but by a combination of two altogether

064. Gottfried Semper, Münchner Festspielhaus Entwurf, 1865.

065. Philip Webb, Red House, Bexleyheath, 1859.

066. Violet Le Duc, *Entretiens sur l'Architecture*, 1864.

067. C.R. Ashbee, Undated Photograph.

new standards: artifactural literacy and taste. You had to know which knife to use and where to sit. To determine the correct course of behavior, you had to use your judgment, but the design of the chair or the knife also expressed its proper use. The designer, in other words, had to represent function in each object. Whether you liked the object had to do with this functional correctness, but also with how well you thought the maker had used function, material, decoration, and place to create a coherent and elegant object. That judgment would draw on your historical knowledge (you had to know how a chair or a knife evolved), your understanding of domestic rituals, an ability to recognize materials, and an elusive sense of proportion and appropriateness that you could gain only through sufficient training and experience.

The elements of the Arts and Crafts aesthetic were not just reserved for the very wealthy. William Morris produced wallpaper and other artifacts, and C. R. Ashbee set up a London store where he sold the products of his utopian community outside of the city. Potteries such as Rookwood in Cincinnati and furniture manufacturers such as Gustav Stickley in upstate New York began producing simplified versions of the high art implements in the farthest reaches of the Western world. The eclectic style and its blended essence, Arts and Crafts, became the lingua franca of culture around the world—it became the way you could recognize a middle-class interior from the salons of San Francisco to a cattle station in Australia's outback.

It was, in fact, outside of Europe's great capitals that this assembly of mass-produced goods and the aesthetic that underlay them transformed itself into something more coherent and more radically different. In the countries and regions of central Europe, then striving to define themselves as independent from Austrian-Hungarian, Russian, German, and even Swedish overlords, the new institutions of the middle class, such as museums, as well as their homes, tried to resurrect what they saw as a peasant culture that predated the colonization they so resented. In Hungary, the style combined Gothic elements with vaguely Turkish influences, as in the Museum of Decorative Arts designed by Ödön Lechner and completed in 1896. You can see a desire to create a pan-Slavic style in this fantastic pile of brick in two colors with tiled roofs (including onion domes). On the inside, however, Lechner went even further afield, combining Persian motifs with classical columns, softening their rigidity into something that perhaps tried to make an argument for Hungary as a meeting place between Eastern and Western cultures. The work of István Medgyaszay and especially Károly Kós took the desire for a national style even further into the realm of wooden houses and churches that tried to meld traditional building practices with a more symmetrical, classical plan.

The style came from often liberal interpretations of what a particular area's past might have been. The Vienna-trained Josef Plecnik returned to his earthquake-ravaged home in Ljubljana after a successful career in Prague to knit the small city back together again with a series of public projects. Starting with the market halls and "Triple Bridges" between 1927 and 1932, he inserted a classicism that looked as if it had been dug up in ancient ruins of the Roman civilization to which the city traced its founding. In Copenhagen, Ragnar Östburg's City Hall of 1911 claimed a tradition of brick building, now disciplined by classical elements, but stretched into an abstracted and elongated version of its medieval sources. In the Netherlands, the "Golden Age" of the seventeenth century reappeared as cleaned-up canal houses built on the site of the ruins of former merchants' homes. Amsterdam's Rijksmuseum, designed by State Architect Pierre Cuypers as a neo-Renaissance mixture of brick and stone trimmings, opened in 1885 as a celebration of what the architect saw as the national style of a nation that had formed only a few decades earlier.

068. C.F. Stickley, Chair, Undated Photograph.

069. Ödön Lechner, Museum of Decorative Arts, Budapest, 1896.

Together with the music, visual arts, theater, and literature of the time, this architecture tried to literally con-

070

struct a native culture that would be both independent of the ruling superstructure and rooted in a place. Nevertheless, the spatial arrangements of these buildings were remarkably similar. Almost all European architects of note had been trained either at the École des Beaux-Arts in Paris, the central and completely dominant academy for the profession around the world, or by schools that imitated its methods. They had learned that the organization of space was based on certain pseudo-scientific rules, as well as on an aesthetic of symmetry, hierarchy, and progression that had been established under Louis XIV by the Académie des Beaux-Arts. Whether a town hall was in Copenhagen or in Budapest, it would have the same elements. All that changed from place to place was the cloak: the "character" of the building could be different, depending on the material you used, the ornament you applied, the way you manipulated certain proportions, and how you furnished the building.

Of these elements, ornament was the most widely debated, and was seen by many architectural theoreticians as the key to the establishment of the style and character of a building. However, it was the integration of that ornament into Gothic or Moorish arches, and the continuation of these elements into chairs and cabinets, that really set the tone for these new environments. The most successful projects, such as the Rijksmuseum, relied on the ability of the architect to design every single element in the building, from the newel posts to the spire, and from the benches to the wall coverings, in order to create a complete sense of another place.

In the works of Edward Lutyens in the United Kingdom, Eliel Saarinen in Finland, Henri van de Velde in Belgium, and Hendrik Berlage in the Netherlands, to name but three prominent examples, all of the Arts and Crafts influences melded into deformations of standard types. They made houses and buildings that were not only *Gesamtkunstwerke* (total works of art), in the phrase Wagner had coined in an essay of that title in 1849, but also were fluid in the ways they combined both forms and historic references. Lutyens' country houses resembled melted versions of medieval castles or Queen Anne style homes, while Berlage reinvented the Amsterdam Stock Exchange in 1903 as a combination of a church—complete with a bell tower and the exchange as the nave—a row of brick houses, and an urban office building with a grid of windows.

In the United States, architects begin to push and pull at the Beaux-Arts models. Though American monuments followed all the rules, after the Civil War, houses began to appear that had a rambling, free-form organization. Because they often sheltered under exaggerated roofs covered with shingles, this form of architecture came to be known as the Shingle Style. These houses—such as Peabody and Stearns' Kragsyde, built in Manchester-by-the-Sea, Massachusetts, in 1882, or McKim, Mead, and White's 1887 William Low House built in Bristol, Rhode Island—seemed rooted to the ground, their base often consisting of abstracted versions of the rocks on which they sat. The roofs mirrored the land, providing a shelter-

070, 071. Jože Plecnik, Market Hall, Liubljiana, 1931–1939.

072. Pierre Cuypers, Rijksmuseum, Amsterdam, 1885.

ing cloak. Between these two planes, the house developed as a rambling assembly of rooms, each open to the other and most of them open to the outside, often with windows so large that you could step out of them onto surrounding porches.

The free-flowing space of the Shingle Style house was the result of the assimilation of Asian influences to a degree that European architects had not dared, or, because of the constricted sites in which they worked, had not been able to pursue. Its roots in fact lay in India, where the "bungalow" was a form of colonial dwelling based on native traditions suited to a warm climate. It had come to the United States by way of the West Coast, and was perhaps the first example of a complete building type from the colonies that had become the basis for a domestic form of construction. That itself marked the Shingle Style as a strange confluence of traditions in an increasingly global culture. Yet, it was also American, both in that it integrated elements in a way that was free from some of the preconceptions still governing building in America, and in the way it was designed to make use of a standard building lot. Finally, it was also the result of mass-production and new technology: mill-cut lumber in standardized sizes ("two-by-fours") that were assembled into structural plates and assembled on-site to create a "balloon frame." Here architecture began to dissolve the difference between structure and infill and started to resemble an open web in which one could shelter. The architect had only then to exploit that freedom and express the moment of sheltering.

With Frank Lloyd Wright, the middle class truly learned how to be at home in the nervous, fractured, indeterminate space of the modern world. His houses literally brought them home. Wright took the strong roof and base, the rambling rooms, and the extensive spaces of the Shingle Style to their logical extreme in designs that collectively became known as the Prairie Style. In a series of house designs that culminated in the elongated lines of the 1908 Robie House, he used a central fireplace as a pivot around which the house could spin out to take possession of its suburban lot. To Wright, the fireplace was the place of gathering imbued with a mystical sense of belonging that, like so much inspiration for designers at the time, went back to primeval times. Its chimney also served to pin the house down to its site. From there, rooms moved out to the light and to the edges of the fraction of the Jeffersonian grid the architect could command. They did so freely, in geometries that did not form a closed grid, but that consisted of elongated lines slipping by each other in space. Along the way, levels might change both above and below you, and rooms might bleed into each other or have strange knuckles of space that acted as miniature anterooms or shrines. It all added up to a flow of solid and void, of space focused, constrained, and released in a structure that came in and out of focus.

Wright wanted to tame and contain the new world, rather than isolating its inhabitants from its realities. He wanted

073. Hendrik Berlage, Amsterdam Stock Exchange, Amsterdam, 1896-1903.

074. Peabody & Stearns, Kragsyde, Manchester by the Sea, 1883.

075. Frank Lloyd Wright, Robie House, Chicago, 1905-1910.

to give it a place, a measure, and a sequence, as if time also could be allied to space. His architecture became a bulwark against the modern world exactly because it was able to let his clients live in the spaces out there in the suburbs that modernity made possible.

In Europe, where such freedom was not popular or possible, architects instead pushed the Arts and Crafts style continually further until all its elements began to meld and even melt together. In Barcelona, one of the cities that benefited most from industrialization in the Mediterranean area, and that had a long tradition of middle-class culture, the "modernisme" style developed out of the same medievalizing roots of so many of the regional variants of the late nineteenth century. Here, however, architects such as Antonio Gaudi stretched the relation between medieval forms and nature even further. If the Casa Vicens, of 1885, was still a more or less conventional Arts and Crafts effort, distinguished by the elaborateness of its mainly ceramic decorations of birds, vegetative matter, and Moorish patterns, in the Guell Palace of 1889 the walls began to melt, decoration and structure becoming difficult to distinguish. Gaudi's most famous middle-class dwelling, the Casa Mila apartment building of 1910, took the standard arrangement of such multi-unit structures and smoothed all the edges, both inside and out, into an object that looks more like a rock worn down by the Mediterranean Sea only a mile away.

Gaudi's most remarkable design (other than the Sagrada Familia, a fever dream of a Gothic cathedral, still under construction and slowly turning into the mystical rock of Montserrat outside of Barcelona) was not a building, but a park. It was part of a real estate development by the wealthy industrialist Eusebi Güell, who commissioned Gaudi to design a green center for a grouping of new homes on the edge of town, as was common in this period. (For example, Cuypers, the architect of the Rijksmuseum, designed his own house in a development he helped finance next to the new Vondelpark in Amsterdam.) The Parc Guell, however, turned from an excuse for real estate speculation into an exploration of how far an architect could dissolve the boundaries of architecture into nature, along the way melding the resulting stew of elements into a fairytale land. You enter the park by climbing up broad stairs that swell and rise with the landscape, which is made lush through extensive irrigation. As you climb, you pass by the sculpture of a monster covered in multihued ceramic tiles and spouting water. You wander on paths defined by rippling walls and small pavilions that seem to be covered with vegetation which turns out to be more artificial ornament. In the hillside, Gaudi carved a cave supported by twisting and leaning columns that resemble stylized tree roots. In this enclave, where the new owners of the homes and their friends could meander through their native land regained and disciplined by architecture, an artificial landscape opened up—one that contrasted the hard world of the city with an imagined world of fluidity.

That melting sensibility became known all over the Western world as the "new style." It was called "Jugendstil" in Germany, "art nouveau" in France, and "modernisme" in Spanish-speaking countries. Its most accomplished practitioners were the designers of furniture and furnishings. In France, Louis Majorelle based his designs on rococo models, but carried them out in wood, as used in Arts and Crafts, and deformed the curls and whiplash curves of the originals into lines that rose and fell up the body of the chests and chairs. At the same time, Émile Gallé used new materials, mainly metals, in combination with age-old glass-making techniques, to create forms in which flowers and plants turned into waves of pure color.

Art nouveau found its richest outlet in jewelry and toiletries, the elements of a middle-class woman's most personal space. Here precious jewels, silver, and gold could imitate natural forms with abandon, while adapting themselves to the skin and limbs of the body. It was as if that body itself was being extended out into space, while the deco-

076. Frank Lloyd Wright, Robie House, Chicago, 1905-1910.

077. Antoni Gaudí & Josep Maria Jujol, Parc Güell, Barcelona, 1914.

rative schemes of the home, the museum, and the department store were attaching themselves to their inhabitants. In the hand of such designers as René Lalique in France or Louis Comfort Tiffany in America, new techniques in enameling and the availability of exotic objects such as pearls enabled the creation of pieces of jewelry that were miniature fantasy environments where strangely beautiful insects crawled through thick forests only a fraction of an inch thick. People, their places, and their landscapes were becoming an integrated, artificial, and yet organic unity, a gilded version of the monster Frank Lloyd Wright had imagined the city becoming.

While jewelry made art nouveau more personal, graphic arts spread the style with ease throughout the Western world. New printing techniques, such as mechanized lithography, let companies create colorful images of their wares or services that could be plastered all around the city. Theaters and circuses led the way, in Paris employing the services of such luminaries as Toulouse-Lautrec. A new kind of artist appeared to create these images: the graphic designer. Trained in either woodcutting or fine arts, and sometimes in both, designers such as Aubrey Beardsley and Alphonse Mucha took the precepts of the Arts and Crafts movement, in which every object had to be beautifully designed, and extended it into the most ephemeral of media, that of the printed page. In Vienna, Koloman Moser reduced forms to heavy but also softly outlined blocks in designs such as the 1899 Fromme's calendar. Berthold Löffler created posters that were more fluid and evoked aquatic imagery, while the painter Gustav Klimt, especially in his 1898 poster for the Sezession, imagined a dreamlike classical civilization in which architecture, human bodies, and vegetation melted into each other.

Private presses, such as William Morris's Kelmscott Press, paved the way for further experimentation. Soon designers were melting what had been illustrations in the margins or at the beginning of a story into mere decorations and then into the text itself. Aubrey Beardsley's sexually tinted designs evoked a true fusion of the body and the world around it in the most abstract of media. In the Netherlands, Jan Toorop designed book covers such as that for Louis Couperus's 1898 *Psyche*, in which border and image blended together into a hallucinatory image. His posters for the Delftsche Slaolie Company of the same period did the same for humble products such as mayonnaise, mimicking their fluid nature in graphic forms.

Many of these arts came together in stores and in workshops. Liberty in London became so identified with the style that the style is sometimes named after the store. One of them even made its own world. Louis Comfort Tiffany, who became wealthy through the production of his stained glass and decorative objects, created a haven for himself outside of New York called Laurel Court. Finished in 1905, the house was a stone monolith that dissolved once you entered into it and Tiffany's stained glass proliferated in its windows and skylights, while ceramic decorations, plaster, and woodcarving further elaborated the paradisiacal motifs (with strong Arab influences). Tiffany both sold his aesthetic and made himself at home within it.

In Austria, the Wiener Werkstätte, which included such luminaries as Hans Hoffmann, began creating housewares that had the primitive form of peasant implements. With the help of theoreticians such as Adolf Loos, they also helped to push the notion of design beyond neo-primitivism or organicism toward a discovery of some more eternal and basic truth they felt lay underneath those forms. Their designs became elongated and simplified into abstract objects often made out of or adorned with precious materials.

The Werkstätte came out of the so-called Secession movement, one of the bands of artists who had been rejected by the official salons in Europe at the end of the nineteenth century. In Paris, they became the Impressionists and

078. Louis Comfort Tiffany, *Venetian* Desk Lamp, 1910.

079. Louis Majorelle, Cabinet, 1859-1926.

080. William Morris, Snakeshead Printed Textile, 1876.

081. Alphonse Mucha, *Bieres de la Muse*, 1898.

082. Koloman Moser, *Fromme Calendar*, 1899.

083

helped bring modernism to painting. In Vienna, they started a movement that turned inward toward the creating of a new environment. Their home became the 1898 Secession Building, designed by Josef Olbrich. It was a white building, almost unornamented, and unlike any other building along the Ring. Its most remarkable feature was a sphere made of what looked like metal string. Instead of the solid globe held up by Atlas, a trope of neoclassical buildings, it presented a geometric abstraction, almost dissolving into the air around it, held up by the piers of the building itself. Inside, artist Gustav Klimt created murals in which the distinction between figure and ground, between form and space, and between what was living and what was mineral began to dissolve into an overall pattern that resembled nothing so much as the ancient tapestry that Gottfried Semper had seen as the beginning of all architecture.

Olbrich and fellow architect Josef Hoffmann became part of the Werkstätte in an attempt to take this modernist aesthetic into the realm of mass production and thus into every home. They organized exhibitions and designed objects. Their tableware became especially popular and influential. Based, like the designs of so many of their contemporaries, on primitive or peasant forms, the tableware evoked a time before aristocratic styles, but also moved implements forward into a realm of pure geometry. Simple bowls became almost spheres; the long, straight, and unadorned stem of a fork could become a pure line.

What was important to these designers beyond the design of each individual object was their relation to each other and to the environment in which they were situated. Ideally, Hoffmann and his compatriots wanted to design everything, down to the clothes their clients wore. Only in one case, the luxurious Palais Stoclet, built in Brussels between 1905 and 1911, did Hoffmann truly succeed, but others picked up the notion of total design. Henri van de Velde not only designed chairs, which looked like the heavy, oaken furnishings of the Middle Ages—here drawn out into tapering arms, legs sweeping back, and backs rising up above the seated figure—but also drew everything from tea services to lampshades to carpets. In all of these objects, geometric forms dominated over direct references, proportions were broad and stretched out, and the scale was slightly larger than the use of any of the objects might merit.

In 1908, the Viennese architect and critic Adolf Loos wrote his own manifesto for modern architecture, "Ornament and Crime." In it, he criticized the very element by which architects of the nineteenth century had tried to make their buildings both up-to-date and part of a grand tradition as being the mark of a decadent society which has not learned that true culture is expressed clearly, honestly, and self-consciously. Embellishment or the mimicry of nature, said Loos, is an irrational waste of labor and a style for primitive cultures. The modern person must face the reality of his world, which is one formed by machine production, anonymous spaces, and the ability to shape one's life through logic. The modern man is a gentleman and bureaucrat, a "man without qualities," as Loos's friend Robert Musil put it in his 1921 novel of that title. He should have an architecture to match.

In 1900, Loos had made fun of van de Velde and his ilk by describing a middle-class client who is so in thrall to his architect that he has him design everything, down to the slippers. Unable to keep the cacophony of the outside world at bay, the owner arranges to have the tram outside roll by to the rhythm of a march. Yet, he fails in the end: on a visit, the architect is deeply offended when the client greets him in the salon while wearing clothing the architect had designed for the bedroom. The cycles of interior design, but also those of production and consumption, are coming to an end:

083. Joseph Maria Olbrich, Secession Building, Vienna, 1897.

> Then a transformation took place in the rich man. The happy man suddenly felt deeply, deeply unhappy. He imagined his future life.

No one was allowed to give him pleasure. He would have to pass by the shops of the city impervious to all desires. Nothing more would be made for him. None of his dear ones was permitted to give him a picture. For him there were to be no more painters, no more artists, no more craftsmen. He was precluded from all future living and striving, developing and desiring. He thought, this is what it meant to learn to go about life with one's own corpse. Yes indeed. He is finished. He is complete. (Loos, "The Poor Little Rich Man")

The middle-class interior had reached a point where its fullness turned into emptiness. Through gradual liberation and unification, but also through its isolation from the realities of modernization and its domestication of its elements, the middle-class interior became the place that reflected on or gave shape to modernity: it became the realm of modernism. Representing social and economic mores as well as aesthetic ones, the domestic interior became the distinguishing mark of the middle-class person who had arrived into a true possession of that status—the lack of which marked you as someone who was not yet ready to enter into the new bourgeois realm. It also marked what was supposed to be the end of the processes of modernization and their fulfillment, a kind of ideal stasis.

The empty space of the Ringstrasse became ringed with these enclaves of good taste, as did the new boulevards of Paris and the squares of London. Soon enough, taste spread from the interior back out into this public realm, causing a change of attitude about the home, which in retrospect were rather bombastic statements of the middle-class power that had been erected there. Good taste and later good design became the cloak that hid the origins of the goods and places the middle class inhabited from them. It turned real places into nebulous webs of aesthetic relationships that only the true connoisseur, the high priest of middle class-taste, could discern. Out of an artificial and artifactual space came a new kind of space, that of true modernism.

084. Henry Van de Velde, Office of the Havana Tobacco Company, Brussels, 1898.

085. Henry Van der Velde, Tea and Coffee Pots, 1904-1910.

4. AT HOME IN THE BRAVE NEW WORLD

By the time Adolf Loos was making fun of van de Velde and the completely designed interior with all of its crafted furniture, textiles, and objects, that kind of middle-class environment had become a mark of conservatism. The nostalgia for other times and places inherent in its eclecticism, along with its impulse to close its inhabitants off from the outside world, made it into a bastion of inward- and back-looking thinking and living. The place the middle class had made for itself became a retreat. Every man could have his castle, and imprison his woman inside it to bring up the children and create order in his life.

As the outside world kept growing in complexity and as technology created more and more ways to be connected to that world, it became more difficult to maintain that isolation. Some clients didn't even want to hide from the world they had helped to make; they wanted to embrace the modern world, even in their most private moments. A growing number of architects and designers felt that the only logical response to modernization was modernism: the representation of that new and continually emerging world.

Throughout the first few decades of the twentieth century, designers and their clients began experimenting with new forms of living. The middle-class home became the laboratory for modernism. It was a controlled environment, small enough that everything could be designed, and without a program that was too complex. It was a place where designers could experiment, and where inhabitants could develop their private visions. It was here that modernism made itself at home.

It was in a home that I first came to know modernism consciously when I was about fourteen years old. I was living in the Netherlands, and was writing a high school paper on the early-twentieth-century art movement named after its house organ, *De Stijl* (The Style). That magazine, which was published between 1917 and 1931, was the brainchild of Theo van Doesburg

086. Theo van Doesburg, *Composition VII*, 1917.

and several of his fellow artists, including the great manipulator of painted grids, Piet Mondriaan. They believed that in "neo-plastic" art the artist would reduce forms, colors, and spaces to their most basic elements. The reality of things as the artist portrayed them would disappear in favor of the most basic colors and geometries. Paintings would become abstract compositions. Then painting itself would disappear, dissolving into architecture. That architecture would in turn dissolve buildings into their most fundamental and abstract elements and then it, too, would disappear. In the end, the whole world would melt away, and pure spirit would reign. The artist was a revolutionary who would paint away reality in order to have a completely spiritual utopia appear.

Intrigued by this vision, I asked my teacher how far they had gotten in their dreams. I had seen their paintings in museums, but I could not imagine how those reds, blues, and yellows suspended in their black gridlines could turn into buildings. "You must go see my old friend, Mrs. Schroeder," she said; "she lives in a three-dimensional Mondriaan." She made an appointment for me, and one sunny spring morning I rode my bicycle five miles to Mrs. Schroeder's work of art.

What I found astonished me. The long row of brick houses I was bicycling along suddenly gave way to a composition of white and off-white planes that seemed to float in space, tethered to the ground only by sticks painted in yellow and held together by red-painted balconies. It was as if the basic elements inherent in all those brick houses had been pulled out of their brick confines and set free. The planes opened up to their surroundings, which, I learned later, had originally consisted of meadows sliced into equally geometric planes by irrigation ditches. Now an elevated highway cut the house off from the countryside, but not from the light and sky all around it.

I rang the doorbell, and the elderly Mrs. Schroeder let me in. The ground floor of the house was rather conventional, consisting of a few small rooms that had become crammed full of the kind of unused things a person who has lived in one house for what was then five decades collects. I did notice what became my favorite detail: one of the geometric planes became a black seat outside the window of what had been Mrs. Schoeder's son's room, so that a friend could sit outside and talk to him through the window. Probably because I was a rather lonely teenager, I loved the idea that architecture could make a new form of social relation possible.

Mrs. Schroeder led me upstairs, and there the world opened up. The whole second floor was one large room where the intersecting planes multiplied and intensified. I marveled at the intricate composition of the strips and stripes on the floor, ceiling, and walls, but quickly learned they had a function: the planes folded, slid on tracks, and clicked into place so that the room could be divided into two, three, or four separate spaces. Once Mrs. Schroeder had performed the miracle of subdivision, each of the spaces had its own integrity as a three-dimensional composition. Storage, beds, and furniture turned out to be integrated into the whole so that there was no distinction between what was fixed and what was moveable. In fact, the whole house was a mechanism for living that adapted itself to the needs of its inhabitants and that yet somehow, through the force of composition and ingenious manufacturing, managed to remain a beautiful whole of abstract colors and forms. The De Stijl artists had gotten much further than I imagined.

What I realize now, but perhaps did not as a teenager, was how radical the vision was not only visually, but also conceptually. In the Schroeder House, the intricacies of modern life combined, changed, and recombined to form patterns, rather than fitting themselves into an overall, pre-existing framework. The house was a giant piece of furniture, drawn up by a furniture designer. Its architect, Gerrit Rietveld, had little experience designing homes; until then his three-dimensional work had consisted of furniture and a few shop interiors. His most famous creation was a chair he designed in 1918 as the most reduced machine for sitting that you could imagine: the seat and the back were both straight, rectangular planes of plywood sitting on a nest of horizontal and vertical posts, all of the same square circumference. Two more slats for armrests completed the chair. A few years later, he painted the piece in primary colors, making the back red, the seat blue, and the posts black with yellow ends. The resulting "Red Blue" chair took an object of use into the realm of completely abstract and primal composition. You could sit in the most basic reduction of form and color.

Rietveld performed the same operation on chests, tables, and even children's toys. They all came out of the gathering of geometric solids, often painted in bright colors, to create things that were both objects of utility and completely self-sufficient compositions. Rietveld's architecture was an extension of that act of reductive composition. He extended the lines and planes out into space to create the

087. Gerrit Rietveld,
Schroeder-Schrader House,
Utrecht, 1924.

vitrines and the other elements in shop interiors. One of the shops he designed was for Mrs. Schroeder's husband, and thus he obtained the commission for this house.

In this way, Rietveld produced a "proof of concept" of the "plastic architecture" proclaimed by his friend and fellow member of the De Stijl movement, Theo van Doesburg, in an article in that magazine in 1924:

> Elimination of all concept of form in the sense of fixed type is essential to the healthy development of architecture and art as a whole. ... The new architecture is elemental; that is to say, it employs its elemental means as effectively and thriftily as possible and squanders neither these means nor the material. ... The new architecture is open. The whole structure consists of a space that is divided in accordance with the various functional demands. This division is carried out by means of dividing surfaces (in the interior) or protective surfaces (externally). The former, which separate the various functional spaces, may be movable; that is to say, the dividing surfaces (formerly the interior walls) may be replaced by movable intermediate surfaces or panels (the same method may be employed for doors). (van Doesburg, "Towards a Plastic Architecture")

Rietveld indeed did not enclose his box of wonders in a normal shell with a main facade facing the street. Instead, the Schroeder House became an intersection of planes and lines in primary colors that had a vaguely cubic shape, but that had no base, no front, and no roof. It was pure composition in space. It was as if Rietveld had turned the whole house into a sculpture you could use, but at the same time the lines brought out the structure and the planes inherent in the more normal row of houses that his design ended. He dissolved that construction into its essence, or into the gridded meadows and irrigation ditches onto which the house fronted beyond the row houses. The city and its architecture were falling apart into something so basic that it was dissolving into both the acts of daily life and nature at the same time.

"All that moving has made me hot," Mrs. Schoeder said. "Sit down and I'll make some tea. But let me open a window first." With that, she walked over to the small dining corner where a plain wooden plane served as one of few identifiable and sculptural elements, a table, with zigzag-shaped chairs that were folded planes producing something one could imagine could support the body. She reached over to the corner, undid a latch, and opened out two long, narrow sections of window. Suddenly, the corner of the room was gone, and, with a rush, I felt all the space around me open up and continue out into the garden. It was as if somebody had dissected my body and freed me to go floating out into space. Right then and there, I decided I wanted to be an architect.

Mrs. Schroeder deepened the desire by pouring me tea and telling me hours worth of stories about the members of the De Stijl group, many of whom had been her friends, some of whom apparently were her lovers, and all of whom had invented a new world in which she still lived. She herself had helped Gerrit Rietveld to design the house. "We were all revolutionaries, of course," she explained. "We all believed that we were changing the world." She spoke of epic fights among the artists, of exhibitions they had held, and the trips they had made to see the best new artworks and buildings everywhere in Europe. She told me of all the visitors, most of whose names I didn't recognize, but all of whom she made sound like romantic heroes of the modernist myth, who had made the pilgrimage to her little house on the outskirts of a provincial Dutch town.

I was sold. I was convinced by the architecture, but also by the dream that it was a way toward a new and better world. I was seduced by the romantic myth of fighting the establishment, the solidity of the world around one as well as social and aesthetic prejudices, in order to build a better, newer, and more honest world. I wanted to live, like Mrs. Schroeder, in that world.

I had the chance, though only briefly, several decades later, when I shared a small apartment in the back section of the Schindler House in Los Angeles with my husband. The Schindler House was never really a house in the traditional sense of a sheltering structure inhabited by one family. Rudolf Schindler, an Austrian émigré who had come to Los Angeles to work on some Californian projects for Frank Lloyd Wright, designed the building at the same time that the furniture maker Gerrit Rietveld designed Mrs. Schroeder's house for her. Schindler envisioned his structure not as a house, but as an open abode or shelter in what to him was the almost paradisiacal landscape of Southern California. The Schindlers were to share the house with the Chace family (Clyde Chace was a structural engineer), and it was to occupy a double lot in what were then the empty fields of West Hollywood. Schindler laid the house out not with function-specific rooms, but with person-specific spaces: a multipurpose studio for each of the four inhabitants, and a shared kitchen. The idea was that these were places where each inhabitant could do whatever they wanted to realize themselves: work, make music, read, or exercise. There were no bedrooms; instead, Schindler designed "sleeping baskets" on the roof: these were hammocks surrounded by a latticework of wood and stretched canvas.

The house's walls were concrete panels that were poured on the ground and then lifted into a vertical position (a technique called "tilt-up" that became quite popular in Southern California). A network of redwood beams held them in place. Sliding glass doors, also framed in redwood, made up as much of the wall as the concrete panels. The four rooms and the kitchen, along with a garage and guest room, zigzagged through the large lot, intersecting landscaped plots Schindler also designed as outdoor rooms.

Schindler's model was a camp where he had stayed in Yosemite Park. He saw the house as the thinnest possible armature for the social relations between its inhabitants, while also being a shelter or shade that would not cut them off from what he considered to be a completely benign nature. Architecture almost disappeared, serving only to mark space and to let you understand in a visible manner how to occupy that territory.

In reality, the winters proved too cold for the sleeping baskets to be practical, the two couples soon quarreled, and before long the compound became more like a regular house. But Schindler continued to build homes in Southern California that abstracted the landscape into horizontal and vertical planes, elaborated those elements to provide only minimal shelter, and then tied them together with a latticework of wood slats that helped define and articulate different spaces.

To Schindler and his fellow occupants, the Schindler/Chace House was an emblem of a new kind of life and a new society they saw arising in Southern California. Far away from the burdens of the past and all its prejudices, they imagined something that was not a city, but a concatenation of open grids cohering loosely as buildings that dissolved into nature. Like the members of De Stijl, they thought society and architecture would fall apart, but Schindler's version of that process was more concrete, quite literally: all that would be left would be a few concrete slabs and wooden frames, through which we would all wander, as naked as possible, through a landscape that technology let us inhabit.

Architects built such moments all over the world. In 1925, the Swiss-born architect who called himself Le Corbusier built a prototype for this new kind of dwelling as the "Pavilion of the New Spirit" for an exposition in Paris.

088. Rudolf Schindler, Schindler House, West Hollywood, 1921-1922.

He outfitted it with furniture he had designed with Charlotte Perriand or that he had gathered from other modernist architects. The pieces (other than a few Thonet chairs) were made out of bent metal and were as geometric and reduced as the planes that defined the double-height living room and the small bedrooms of the dwelling.

Le Corbusier had ideas and rules for these structures. In 1927, he published his "Five Points for Architecture" in the magazine he had helped found, *L'Esprit Nouveau*. A house, he said, should be lifted off the ground to disassociate it from the confusion and the disease he felt was inherent in the old city from which he wanted to escape. The columns that would raise the house up would form a regular grid of round points he called "pilotis." The land the house took up should be replaced on its flat roof as an artificial Eden, a roof garden devoted to sun, light, and exercise. Around the abstract geometry of the pilotis and between the horizontal planes, the plan could flow in complete freedom, adapting to the needs of each room. The facade itself would be free as well, as the pilotis and the stacked horizontal planes were the structure. However, the relationship with the rest of the world should be established by a *fenêtre en longueur*: a ribbon of windows at eye height that would connect the middle-class inhabitant to the horizon line and thus the larger world.

Between 1925 and 1929, Le Corbusier built three houses that perfectly illustrated his theories: the Villa Stein in Garches, the Villa La Roche in Paris, and the most fully realized of them all, the Villa Savoye in Poissy. That house was more than just a building that stood by itself—it was the end point of a journey that started when the owner left his Paris apartment and set out in his motorcar to his vacation home. Arriving at the house, the car swung around into the lot, drove between the pilotis and parked at an angle under the house. The owner would get out of the car, walk into a bull-nosed entry foyer enclosed in glass, and move up switchback ramps that continued the motion of the car into the domestic realm. Arriving on the house's single living floor, he would find a loft-like living area separated from the bedroom area by an internal courtyard. If he continued his motion up through the house, another ramp would take him up to the roof garden, where he would be liberated into a world of geometric forms that shaped an abstracted garden high above the ground and screened from the surroundings by a white windscreen.

The Villa Savoye was no more and no less than a line unfolding from the movement that was at the essence of modern life. It was not a place of static rooms, of the presentation of facades and the sequence of events that happened in either the rhythms of daily life or the receiving of guests, but was just the pure development of a new kind of space around a collection of columns, ramps, planes, and occasional objects. From the outside, the Villa Savoye was a box lifted up off the ground, without bottom or top and with no formal facade. It was at the same time a fragment of some urban machine and a piece of sculpture. If it had a heart, it was not the chimney or the central salon, but the bathroom, a place where the naked body would finally come to rest literally on the architecture: Le Corbusier designed a tile-covered chaise longue that split the bathroom down the middle, where you could repose, surrounded by columns and white walls under a skylight, and become completely part of the order Le Corbusier had established.

While Le Corbusier's other houses were not quite as extreme as the Villa Savoye, they all shared the same radical idea that, as he famously said, the "house was a machine for living in." As the domestic part of the world of technology and science, the house should be mass-produced and be as efficient as possible. It should look, if not like a machine, like something that a machine could produce. All this meant that the house should be a collage of abstract elements grouped into a composition that operated

089. Le Corbusier, Pavillon de L'Esprit Nouveau, Paris, 1925.
090. Le Corbusier, Villa Savoye, Poissy, 1929.

like a piece of machinery. Its components were pure structure, pure enclosure, and pure implements. No longer was there any question of decoration, or what style to use, or how you might respond to the building's given conditions, whether in terms of site or of people's expectations. There was only the arrangement of elements in space, with each class of components holding up or shaping space, or filling space with functions. That the actual houses still had recognizable traits was as much chance as anything; Le Corbusier was not trying to make houses or any other familiar type. He was trying to build the modern in such a way that you could see, understand, and inhabit it.

In the confines of Europe, the production of such a free space involved a lot of pushing and pulling and a lot of slipping and sliding in order to get free space. The master of such movements was the German architect Ludwig Mies van der Rohe. Trained by Peter Behrens, he started stripping away all that he felt was extraneous from his very first houses and on, while trying to free up as much space as he possibly could. In 1923, he designed a Brick Country House that was no more than lines moving through space without touching. He indicated no enclosure, no division, and no function. It was an abstract diagram of a house, the essence of a Prairie School design without any reality. It was architecture reduced, as he liked to say, to "almost nothing." When he did have a chance to build a villa that represented his ideas of what a modern house should be, he held on to the rectangular enclosure as the basic form, but then eliminated as much else as he could.

By the time I saw his Tugendhat House, in 2003, it was an almost ruinous empty structure, though it had been renovated several years before (it has since been meticulously restored, so that it, like the Schroeder House, is a bit of a frozen museum piece). Built for a Jewish family, it had housed both German and Russian soldiers, and then sat empty for many eras. Yet, the clarity of its singular statement remained. Van der Rohe designed the house for a

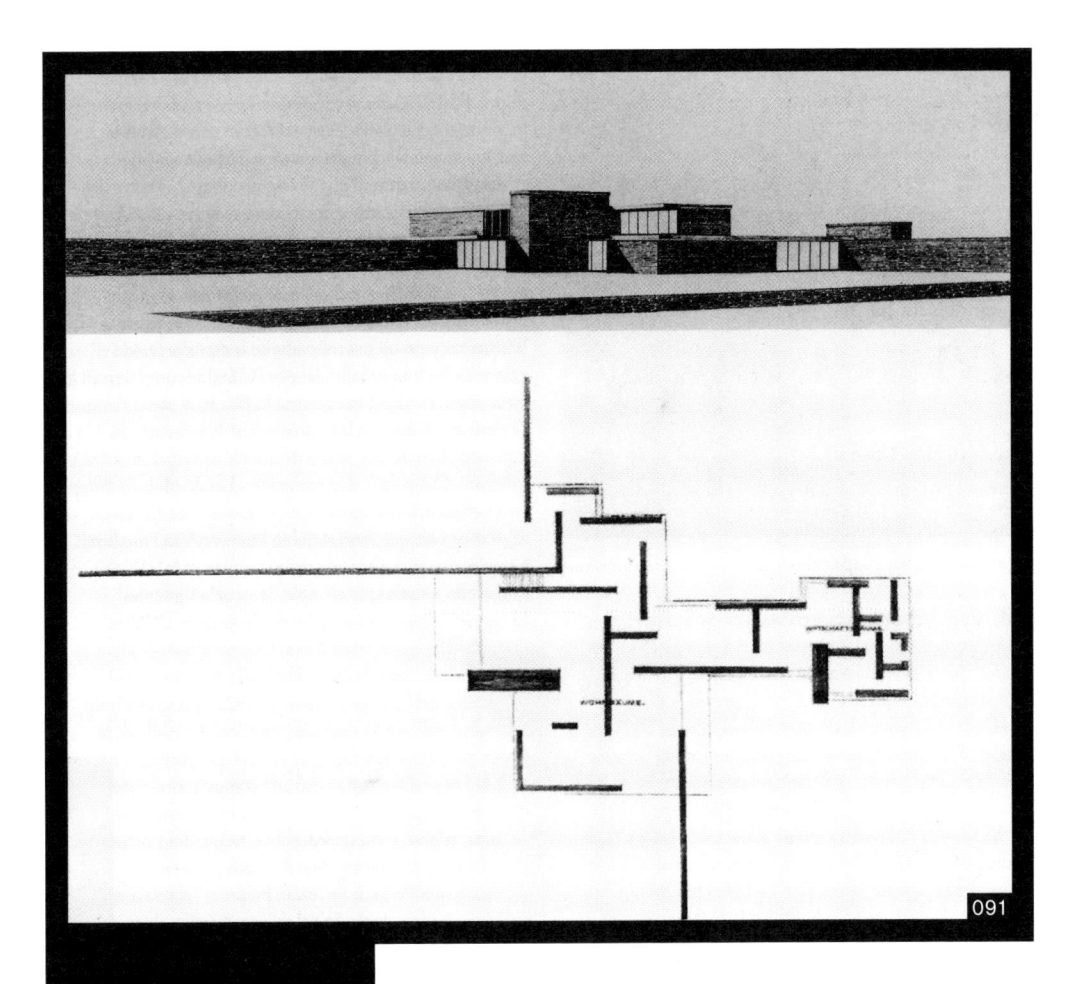

91. Mies van der Rohe, Brick Country House, 1923.

hillside overlooking the Czech town of Brno in 1930. It is essentially only a plinth and a row of bedrooms overlooking a roof garden. Between these white stucco volumes there is a large living room looking out over the city. To make sure you were not fooled into reading any structural continuity or formality, Mies van der Rohe cut openings for windows and walls in a syncopated, seemingly random pattern. In a final rhetorical flourish, an immense section of the floor-to-ceiling wall of glass that encloses the living area and the surroundings can slide into the ground with the push of a button (and a powerful machine in the basement), creating true continuity of space.

Within this open space, Mies van der Rohe's structure danced rather than being structured. It consisted of columns he clad with aluminum and made into cross shapes, as if they were X's marking the spot of support while almost dissolving into reflections. Between these columns, a half-circle of raw silk demarcates the dining area, its sensual shape standing between the house's abstract geometry and the curve of the body as it might lean over to listen to a dinner companion. If the house has a movement, it is a spiral curled around a music room in the house's rear that unfolds out through a greenhouse, out past the view, and then into the curved dining area. Along the way, every door handle, pulley, and cabinet was handcrafted to enforce the idea that this was a sensual machine for social gathering and viewing.

In the Tugendhat House, architecture doesn't quite disappear. It states what is important—the site, the view, the order of the house, the moments of gathering—and leaves everything else as blank expanses of white or transparency. What it leaves became the essence of an architecture that saw its sole task as defining our relationship to each other and our place.

The other side of such freedom in form and openness of space was a hollowing out of existing forms. No one did that better than that acerbic critic of the certainties of the older middle-class home, Adolf Loos. In 1930, he completed the Villa Mueller in Prague (also fully restored). It is a white, cubic object, but one that remains closed and compact. Windows framed in yellow-painted wood puncture the white expanse in what appears to be a random pattern, giving you no sense of the hierarchy of rooms or spaces inside. The house deliberately frustrated any attempt to try to figure out what kind of building it is, who might live there, or what might be taking place behind its blank facade. It is not just anonymous, but posed deliberately against the social setting in which it existed.

On the inside, Loos concentrated on creating ambiguity. The Villa Mueller's central space is neither a defined room nor the open loft favored by other modernist architects. Instead, it is a one-and-a-half-story space that is symmetrical and proportioned in a classical manner, except for the fact that one of its long walls is a half-height expanse of heavily grained green marble extending up in two places to become the columns that support the ceiling, while eroding at the other end to become the staircase leading down from the hall that forms the real heart of the building. All of the public spaces are at different levels, spiraling around this hall, which is something between a circulation space and a room. Marble and wood cut through these rooms, wrapping around corners to define space or jutting out to stand as screens. These materials and rooms define a moment of high luxury without formality, denoting wealth rather than surrounding you with it. You are never sure when you have arrived at, or what is, the true core of the house. There is a sense of suspended motion built into the half-level rooms looking out over each other, as if you should always sit on the edge of your chair, waiting to move on to the next room.

Loos's design tried to capture the in-between character of the modern middle-class family, suspended between inherited traditions and forms of behavior on the one hand and a sense that the world they inhabited was loosening all ties and proposing new modes and models of behavior on the other. The house was a harbinger of the suburban split-level, still clad in the abstracted remnants of palaces. Its exhilarating vistas are all internal, leading the eye not outward to the landscape or up into the sky, but, if anywhere, to the dark bedrooms up above. This is modernism turned inward, not so much making its inhabitants at home in the modern world, as bringing the uncertainties of that ever-evolving reality home.

092. Mies van der Rohe, Tugendhat House, Brno, 1929-1930.

093. Adolf Loos, Villa Müller, Prague, 1930.

094

Between the Tugendhat House and the Mueller House, the experimental parameters for modernist living were set for the next few decades. Architects around the world created countless examples of structures that let the upper middle class live in the kind of free, if sometimes unsettled and nervous, space they had conquered—and paid for. The home was also becoming a machine, and architecture sought to become like industrial design, churning out logical cubes around the world. The perfect symbiosis of furniture and architecture was achieved in the Maison de Verre, or Glass House, designed by interior designer and architect Pierre Chareau in 1935. In this renovation of an old Parisian courtyard home, Chareau created a giant void faced with an enigmatic glass-block facade. Inside, the steel columns that supported the new space rise up among a sea of both built-in furnishings and structure that also consist of riveted, soldered, and bent steel. Many of the house's rooms are hybrids of walls and storage spaces that never quite close one space off from the other. Public and private, as well as the various rituals of daily life, weave through this open web of highly stylized machinery. The Maison de Verre as a piece of machinery and the Schroeder House as a pure spatial arrangement come as close to creating a crystallized version of domestic modernism as anything that was ever built.

But the standard form in which people came to inhabit modernism was the white villa in which machine-style furniture had its separate place. During the boom years of the 1920s and into the last years before the Second World War, architects all over Europe and America, and even in outposts of Western culture around the world, built white villas. Those designs veered between the open optimism epitomized by the work of Le Corbusier and Mies van der Rohe and the inward-turned, more complex structures both Schindler and Loos produced. In Paris, architect Robert Mallet-Stevens filled a whole street around the corner from Le Corbusier's Maison La Roche with white structures of his own design. Though they are not as radical in their spatial experimentation, they are elegant and, above all, white, abstract alternatives to the more-traditional bourgeois villas all around them.

094, 095. Pierre Charreau, Maison de Verre, Paris, 1932.

096. Fritz Molnàr, Dalnoki-Kovats Villa, Budapest, 1932.

In eastern and central Europe especially, there were whole neighborhoods of such villas, usually situated on hillsides just outside of the old city, along the tram or bus lines leading out to the suburbs. In Zagreb, architect Stjepan Planić built several houses for an elite then growing rich from manufacturing. Planić incorporated some of the Turkish and Slavic traditions that still persisted in this edge of the Austro-Hungarian Empire, designing courtyards and pergolas that gave his designs a decidedly romantic flavor. He even used stone, wood, and other more traditional materials. The villas stood like human-made rocks on the steep hillside, creating a sense of modern wealth growing up toward what was then becoming the fashionable resort of Bear Mountain.

In Budapest, Fritz Molnár created houses in much the same manner on a site that was only a little bit less steep. Molnár delighted in emphasizing the elements that broke the white box, including curved staircases that seemed suspended over the ground, equally curved living rooms extending into the garden, and balconies angled to the view. He pushed and pulled at the box, creating a complex geometry while holding on to the white and minimal shell that gave these structures a sense of both newness and unity.

Molnár was not the only one to do this. In 1931, Italian architect Alberto Sartoris published a collection of house designs from all over Europe, ranging from England and Scandinavia to Greece, in which he included what often looked like interchangeable studies in black and white. Each design was an essay in blank planes punctured by glass windows that in the black-and-white photographs looked like voids; each had a flat roof; many of them extended into the landscape with pergolas and balconies; and none of them looked anything like a traditional home. Looking at the photographs, you would think that a new world was being built all over Europe, but in fact

097

these were isolated experiments. Building a white villa was the mark of your progressive taste as well as your command of enough resources to commission such a freestanding structure. It became the mark of the upper-middle-class elite whose money came either from manufacturing and trading enterprises or from plantations in Asia. As it became easier to identify modernism, at least in its domestic variant, that modernism was also gaining a very particular social and political status.

The most extreme example of the political nature of domestic modernism was Tel Aviv's White City. With the rising power of the Zionist movement and later the shadows of the Nazi regime beginning to fall on Germany, more architects moved to what had until 1909 been a stretch of sand on the Mediterranean coast. In 1925, the Scottish planner Patrick Geddes laid out the city along a set of boulevards that made use of what natural landmarks there were and established others around major traffic intersections, leaving blocks that Geddes hoped would preserve green space on their interior. Starting in the early 1930s, these blocks began to fill in with the kind of white cubic structures that marked them as the building blocks of the new world the Zionists wanted to build here.

Private homes such as the Kraskal House, designed by Richard Kaufmann in 1931, look like a combination of Le Corbusier's Domino House and one of Adolf Loos's villas. Other houses, such as Dov Karmi's 1936 Liebling House, are even more open, appearing to be no more than layers of balconies held together at the corner. This was especially true of the many apartment blocks that soon began to rise between the private homes. Most refugees did not have the means to commission a stand-alone structure, so instead they gravitated to roads such as Petah Tikvah, where row after row of white-painted apartment buildings present their combinations of rectangles, cubes, and curves to the viewer. Often these small apartment buildings were designed in series, so that there are a remarkable number of "twins": identical designs placed

097. Yehuda Magidovitch, The Cinema Hotel (former Esther Cinema), White City, Tel Aviv, 1938.

side by side, or two buildings designed to complement each other. The result is a new kind of urbanism, in which the private living spaces begin to create a coherent neighborhood not in the red brick walls of solidarity, but in the fragmented geometries of what promised to be a more rational society. Ironically, that new society is based on a romantic notion of history and belonging that brought people from all over Europe to a place that was completely alien to them and that they saw as an empty territory.

Thus, experiments arose all over Europe and beyond, and the (upper) middle class made itself at home in them. But what about the rest of the population? Most of the architects creating such bourgeois experiments saw them as laboratories for what they thought was the central task of modernity: creating housing for the masses. That was not just an idealistic notion. Because of the rapid growth of urban centers, millions of units of housing were needed across Europe and the United States.

The first experiments in social housing were not pretty. They were often carried out by rapacious developers trying to cram as many of the former peasants crowding into the cities to work in the new factories into as little space as possible. It was the sight of such dwellings in Manchester that had inspired Karl Marx and Friedrich Engels to write their first political tracts. Sometimes, enlightened factory owners would try to create more utopian housing for the masses, as in the company town Saltaire, designed in 1853 by Lockwood and Mawson for Sir Titus Salt, or the 1888 Port Sunlight, commissioned by Lord Leverhulme for the workers in his soap factory. In less utopian situations, all the authorities could do was try to restrict the developers, as they did when they passed the 1879 law that created the "dumbbell" apartment type in New York, whose mid-block indentation at least gave everyone access to some daylight.

It was not until after the passing of the 1901 Housing Act in the Netherlands, however, that the first real attempts were made to create social housing that was part of the city's fabric and that aspired to be more than slums. The Housing Act mandated that each municipality establish rules for housing construction, including maximum height, width, and building materials. It also instructed local authorities to plan for the expansion of their cities and gave them the power either to work with developers or to create their own neighborhoods through eminent domain. Finally, and what turned out to be most important, it offered subsidies to the municipalities which they could either use themselves or pass on to collective building associations to promote the construction of affordable housing.

The Dutch approach thus combined incentives and restrictions. It empowered a new entity, the city planning or housing agency, and it created opportunities for diverse social housing experiments, partially paid for by the state, within clearly defined outlines. As such, the approach became a model alternative to the instant slums that developers produced, as well as to the notion that you had to create utopian communities out of nothing. By the 1920s, most European countries had adopted similar approaches, though they were by no means all based on the Dutch model.

The most successful proof of the 1901 Housing Act's approach came with H. P. Berlage's 1917 Plan South, which laid out an entirely new district to the south of Amsterdam's historic core. Berlage turned compromise into form, finding a way to combine the familiar with the new. He based his plan on the existing landscape, which consisted of a grid of meadows separated by irrigation ditches. Combined with existing street patterns and an extrapolation of the semi-hexagonal plan of Amsterdam's "canal zone," this gave him a complex grid that he proposed turning into three dimensions, in a residential version of the American business structure, by mandating that the outlines of each block be built up with solid apartment buildings. The interior of the blocks would be left open for a combination of shared gardens or playgrounds and communal buildings such as schools. Berlage then used the complexity of the plan's different geometries, which he accentuated by cutting several large axes connecting major plan elements to each other through the grid, by asking the developers of certain blocks to emphasize corners or transitions from one geometry or the other. He thus replaced the age-old distinction between public monuments as place holders for both power and visual interest and background dwelling units with the unified expression that came from a collective of housing units whose ornamental flourishes and height variations integrated a sense of grandeur into the complexity of the neighborhood itself. For Berlage, this approach also had a distinct ideological aspect: a convinced socialist, he believed that the red brick he mandated for the buildings of the Plan South represented the workers coming together into a unified wall that would build a new, more just community.

In keeping with the Housing Act, Berlage did not design any of the actual housing blocks. Instead, he worked with the City of Amsterdam to establish a committee of overseers. Developers—whether private or corporations formed by worker's associations or pension unions—

098, 099. Hendrik Petrus Berlage, Plan Zuid, 1917.

could buy a plot from the city, and then had to design their blocks according to Berlage's guidelines. Architects also received a detailed list of guidelines. The committee ensured a certain degree of harmony between the various elements in the plan by reviewing every design. The result was a large new neighborhood whose unity, variety, and monumentality all came from the manipulation of the same four- to six-story blocks of red brick housing. With no monotony and no jarring sense of discontinuity, Plan South is as ideal an image of what the modern metropolis could become as has ever been built.

At the other end of Amsterdam, architect Michel de Klerk designed the most radical example of what was possible under the Housing Act and built with materials common in the Netherlands. The Eigen Haard (Own Hearth) block, completed in 1919 in the northern part of the city, follows its trapezoidal plot with a housing block whose lines are as sinuous as anything Antonio Gaudi had cut out of stone. Each detail, from mailboxes to house numbers, is an excuse for stone carving and complex manipulation of brick courses. The block's focal point is a small tower, placed back from the street at the blunt end of the trapezoid. Without any particular function, the tower marks and celebrates the housing estate, acting in the role of a church steeple to this church of the home.

The Dutch continued to design housing estates that not only gave adequate shelter to the inhabitants of the industrial city, but also broke down the empty and amorphous space the middle classes had created for themselves in the century before. Instead of empty squares and boulevards, architects created sheltered courtyards and axes that turned on pivots of housing. The building blocks of these neighborhoods were small flats or row houses, each with its own public and private spaces and a guaranteed amount of light. Even office buildings and schools looked a bit like these housing blocks, as they were clad in brick and had a small scale. The domestic ideal that had been at the heart of the middle-class revolution that started in 1848 here permeates the

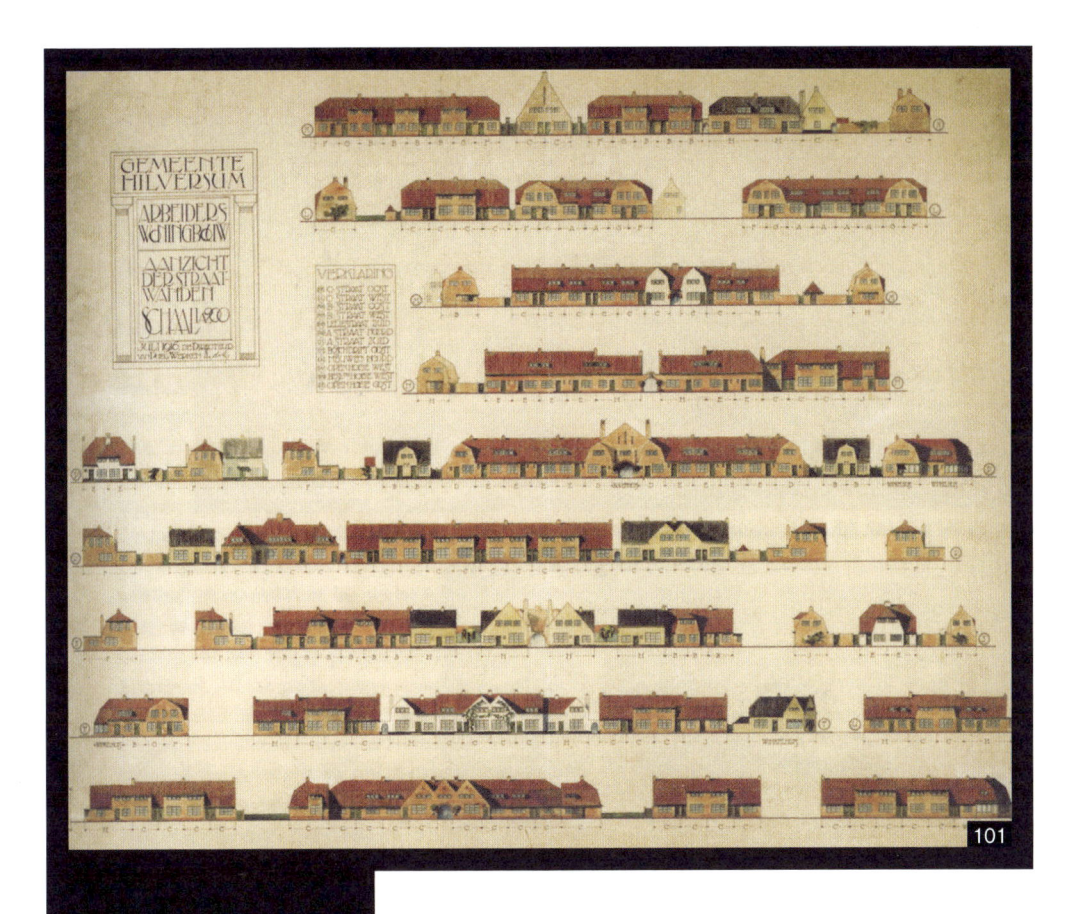

100. Michel de Klerk, The Eigen Haard, Amsterdam, 1919.

101. Willem Marinus Dudok, Social Housing Blocks, Hilversum, 1916.

whole built environment, turning the city into a landscape of human dwellings without monumental core or hierarchy.

The most successful example of the integration of public and private housing with monumental form and public amenities is the series of neighborhoods designed by Willem Dudok in the small city of Hilversum, where he was director of public works from 1915 onward and municipal architect starting in 1928. The first projects, designed right at the end of the First World War, are rather conventional assemblies of brick houses with tile roofs, grouped together to make small courtyards, squares, and

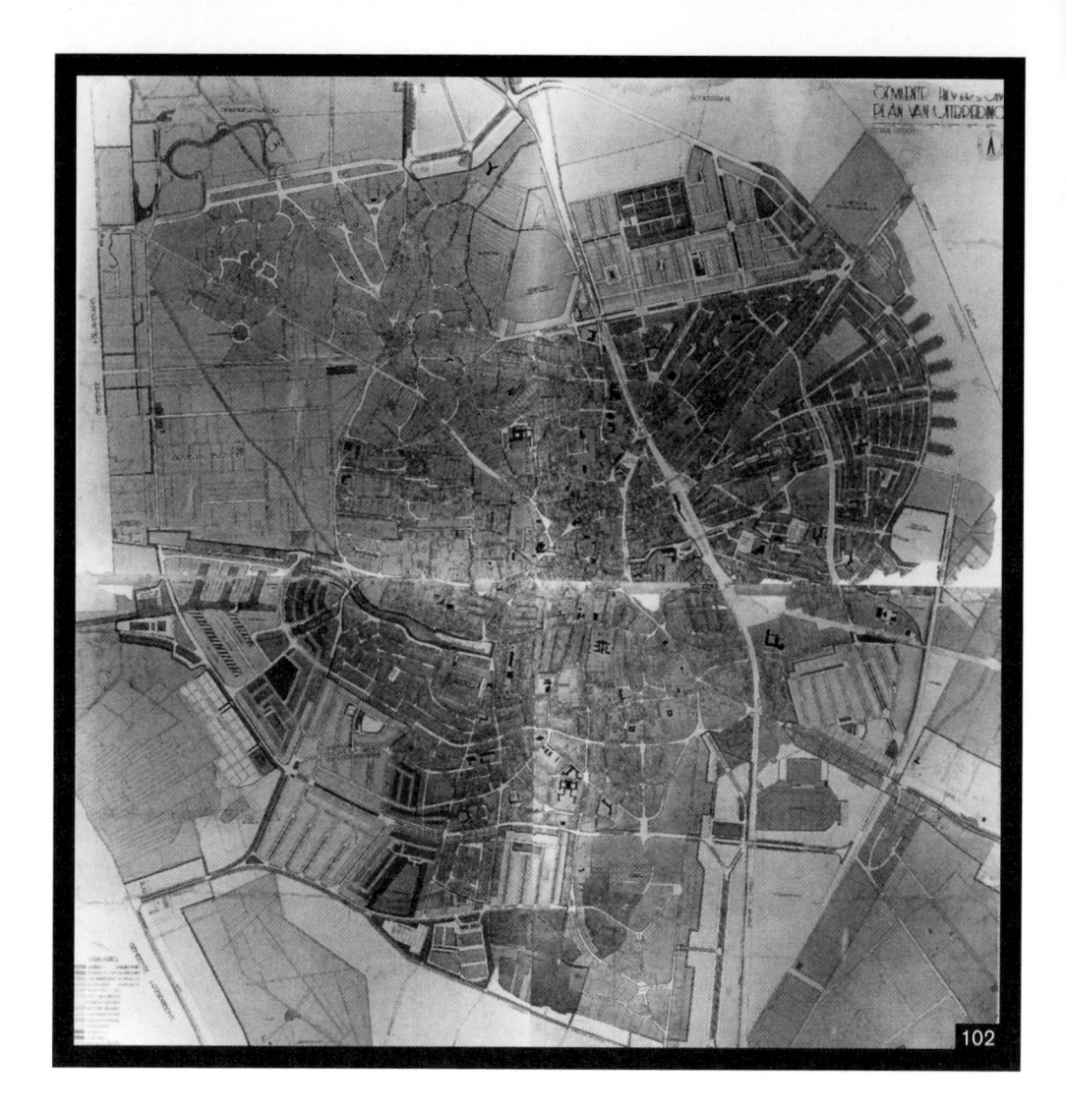

alleys. As Dudok's commissions became larger and his own style developed, the blocks became larger and more monumental. By the time the Eighth and Ninth Social Housing Blocks, designed between 1919 and 1924, were constructed, Dudok had begun to elongate the roofs so that they became multi-unit, social equivalents of the sweeping roofs of the American Shingle Style homes, and pinned them down with oversized chimneys in the manner of Frank Lloyd Wright (who was a major influence on Dutch architects at the time). Dudok used techniques that Berlage had developed, but in keeping with the smaller scale of the buildings in Hilversum, he broke the elements apart so that the results seemed more like a suburban development than collective housing.

The modern port city of Rotterdam chose to build its housing using less familiar elements. Under the leadership of City Architect J. J. P. Oud (brother of the city's mayor), Rotterdam sanctioned such modern blocks as Brinkman and van der Vlugt's 1921 Spangen block. Here concrete slabs that the architects made little effort to hide surround the communal block. Both buildings and blocks are larger than in most other Dutch cities, in keeping with Rotterdam's sense of itself as a metropolis of great future and scale. At mid-level, the architects inserted a "street in the air": a broad, outdoor corridor connecting the various blocks by an elevator so that merchants could ply their trades and mothers could get their baby carriages up there.

Oud himself took further the idea that you should create a truly new city out of the basic elements of the Housing Act when he designed the housing estates at Hoek van Holland in 1924 and Kiefhoek in 1925. The latter consists of rows of white-painted houses of only two stories arranged in an intimate geometry. It presents a smaller-scale alternative to the massive blocks developers had built for workers nearby. In its lightness, it also is meant to present something new: a world of reason and open space, disconnected from the past. Here the worker would live inside a kind of machine, rationally constructed to give each family the maximum amount of usable space for the minimum amount of money. What ornament there is comes out of the designs of bits and pieces surrounding the doors, the windows, and the eaves. The geometry of the blocks themselves provides the rhythm and logic that hold the whole neighborhood together.

102. Willem Marinus Dudok, Hilversum Plan, 1915.

103. J. J. P. Oud, Block VIII, Spangen, Rotterdam, 1919.

104. J. J. P. Oud, Model Living Room, Spangen, Rotterdam, 1920.

In Hoek van Holland, a harbor workers' colony more than ten miles away from the center of Rotterdam, Oud streamlined the low blocks into rounded white lines that curve around from one street to the other. He set up a strong symmetry merely by posing two of the sharp angles of triangular blocks against each other, and let the rest of the neighborhood flow from there into tight lines that open up and fracture at the project's edges. This complex not only was home to the workers who were building the modern world; it also housed the ideal of a world of machine-like, scientific precision that architecture could represent.

Few other countries were able to develop housing projects of equal clarity. The most ambitious and rhetorical project was Karl Ehn's Karl Marx-hof, built in Vienna in 1927. Designed specifically to house socialist workers in opposition to the right-wing government, its main facade sports large brick arches that rise up to towers, shooting out a connecting base and balconies along the way. These gate and tower assemblies are clearly anthropomorphic: they represent workers standing with their legs splayed and their arms linked, their heads proudly lifted up. Behind these figural elements, the housing block is a logical block of apartments clad in stucco. When the right wing took over Vienna's city government a decade later, the workers indeed barricaded themselves, to no avail, in this socialist sanctum.

The rebuilding of Germany after the First World War produced the largest variety of housing experiments in Europe. Most of them took the form of *Siedlungen*, or colonies: blocks of

106

105. J. J. P. Oud, Housing Development, Hoek van Holland, 1926-1927.

106. Karl Ehn, Karl Marx-Hof, Vienna, 1927-1930.

housing built either by the municipality or by private companies at the outskirts of town (or beyond) to house industrial workers. As a result, few of them contained public, shared spaces behind closed facades in the manner of the Dutch examples. Instead, most of them were single blocks, almost always covered with white stucco, that were grouped freely in the landscape, as if in a collective version of the middle-class suburb. The rhetoric around such developments reinforced that sense of creating a "worker's suburb": the planners' goal was to give those who could not afford a single-family home access to space, light, and air by collectivizing those phenomenon. With their housing blocks placed in open space at a distance from each other and outside of the crowded city, workers could command an undefined and fragmented, but still open space, only partially marked by the presence of neighboring blocks.

In the neighborhood that the Siemens Company built in Berlin starting in 1921, called Siemensstadt, the architect Hugo Haring still placed the buildings in a relatively orthogonal relation to each other. The blocks he designed, along with luminaries such as Walter Gropius and Hans Scharoun, are modest, four- to eight-story white boxes, their geometries emphasized by the banding of windows and the rhythm of balconies and entrance pavilions. In the Bruchfeldsiedlung outside of Frankfurt, designed under the direction of City Architect Ernst May and built in 1926 to 1927, the buildings begin to fan out and terrace up. May oversaw the planning of a number of different housing developments in and around Frankfurt in these years, designing some of the most abstract housing blocks himself. He went beyond the creation of overall neighborhoods, however. In 1926 he commissioned a group under the direction of Margarete Schütte-Lihotzky to design a compact kitchen that would be as efficient as possible. The "Frankfurt kitchen" became a model of how, through a scientific study of a person's movements and then engineering a space to respond to and discipline those movements, you could create the machinery by which the activities of everyday life could enter the world of modernization, and vice versa.

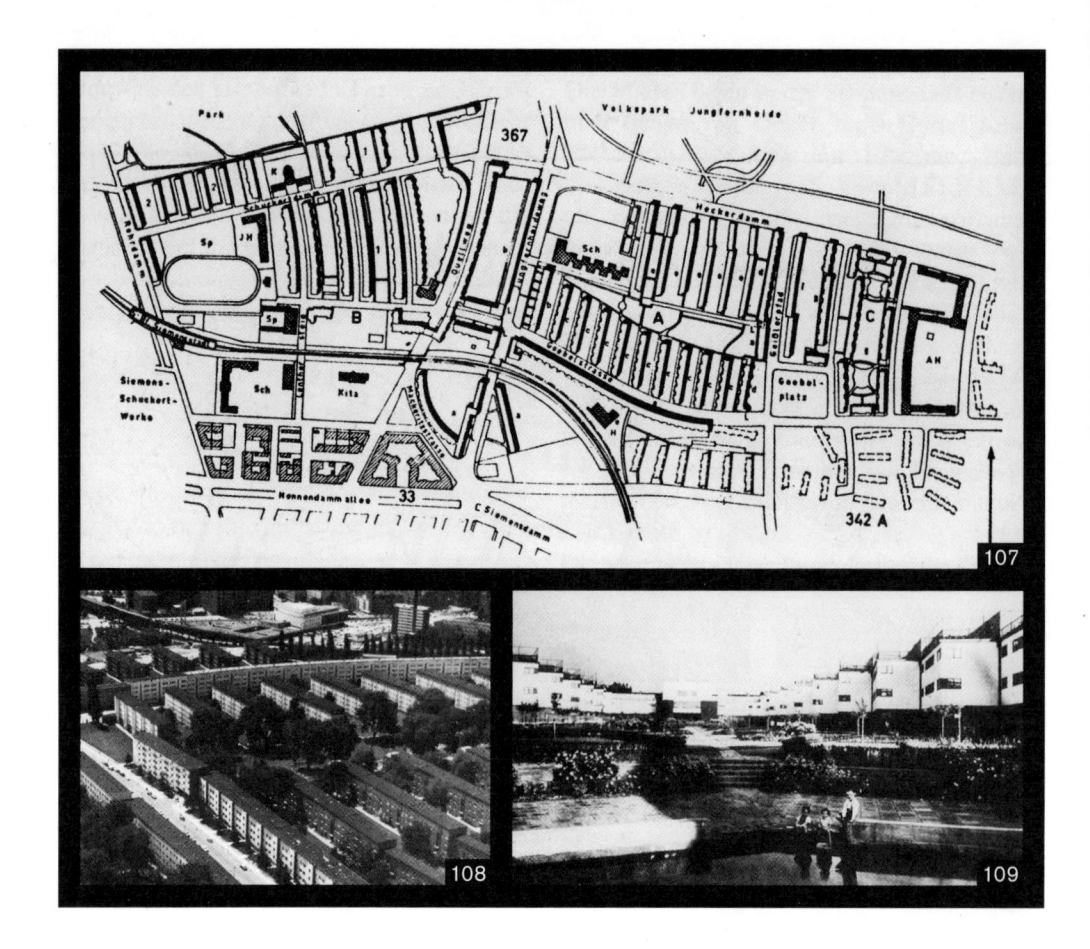

The showcase for the *Siedlung* movement, and for much social housing between the two World Wars, was the Weissenhof Siedlung, constructed in Stuttgart in 1927. Though it is a modest array of blocks loosely arranged along a hillside at the edge of town, it is remarkable because some of the most famous architects of the time contributed designs. Ludwig Mies van der Rohe came up with a simple slab of apartments whose grid of windows emphasizes the horizontal flow of the apartments rather than the fact that they are stacked one on top of each other. Hans Scharoun sculpted small housing blocks to respond to their

107, 108. Hugo Haring, Siemensstadt Housing, Berlin, 1929.

109. Ernst May, Bruchfeld Siedlung, Frankfurt am Main, 1926–1928.

110, 111. Le Corbusier, Weissenhoffsiedlung, Stuttgart, 1927.

112. Moisei Ginzburg, Ignaty Milinis, Narkomfin, Moscow, 1928-1932.

sloping sites and to each other in a free composition in space. J. J. P. Oud appended smaller elements at right angles to the rear of his smooth row houses, letting them catch private courtyards between their simple shapes. Le Corbusier designed a villa of glass, steel, and stucco that is in actuality several apartments grouped together to create a grander appearance. In all of these structures, the simplest groupings of rooms together create flats and produce variations on geometric blocks that, through the placement of windows, doors, and balconies, are broken down further into what to the commissioners and the architects (though perhaps not to the inhabitants) were the building blocks for a new society.

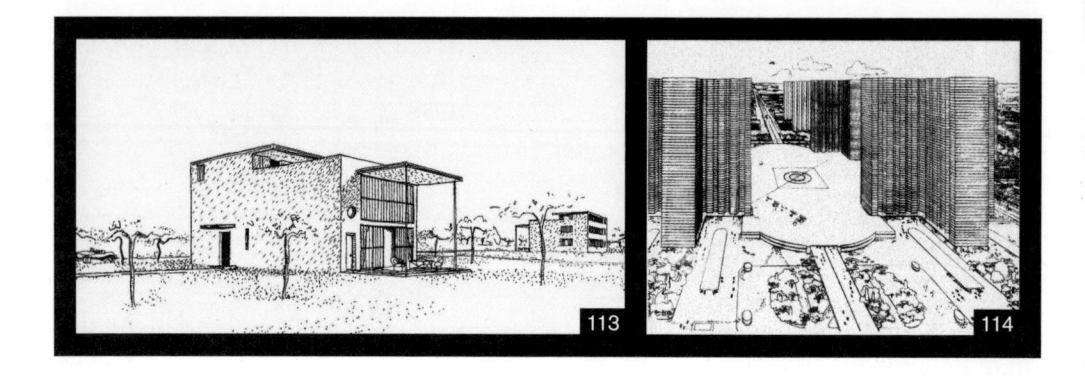

While the Dutch and the Germans were building a new society out of and around their cities, architects in other countries were mainly dreaming. Yet, their proposals were on the whole more radical. Only in the newly communist Soviet Republic were some of these experiments constructed, though even there the most daring ideas were never realized. Moisei Ginzburg dreamed of a mile-long housing block with communal kitchens and nurseries. It would not only be an immense line shooting out into the landscape, but its architecture would also emphasize that linearity, reducing itself to the purest and most minimal shape possible. The two blocks Ginzburg constructed in Moscow, the Narkomfin of 1930 and the Communal House of 1929, are both no more than fragments of that ideal. Similarly, in Berlin, Ludwig Hilberseimer imagined a completely integrated city in which all the old buildings would disappear and the new housing blocks, perfect geometric solids with dark bands of windows dissolving into an overall grid, would hover in serried rows over massive highways, which would take the place of the parks in providing light and air in the suburbs. The blocks Hilberseimer did build have some of the idealism of that vision, but none of its scale or radical reduction.

The most coherent and grandest, though unrealized, schemes came from Le Corbusier. In 1915, he had proposed that houses could be built like cars, just as he would propose in his 1925 manifesto. The Domino House was a skeleton of concrete posts and slabs that could be filled in with mass-produced elements at will. In the Maison Citrohan of 1920 (the name was a pun on the Citroen car), he designed the whole package, showing how the structure could contain an efficient arrangement of spaces. In the Plan Voisin of 1925, he proposed replacing the historic core of Paris with towers standing in an open park landscape. Le Corbusier specified his vision of the ideal city in his plans for the "Contemporary City" of 1922 and the Ville Radieuse of

1931. The city should be made up of a grid that could be logically developed, crossed by major infrastructural lines that would also become monumental boulevards. Workers would be housed in towers where their small apartments could be piled on top of each other for the least amount of money. The middle class would live in shorter apartment blocks that would contain private courtyards. Each apartment would also have its own hierarchy: the living room would be two stories tall, with a large window looking out at the new world, while the bedrooms would be stacked up behind it. Corridors that ran only every other floor, thus reducing costs and emphasizing the individuality of each unit, would service the whole apartment.

Le Corbusier drew these building blocks of the new city with great verve. Each building, illustrated as a few black outlines, was an intricate intersection of lines that together created solid, white blocks which he believed, as he had noted in his manifesto, *Towards a New Architecture* (1923), would appeal to the eye's search for aesthetic balance. Taken together, the blocks showed a world in which the classes and functions that allowed the modern metropolis to work would be analyzed, measured, and each given its own space. It was a city of separate elements, connected to each other by a largely invisible infrastructure and given a sense of coherence because the architect had designed the whole as a relationship between the different parts. The vision was so powerful that all the small-scale experiments of the Netherlands, all the Siedlungen, and many of Le Corbusier's other ideas were largely forgotten. After the Second World War, what we got were giant versions of the Ville Radieuse. They became the *banlieue* of Paris, the New Towns of the Netherlands and Scandinavia, and the housing projects of the United States. Rather than liberating landscapes, they turned into holding tanks for the poor. The dream of living in a free environment turned into a nightmare of empty, vast spaces in which nobody could be at home.

113. Le Corbusier, Maison Citrohan, 1920.

114. Le Corbusier, *Ville Radieuse*, 1931.

5. BUILDINGS LIKE CRYSTALS, FORMS AS COLD AS ICE
the styling of modernity

At the beginning of the twentieth century, it became clear that a third element had joined the opening of space and the abstraction of form as one of the prime hallmarks of modernism: plasticity. The experiments architects and designers pursued as they tried to represent modernization and to make the middle class at home within its upheavals shared an important characteristic: they assumed the world had become plastic. The forms and orders we inherited from the past were no longer fixed, but malleable. With new forms, new images, and especially new materials, you could express a more fluid reality. The modern world was framed in steel, a material that was a condensation of iron ore, carbon, and various chemicals you could extrude into a number of shapes. By the end of the century, concrete was perfected so that walls could be shaped into compound curves. Machines could stamp metal into any number of shapes. In the twentieth century, human-made materials became readily available, including what we today know as the most plastic of all building blocks of the modern: polycarbonates, or common plastic.

Today, metal is all around us. So is plastic, and myriad other artificial materials. Most of the objects we use every day are streamlined, smooth, and designed to be ergonomic. Machines and tools fit in our hands, controls conform to our grip, and shapes cocoon us everywhere. Even the computer on which I write these words is a smooth, white container, its corners rounded, its innards hiding somewhere behind the screen. We have shaped an artificial world for ourselves, and we have filled it with things that help us live in that world, from automobiles to houses.

Some of those objects are still remnants of an older age—we call them antiques, or relics, or perhaps traditional. We still use materials such as wood for everything from the boxes in which to keep things to the boxes in which we live, though most of the lumber today is mass-produced in fast-growth forests. Overall, however, every surface we touch and every form we see is machine-made. The modern world we experience is one in which our senses are suffused with artifice.

115. Peter Behrens, AEG Clock, 1908.

The spread of such designed surfaces and forms came after the emergence of abstract and empty space. It was the result of mass production as well as of scientific inventions, and fed the middle class's need to make a world in which they could manipulate every aspect of their environment. The shaping of modernity meant also a styling of modernity: things had to look as if they had been machined and were ready to use, without revealing the messiness that made it all work. Through architecture, industrial design, and graphic design, the modern world took on the look and feel we associate today with modernism.

In 1907, the industrial giant AEG hired Peter Behrens as its in-house designer. Behrens had a few years earlier helped found the Werkbund, whose exposition Bruno Taut was later to adorn. The Werkbund was a society not unlike the Wiener Werkstätte, and Behrens subscribed to similar notions of creating an integrated, modern environment. As a test, he had designed every aspect of a house for himself, including its interior, at the Werkbund artists' colony in Darmstadt. At AEG, he had the chance to expand on what was essentially an Arts and Crafts sensibility at a vast scale. He designed the company's graphic identity, creating a new logotype that had hints of a primitive German script but relied on clearly expressed geometry to construct the letters. He also designed many of the company's products. His clocks were the essence of such objects: they are black metal circles surrounding white dials in which every number and every element has been disciplined to create clear legibility. When he designed the first electric teakettle, in 1908, Behrens emphasized its stretched and slightly deformed geometry so that it hovers between being a piece of machinery and a household implement familiar to its users. That combination of an industrial sensibility, which he often expressed with visible fasteners and slightly overscaled metal frames, and abstractions of familiar shapes to make them easier to use and simpler in appearance became the hallmark of Behrens's design.

116 117 118

Behrens also set the standard that designers in other German firms, and later firms around Europe, would imitate for the next half-century. For, Germany had by then become the powerhouse of industrialization, turning out products that rivaled those of the British in their reach but were altogether more modern in their design. Such technical implements meant for mass production as the 1913 Leica camera, a marvel of intersecting circles on a simple rectangle, were typical of the ways in which the design sensibility developed by the Arts and Crafts movement began to pervade everyday objects. Yet, there was also logic to their design that had little to do with aesthetic preferences. The clocks, watches, cameras, and electric implements had to look the way they did because of the way they functioned. This "engineers' aesthetic" entered into daily life because applied ornament was expensive and cumbersome, and thus was eroded away by the logic of a marketplace looking for ever cheaper and better products. The light bulb was an essay in spherical geometry, transparent and thin, but elongated into something new, not because a designer had shaped it, but because Thomas Edison and his craftspeople had developed the best way to distribute light while encasing the filament in a shell they could mass produce.

You can see this kind of "engineers' aesthetic" especially clearly in furniture destined not for the home, where for a long time consumers resisted the industrial aesthetic, but for the workplace or public spaces such as cafés. In the 1840s, Michael Thonet had developed a technique of steaming, laminating, and bending layers of plywood to create a very cheap, light, and sturdy chair he patented in 1850. The so-called Thonet chair and its many variations and imitators became a staple of European cafés and public spaces. Its forms echoed the curves of the "styles of the Louis," but in such a simple and abstracted way that they are no longer recognizable as such. In 1912, designer Charles Jourdain patented a system of making office furniture that is modular: a collection of geometric solids that you can stack in various ways to house all your work needs. Office chairs became equally interchangeable and simple, evolving from a smaller version of the ornamental desk chair to something a bit closer to the peasant's assembly of a few pieces of wood. Designers began introducing curves and geometric devices that are not so much ornamental as meant to accommodate the body through their various curves and extensions, thereby developing a more efficient response to the needs of the working clerk. Soon mechanical elements began to be used in the chair's construction, letting the occupant lean back, turn, and even move across the floor on casters. The sitting-machine came very close to the middle-class body, but in a smoothed-out and tasteful version unlike the naked machines factory workers had to use.

Yet, in many ways, firms such as AEG or Thonet did not represent the most advanced form of industrial production in the world. In 1908, Henry Ford had produced the first Model T, a marvel of industrial *bricolage* that threw out most of the attempts to make the car look like a mechanized version of a traditional buggy. Instead, Ford just put together all the different elements that it would take to house people while moving on wheels propelled by an engine as efficiently as possible. The Model T became the prototype for most industrial design for the next century: a collage of different elements piled up on top of each other, usually painted in one color (black, in this case) and connected with various lines arching or angling through as little space as possible. Each element often combined various geometries following the logic of the light bulb, but there was no overall order, hierarchy, or even coherent scale to the assembly.

Architects and designers also began adapting the materials and techniques of the factory to domestic furnishings. Gerrit Rietveld used plywood, which was then a relatively new way of utilizing wood products and one that certainly was not seen as proper for a middle-class interior. His 1934 Zig-Zag chair took the material to its furthest extreme, making one line that is support, structure, and image at the same time. Alvar Aalto, living and working in Finland, the center of Europe's new wood,

116. Oskar Barnack, Leica Camera, 1914.

117. Thomas Alva Edison, Light Bulb, 1802.

118. Henry Ford, Ford T-Model, 1908-1927.

119. Thonet Brothers, Chair Thonet Model no. 14, 1859.

120. Gerrit Rietveld, Zig Zag Chair, 1934.

121

122

plywood, paper, and pulp industry, combined this new material with Thonet's technology to produce bent plywood furniture. This included a chair he designed in 1930 for the Sanatorium in Paimio and the small stools, no more than four plywood legs supporting a perfect plywood circle, that he started producing a few years later.

Most designers, however, were interested in pure geometries and new materials. Designer Anni Albers took weaving into the realm of geometric abstraction. Her rugs weave horizontal lines in primary or bright colors past and through each other, eschewing any of the flowers or decorative borders that marked earlier textile design. In such rugs as the Smyrna of 1925 and the Goldrose of 1926, she also began to let rectangles and squares of pure color enter into the striated fields. As her work progressed, it began to imply more of its own spatial presence, even as it became more and more abstract.

Wilhelm Wagenfeldt designed cutlery and ceramics that also brought a sense of pure forms to the dinner table. His tea set of 1931 consists of various glass bowls, the largest of which is the teapot, in which you can see the tea steeping. The glasses and saucers are as perfectly round as he could make them. The ceiling lamp Marianne Brandt designed in 1926 or the table lamp Wagenfeldt created two years before that took the industrial aesthetic produced by firms such as Siemens, AEG, and Philips and elongated its forms, composed its various bits and pieces, and thus turned the machine collage into a domesticated object.

The equivalent of the cubic villa in furniture became the bent-metal chair or lounge. Probably first invented by Mart Stam in 1923, its origins are still in dispute. What is certain is that in rapid succession Stam, Marcel Breuer, and Mies van der Rohe all produced chairs that are essentially just metal tubes curved, extruded, and run past each other to create a place to sit. The most famous of these became Breuer's Wassily chair, an intricate intersection

121. Mies van der Rohe and Lilly Reich, Barcelona Chair, 1929.
122. Alvar Aalto, Paimio Chair, 1931-1932.
123. Alvar Alto, Säynätsalo City Hall, Säynätsalo, 1952.
124. Wilhelm Wagenfeldt, Tea Set, 1931.
125. Marcel Breuer, Wassily Chair, 1925.
126. Anni Albers, Smyrna Rug, 1925.

of metal lines and slung leather or canvas supports. Mies van der Rohe went beyond steel tubes in the chaise he designed for the 1929 German Pavilion in Barcelona. This broad chair's structure consists of two crosses of metal across which two black slabs, one a seat and the other a back support, rest. The structure made the X-shapes he favored for columns into something you could inhabit, while the seat and back are gridded planes. If this was about as simple as you could make it, Le Corbusier made something that is more expressive. The Chaise Longue he designed in 1928 together with Pierre

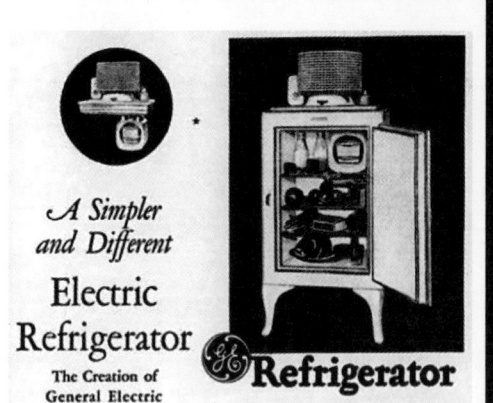

Raymond Loewy, "Coldspot Super Six" Refrigerator, Sears, Roebuck & Co., 1935

Jeanneret and Charlotte Perriand is a complex superstructure of folded metal plate on top of which floats a curve mimicking the body's contours. It is a machine for resting.

Everywhere geometry and abstraction filled the home. Wagenfeldt reduced storage to a cubical stack of glass in 1938. Coco Chanel produced her Parfum No. 5 in a rectangular glass bottle. In the United States, a new specialty was born: industrial design. Practitioners such as Raymond Loewy, Henry Dreyfuss, and Norman Bel Geddes set about containing the machine collage in smooth, simple encasements. It started with office equipment such as the Gestetner stapler, designed by Loewy in 1932, but soon Dreyfuss was making the telephone friendlier to the touch and Loewy was turning the Sears Coldspot refrigerator into a gently curved monolith. Radios, the very emblem of the modern world, transformed from miniature cathedrals or carved oak chests into fragments of the large geometric forces shaping the home. The machine was being domesticated.

127. Raymond Loewy, Sears Coldspot, 1934.

128. Buckminster Fuller, Dymaxion Car, 1933.

What was needed was a form that would create a visual and functional unity of these pieces and would make these machines more acceptable. It should be a frame or an order that did not come out of preconceived notions or add anything, but that fused and optimized machine-produced forms so that they were easier to make, assemble, distribute, and use, as well as easy to consume. What was needed was streamlining. Loewy, who certainly made the term popular both in his writing and in his designs, probably invented that word. His idea was that all of the complexities by which a machine or mechanism (including a house or office building) worked could be contained in a form that offered as little resistance as possible. The question was, resistance to what? At first, the answer was, simply, wind, friction, and gravity. Streamlining was most popular in the design of objects that had to move: cars, trains, and planes. The Twentieth Century Limited locomotive, designed by Dreyfuss in 1938, summed up the idea: every element in the locomotive and in the cars behind it was smoothed out to reduce wind resistance and make the train not only go faster, but look as if it did. The 1934 Douglas Dakota DC3 accomplished the same feat, as did the various cars Detroit began turning out in these years. In 1933, inventor Buckminster Fuller designed the most radical version of an object made for speed: the teardrop-shaped Dymaxion Car.

But streamlining also was meant to reduce another kind of resistance, as Loewy himself acknowledged: the consumer's resistance to objects produced by factories to the specifications of engineers. The collage object might be an honest representation of how machines worked, but it also looked like a machine and therefore seemed alien to most people's daily lives. Moreover, its complex shapes caught dust and dirt as well as the eye. The industrial designers' idea was to encase the mechanism in something that came closer to the forms of the human body or of some notion of nature. The fluid bull-noses, lozenge shapes, or boxes with rounded corners quite literally took the edge off industrialization and made it easier to swallow up into the home.

In a spatial sense, streamlining could also respond to the faster pace and the large scale of modern movement. In the London Underground, everything from the bull's eye logo, created by Edward Johnston, to the system maps (designed by Harry Beck), to the stations themselves were redesigned to ease recognition and thus movement. In department stores, counters became curved, as did stairs and windows, eliding the barriers between consumers and the objects they should buy. Even letters became streamlined, in typefaces such as Paul Renner's 1927 Futura, its fluid forms easing the instant apprehension that constant movement made necessary in the modern city.

German architect Erich Mendelsohn had already tried out this streamlined style as early as 1925, when he designed the WOGA complex in Berlin. This cinema, retail, and office complex still looks like a composition of geometric solids, but Mendelsohn curved the edges and made the windows into stretched bands. In a number of department stores he designed in the following years, such as the Schocken in Chemnitz in 1928 and the Petersdorff in Breslau in 1927, he pushed this idea even further. They are continuous curves of glass with only a minimal amount of stucco to hide the structure that made this gesture possible. It is as if these designs

129. Edward Johnston, London Underground Logo, 1917.

130. Harry Beck, London Tube Map, 1933.

131, 132. Erich Mendelsohn, Woga - Komplex Berlin, 1925-1931.

are no longer buildings that were constructed, but lines of movement that appeared and hover just at the corner of your eye, dissolving the mute masses of the city around them and focusing your attention on the wares on display. Mendelsohn's widely published sketches, both of his own buildings and of natural phenomena such as dunes and waves, make this desire even more clear.

Mendelsohn designed his buildings not because he was trying to create streamlined structures, but out of a desire to express in as minimal a gesture as possible the essence of an institution and a place. His work came out of a movement in Germany and eastern Europe that sought to represent the energy of the modern world, one that recalls the expressionist scenes in the movie *The Cabinet of Dr. Caligari*, which came out in 1920 under the direction of Robert Wiene. There was something not rational about this work; it did not wish to represent modernity, to explain it, or even to make it possible, but instead wanted to draw out its force as an act of a nature that might be new but that these designers believed was deeply connected to an ancient cosmos.

As such, this expressionist approach was essentially a way of styling the world to smooth out distractions so that the inner beauty and energy of forms would come out. That energy could be violent as well as beautiful. It went beyond the human being, even as it appeared to be more sympathetic to the body. It wanted to become an almost nothing, of the kind Mies van der Rohe dreamed, in a manner that would transcend humanity. To many architects, this was a semi-mystical task, but to designers working in other fields, it became a way of making things look new. Many of them came together in what was the White City of this era, the 1925 Exposition d'Arts Decoratifs in Paris. It was this fair that gave its name, in fully modernist abbreviation, to that style: art deco.

Much less ambitious in scope than some of its predecessors, the 1925 fair's main aim was to reestablish Paris as the center of style and fashion in an increasingly international market. Half of the exhibition was devoted to French companies and designers. René Lalique designed a tower completely out of glass as both a beacon and a mark of his design prowess. While most of the exhibitions were standard, Robert Mallet-Stevens's Tourism Pavilion showed how white planes were taking over the world, while Le Corbusier's Esprit Nouveau Pavilion and Melnikov's Russian Pavilion offered a preview of the world to come.

The fair was truly influential, however, in the way it brought together the work of countless designers who were all introducing modern modes of production and appearance in the many

133, 134. Robert Mallet-Stevens, Tourism Pavilion, Expo 1925.

135. Émile-Jacques Ruhlmann, Expo Paris 1925.

artifacts of everyday life. The most photographed and copied of these designs were those of Émile-Jacques Ruhlmann, who installed several room settings at the fair, including a boudoir, a grand salon, and a bedroom. In all of these, he eschewed the more radically reduced and white interiors produced by designers such as Michel Dufet or Pierre Chareau in favor of furniture and furnishings that had all the hallmarks of traditional forms, but whose elided and smoothed edges made for shapes that were more comfortable and simpler than their grander predecessors. Ruhlmann's furniture was elongated like that of Josef Hoffmann or Charles Rennie Mackintosh, but only slightly so. It revealed the wood out of which it was made, but was not afraid to carve into it or to embellish it with a few flourishes. The new world was not a mystical endpoint, but a comfortable resting point.

This compromise between free-floating planes and forms anchored in tradition and gravity became the standard for furniture designers all over the world. The art deco style, as it came to be known, took the vectors by which radical designers sought to escape from the old world and turned them into lines incised on furniture or placed on facades. Often these lines were layered to create a banded effect and were curved at their ends, bringing them into sympathy with the streamlined forms of cars and other pieces of domesticated machinery. Art deco designers also favored luxurious materials. If they could not afford real ebony or marble, they made do with veneers, as they believed the effect was more important than the reality. A curious addition to the art deco look was the presence of jungle imagery. Designers took the stylized plant and animal forms that had been a staple of decoration since at least the seventeenth century and modernized it by making it more exotic. Instead of delicate branches dividing in intricate geometric patterns, they favored lotus blossoms, palms, and heavy, over-scaled foliage. These elements, mixed with motifs that took off from classical Greek vases and decorations, in some ways made art deco another version of the neo-classical revivals that periodically have swept through European fashion.

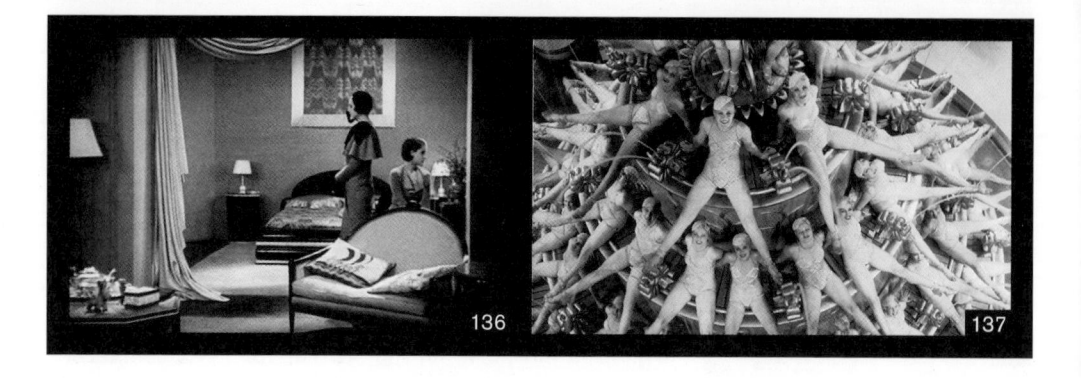

The most effective means for spreading art deco style became the movies. Set designers in both France and Hollywood, and later in England and Germany, began using art deco as the signal of a modern and luxurious life. Cedric Gibbons in Los Angeles was the most accomplished of these designers, creating sets that were a creamy white, their edges blurred by gauzy curtains, but their forms glistening in the studio lights with curved edges and thin planes. In a grander mode, the films of Busby Berkeley and other directors of musicals turned even human beings into the geometric patterns and streamlined forms of art deco. Art deco became the style of the stars. Movie stars were a new kind of aristocracy that was essentially middle class because they were self-made and lived in the world of artifice that popular culture had created; thus, their style became the style of the middle class.

Art deco furniture and implements were soon being mass-produced as the style became the default style not just for stars, but also for the whole middle class. It populated more and more homes, and so became acceptable and expected. Soon it also started to move from the boudoir and the bedroom to the facade and the whole structure of the building. For those architects and for clients who were seduced by the notion they should lead modern lives but were not ready for the white villa, art deco offered a cloak of modernity without changing any of the fundamental aspects of their lives. Streamlined versions of English country cottages and French chateaus, as well as simpler, ahistorically designed blocks, presented planes on which architects would inscribe a few parallel lines ending in sweeping curves to indicate that their structures had some sort of style.

You could see the movement most clearly in new communities then rising up at the edges of civilization, such as Napier, New Zealand. This small town was leveled by an earthquake in 1931, and rebuilt on new land that had risen up out of the sea. Architects such as Louis Hay smoothed over an English neo-classicism into lines that sweep around the modest, but often brightly colored stucco buildings. The town's civic focus is a band shell by the beach: a pure half-dome set in a landscape of simple walkways and low walls, it sums up the simple, but sensuous modernism of the town.

A similar sense of style came to mark the downtown of Bandung in Indonesia. The Dutch, who controlled what they called "Our India," refounded the city in 1917 to be the new capital of their colony. They laid the residential neighborhoods out as garden-city suburbs following the course of local streams and emphasizing the flowing lines of the geography. The central business district became home to businesses and hotels that flaunted the city's new wealth not with columns and pediments, but with sweeps and curves. Architect A. F. Albers designed several of these structures, taking his cues from the design of the social housing blocks of Amsterdam, but opening up the blocks to account for the tropical climate and constructing white stucco models of modern living.

The most remarkable collection of art deco buildings rose in the narrow confines of Miami Beach, Florida. Developed as a winter haven for the middle class of the American East Coast, the city soon became a long strip of whitewashed hotels with rounded corners and parallel layers of balconies that are halfway between the Bauhaus's abstract blocks of modernism and the sensuous lines of art deco. Lawrence Murray Dixon, who had learned how to design hotels while working for the New York firm of Schultze & Weaver, created many of the best examples of this style,

136. Cedric Gibbons, Still from *The Kiss*, Los Angeles, 1929.

137. Busby Berkeley, Still from *By A Waterfall from Footlight Parade*, 1933.

138. Kingsley Anketell Henderson, Temperance & General Insurance Building, Napier, 1929.

139. Lawrence Murray Dixon, Mc Alpin Hotel, Miami, 1940.

140. Henry Hohauser, Crescent Hotel, Miami, 1938.

141

from larger hotels such as the Tides and the Atlantis, to the countless two- to three-story apartment buildings that line Collins Avenue and various side streets. All built between 1933 and 1940, these structures are white, in many cases have rounded corners emphasized by decorative bands, and use paint to emphasize a sense of bands of windows (even though they are just punched openings) as well as monumental openings. Even more remarkable is the way in which many of the small apartment buildings seem to complete each other, the off-center compositions of white planes and colored lines leading your eye from one block to the next. The individual buildings come together to create a shared stage-set for vacation living. Miami Beach was a fluid place for a new kind of life, because a new class of people was being created, free from the places where production took place, free to enjoy the riches of an industrial world as pure consumers.

For, that was what art deco produced: a unified style for a middle class for whom the modern world had been produced, and who were responsible for its production, but who identified themselves more as inhabitants or users of that world. The smoothing over of all distinctions in design mirrored the transformation of a world economy from one based on production to one focused on consumption. This movement started right at the moment the Great Depression set in, was interrupted by the Second World War, and triumphed in the years after that. Design had the role not of revealing how things were made or how the new world might look, but of providing escape. By awaking frictionless desire, design could smooth out the systems of both production and consumption, and, according to historian Jeffrey Meikle, some designers hoped this desire might get the economy humming again.

Loewy and his fellow industrial designers saw their work as part of the selling of products, closely allied to marketing and advertising. One of the most remarkable aspects of art deco was indeed the marketing of the movement itself, in posters for railroads, automobiles, and vacation resorts. While graphic designers at the Bauhaus were inventing new letter types and arranging their blocks of information in geometric patterns, the French national railroad company (SNCF) was commissioning designers such as Constant Léon Duval, Roger Soubie, and L. de Neurac to create streamlined visions of the destinations you could reach with their rail lines. Though these images were still somewhat realistic, designers in the Netherlands (often working anonymously for the Holland America Line) and in Germany (such as Anton Ottomar) produced more abstract images. The most expressive of all of these designers was A. M. Cassandre, whose bold, full-frontal view of the *S.S. Normandie* (itself a floating palace of streamlined form and art deco interiors) became the icon of modern travel.

Car companies such as Citroen in France and Chrysler in the United States followed suit, commissioning poster designers to try to catch motion and engineering in singular images. The result was a frozen kind of machinery that approached the abstraction of high modernism but remained recognizable. Used in the marketing and packaging of everything from cigarettes to soap, the style penetrated every aspect of daily life. Especially remarkable was the appearance of the bull's eye, the center at the core of all this movement. Designers used it to identify, focus attention on, and sell Tide detergent, Lucky Strike cigarettes, and the London Underground, as well as countless other products and services. The pure geometries of modernism came together with the whiplash curves of motion so favored by streamlined designers to make you realize the modernity, availability, and attractiveness of almost anything the producers wanted to sell.

It was perhaps not surprising that soon the buildings of travel, from hotels and resorts to train stations, started to become part of the marketing effort and gained streamlined art deco styling. A magnificent example is Union Terminal in Cincinnati, Ohio. Designed in 1928 by Fell-

141. Citroen Sedan, Designer Unknown, c. 1930.

142. Adolphe Mouron Cassandre, Poster for the S.S. Normadie, 1935.

143. Lucky Strike Cigarettes featured in *Movie Classic* Magazine, April 1935.

144

heimer and Wagner (with the assistance of the neo-classical architect Paul Cret) and opened in 1933, it is a piece of architecture that disappears into lines of motion. The trains were once invisible as they passed by the station to the rear, while cars would sweep up on a grand new boulevard cut through slums, rise up, and then dip down into an underground passage covered in gleaming tiles. The station itself embraced this movement with two curved wings into which the cars disappeared. Its center is a gigantic arch, liberated from the surrounding block in which stations had until then been encased. Inside, what might in a previous era have been a centralizing dome became a semi-dome open to the city, covered with tiles, and surrounded by murals depicting the history of the area as well as the building of the station. As the architecture comes down to the scale of humans, at the base of the dome and in the numerous waiting rooms and offices, it peels off into layers of stone and stucco and tile, each of them curved and often ending in elaborate details that evoke motion.

Union Terminal was not the only such art deco station. All across the Western world, stations, and soon airfields, tried to catch motion in their forms. In many cases, such as the Spanish colonial–style Union Station in Los Angeles, they adapted themselves to what the designers saw as local traditions. In other cases, as in the stations that began appearing in Mussolini's Italy, they were more abstract, answering the ponderous forms of the old city with the introduction of a new scale and speed. Travel, the very essence of change that was the engine of modernization, in these buildings turned into self-conscious movement without a goal and became the place where design could most fully celebrate the appearance of the modern world.

But the streamlining of form and the celebration of the modern did not remain restricted to these more fanciful moments. It became part of the overall fabric of the city, not just in goods and advertisements, but in other buildings as well. During the economic boom of the 1920s, mainstream architects began assimilating the modern forms coming out of the schools of Europe and the isolated moments of the white villas, and adapting them to what remained fairly standard blocks. Everything from apartment buildings to office structures to factories could be streamlined and made to look modern, even if few of these structures were as exuberant in their appearance as what you might encounter in Miami Beach or Napier.

Department stores took the lead in their interiors, though few bothered following the Mendelsohn model of streamlining their exteriors. In the United States, Eleanor Lemaire started working with Bullock's in Los Angeles to create free-flowing spaces based on scientific ideas of how people move through space. Her ideas were picked up around the country, with department stores becoming public versions of the streamlined boudoir.

At the other end of the consumption and production continuum, in factories, Albert Kahn followed the logic of the assembly line, eliminating more and more columns, massive structure, and detailing, as his commissions became larger. His factories became hollow volumes, their

144. Alfred T. Fellheimer, Paul Philippe Cret, Roland Wank & Steward Wagner, Union Terminal Cincinnati, Ohio, 1933.

145. John and Donald Parkinson, Bullocks Wilshire Department Store, Los Angeles, 1936.

146. Eleanor Lemaire, Bullocks Wilshire Department Store, Interior, Los Angeles, 1936.

147

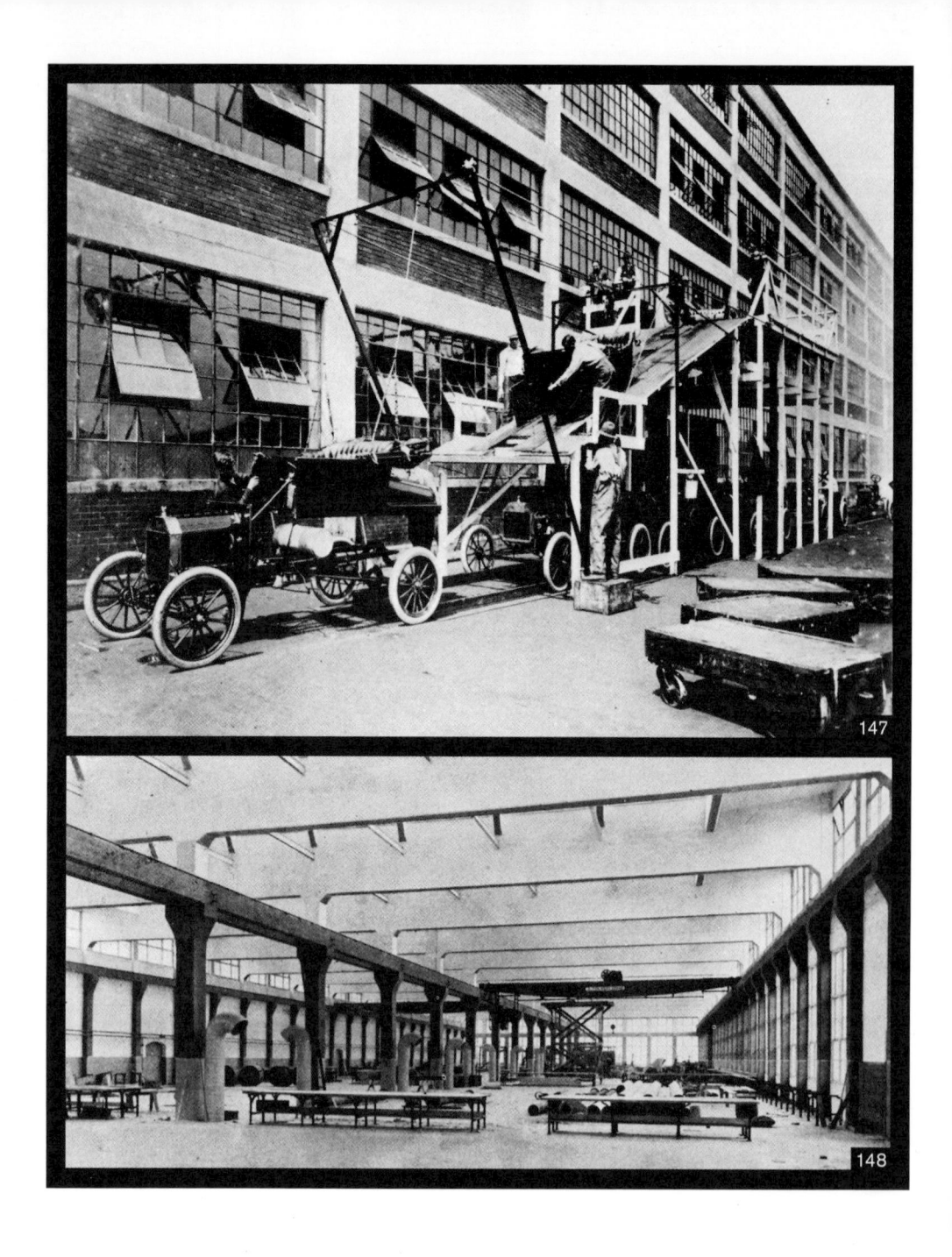

148

147, 148. Albert Kahn, Ford Factory, Highland Park, 1910.

149. Albert Kahn, Ford Engineering Laboratory, Detroit, 1910.

stretched-out facades mainly covered in glass, with roofs that did not spread out, but opened up to skylights and folded to make room for the steel trusses that opened up vast spaces on the inside. If there were facades to the street, Kahn usually streamlined them to resemble brick versions of the production halls behind them.

Frank Lloyd Wright designed the most remarkable streamlined production facility of all. Completed in 1939 in Racine, Wisconsin, the Johnson Wax Headquarters is all curving lines. The main office tower is a triangular structure made up completely of alternating bands of glazed brick and tubular glass. The main office hall below

150

it is also a curved brick structure with no apparent openings. Inside of this sheltering band, the clerical workers sat under skylights held up by splayed columns that resembled streamlined palm trees. This ethereal world presented to the public the notion that Johnson Wax was a company that was all about clean, glistening surfaces and simple, pure lines.

But modernism was able to create its most iconic forms in the design of skyscrapers. Their shapes were already lines reaching out into the sky, the motion of the city turned vertical. The task for designers was to repress the grid that was both their structural and and their functional reality, to use the setbacks and other laws that had begun to sculpt these gigantic office blocks, and to make the results seem even taller than they were. In New York, where the tallest and most beautiful examples were built, skyscrapers were sold by renderings that convinced investors, renters, and the public of the beauty of what was to come. The greatest salesman of skyscrapers was the architect and renderer Hugh Ferriss, who reduced them in his charcoal renderings to dark but soaring masses disappearing into the sky while the world around them faded into softer tones of gray.

In 1929, Ferriss summed up his vision in a collection of drawings not only of real buildings, but also of what he thought all these skyscrapers together could make of the modern city. Entitled *The Metropolis of Tomorrow*, the book showed New York as one mass of thrusting skyscrapers. Most of the objects, such as his image of the Waldorf-Astoria tower under construction, were real buildings Ferriss had drawn for other architects, reduced to what appeared to be almost forces of nature. But in the "Project Trends" section of the book, he presented a solitary figure looking out over an Alpine landscape of ghostly white towers massed together. In the following pages, Ferriss showed a city in which the street had disappeared, or rather had become assimilated into the skyscrapers as bridges and viaducts. He explained that a scientific analysis of the best way to create skyscrapers would turn them into abstract geometric elements with long, pointed tops. In some of the renderings, Ferriss's buildings retained neo-classical elements, but in many they took on the qualities he attributed to one of his fantasy designs:

> Buildings like crystals
> Walls of translucent glass.
> Sheer glass blocks sheathing a steel grill.
> No Gothic branch; no Acanthus leaf;
> no recollection of the plant world.
> A mineral kingdom.
> Gleaming stalagmites.
> Forms as cold as ice.
> Mathematics.
> Night in the science zone.
> (Ferriss, *The Metropolis of Tomorrow*)

Though few buildings could match Ferriss's vision in actuality, in a few short years architects transformed America's largest and most visible constructions from being stretched-

150. Frank Lloyd Wright, Johnson Wax Headquarters, Racine, 1936-1939.

151. Hugh Ferriss, Still from *Metropolis of Tomorrow*, 1929.

out versions of neo-classical temples or Gothic cathedrals into completely modern forms. The true skyscraper was no longer a vertical translation of the grid. It was still a pile of offices or hotel rooms one on top of the other, but the architects streamlined them into singular expressions of height that reached into the sky, along the way shedding the building's materiality as much as possible.

The most famous of these modern skyscrapers is the Chrysler Building. Designed by William van Alen and finished in 1930, it was briefly the tallest building in the world. Van Alen made it into as simple a tower as he could, following the zoning requirements by stepping it up to a central shaft that rises more than eighty stories over the city. At the base, he used black granite to streamline the facades, piling up horizontal planes and lines and then feathering them up the building's mass. On the inside, the lobby is a riot of stylized jungle vegetation in high art deco, much of it carried out in aluminum. At transition points, decorative flourishes refer not only to the vegetable kingdom but also to the hubcaps of Chrysler automobiles. At the top, the building erupts into arches piled one on top of the other. Clad in stainless steel with polished chromium nickel details and lit at night, the Chrysler's top might have come out of some sort of fan palm, but its effect was to turn the Gothic arch and the plant into purely abstract lines that seemed to pull the tower ever higher while celebrating the sheer force of construction.

While the Empire State Building, completed a year later, replaced the Chrysler Building as the tallest structure in the world, it shed much of the earlier building's detailing. The architects, Shreve, Lamb, and Harmon, did this mainly to save money and time, as they did not have a private company as a client but were working for developers who were racing to rent out the space. The architects manipulated the building's mass by carving it into relatively thin planes that dropped off one by one, allowing the central shaft to rise up to a single spire reaching up with even more conviction than the arches of the Chrysler Building. Soon the movies were to adopt that spire, portraying it as the site where the new world of airplanes defeated the jungle world out of which King Kong had escaped.

152. William Van Alen, Chrysler Building, New York, 1928-1930.

153. Wallace Harrison, Rockefeller Center, New York, 1939.

The era of the art deco skyscraper was short. In only a few years, the economic logic that demanded as little investment for as much space as possible stripped skyscrapers of their ornament and their expressive form. Then the Great Depression stopped construction of most, if not all, such bravura buildings. The last great skyscraper, which fragmented its streamlined exultation into something more abstract and modern, appeared during the economic upheaval that halted the great era of skyscrapers. Rockefeller Center started in 1927 as a cultural project: the Metropolitan Opera, with the help of its wealthy supporters, wanted to buy a plot of land in midtown Manhattan as its new home. When the stock market crash wiped out the opera's base of support, its leading donor, John D. Rockefeller Jr. stepped in, bought the lease for the whole area and turned it into a commercial development. Between 1930 and 1939, he built fourteen skyscrapers on the site, as well as Radio City Music Hall and an extensive system of underground walkways and rooftop gardens. When it was completed, Rockefeller Center comprised over six million square feet of space and was a true city in a city.

The very fact that a development of such a scale was possible made it clear that a new reality had arrived. Once you walk down the gently sloping walkway that leads from Fifth Avenue down to the ice rink under the seventy-story RCA Building, buildings that have all been designed in an integrated manner surround you. Everything, from the buildings' massing to the artworks on their facades and in their lobbies, was designed to reinforce the coherence of the whole. That whole consists of limestone facades rising up in what appear to be thin sheets, their vertical lines shedding ornament as they move up. There are cast aluminum details, no flourishes, and not even any crowns on these buildings. Indeed, they come close to resembling the mountain ranges Ferriss had imagined, here turned into the precise contours of office towers filled with arrays

154

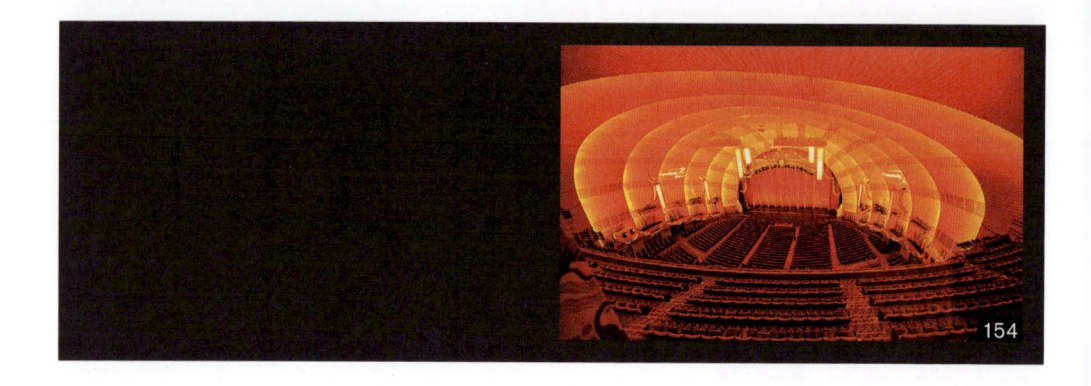

of desks and cubicles. The towers do not follow Manhattan's grid. Instead, they rose up in the middle of blocks behind "paws," lower structures that reach out to Fifth Avenue and define plazas. While the tallest of the structures, the RCA Building, is a thin slab with an east-west orientation, the towers to the north and south of it define the opposite direction, so that the whole forest of towers begins to pinwheel in a metropolitan version of the motion Frank Lloyd Wright had used to open up the suburban home. The composition liberates the city's core, turning it into a place with its own character as well as geometry. It is an abstracted, clarified, and energized version of the skyscraper grid that Manhattan had become.

The core of this new world was the ice skating rink, where Paul Manship's statue of Prometheus stealing fire from the gods hovers over those merely turning in circles. Sunken below street level, the rink removes any sense of there being a datum or reference point. Instead, you inhabit your own world, the skyscrapers thrusting up above you at angles. Even the ground below turns out to be an extension of that world, as mile after mile of stores line walkways connecting the five square blocks into a network that is both infrastructure and place of commerce.

There is a scientific logic to everything about Rockefeller Center. The walkway slopes down to draw people in. The ice rink is there because it proved the only commercially viable use for the space during cold months. The underground network exploits the necessity for a vast amount of service space, which usually remains hidden under buildings. This underground world is paved in black terrazzo and granite with bronze accents. This stylish necessity is a system of caverns that can exploit the captive audience moving in and out of the subways or doing errands between the buildings, by turning them into consumers.

Even the tower's shape is logical: the RCA Building exploits its site to the fullest, starting out as a thick mass around the broadcasting company's recording studios and public spaces.

154. Donald Deskey, Radio City Hall, Interior, New York, 1932.

It then rises up around an elevator core that becomes thinner as it goes up, as more and more elevators drop off, leaving only the high-speed tower service to reach up to the most exclusive (and highest-rent) offices at the top. The building undresses itself, showing the logic of its skeleton, though veiled in sheer stone.

If the skyscrapers and their underground counterparts revealed the logic of modern construction, the decorative scheme tried to create a story about it. The statues of Prometheus stealing fire and Atlas holding up the world speak of the power of modern technology and commerce. Artist Isamu Noguchi depicted the marvels of instant knowledge in his *News* relief. The layered horizontal lines around the tower's bases streamline the whole in response to the movement of the crowd. Abstractions of machines mix with floral elements to give you the sense that Rockefeller Center is rising out of a new kind of nature. Most famously, Mexican muralist Diego Rivera was commissioned to create a painting of the center itself in the lobby of the RCA Building, but his depiction of the real work and class struggle behind this dream of modernity so incensed Rockefeller that he had it painted over.

Such a myth of modernity as Rockefeller Center became was too much for one person to design. Rockefeller assembled a team under the leadership of John R. Todd, though just as important was his counterpart, the public relations and marketing specialist Ivy Lee. Todd's team included Raymond Hood, an experienced master of skyscraper design, as well as a host of other architects. Soon the most prominent of these became Wallace Harrison, who would go on to become one of the most important modernist architects of the postwar era. What is remarkable is that these strong individuals did work as a team, to the point that it is difficult to distinguish who was responsible for what in the final design. Rockefeller Center was the ultimate example of the kind of steel and stone real estate speculation Louis Sullivan had first described—streamlined by a modernist style, shaped by intricate analysis of technical and social issues, and appearing as a singular fact at an immense scale.

The most celebratory moment in Rockefeller Center is Radio City Music Hall. At the time the largest auditorium in the world, it is also the most lavishly decorated example of art deco style. Every inch of its space sweeps together into curves and whiplashes, lines and layers in muted colors that borrow from all times and all cultures to make you feel as if you have entered into an exotic space where anything is possible. When you come into the actual place of performance, a giant layered arch—an interior version of the Chrysler Building's spire or Union Terminal—draws your eye to a stage where the magic of stagecraft allows spectacles of an immense scale occur time after time. Inside Radio City Music Hall, and inside Rockefeller Center as a whole, modernism was able to create its grandest, most popular argument for the arrival of the streamlined, plastic, open, and abstracted new space of the modern world.

And yet, outside of this great capitalist achievement, things were falling apart. The Great Depression had arrived, and construction of buildings as well as the purchasing of new goods slowed down almost to a halt. Streamlining was not enough. America and most of the Western world was in limbo, having laid the foundation stones for a new reality and built its prototypes, but unable to conquer the internal contradictions of class injustice, unequal development, and the sheer wastefulness of its own appearance.

Modernism had its limits. Writer F. Scott Fitzgerald had noted this point when he returned to New York for a visit in 1932 and climbed the Empire State Building. He described his experience in the essay "My Lost City":

In the dark autumn of two years later we saw New York again. We passed through curiously polite customs agents and then with bowed head and hat in hand I walked reverently through the echoing tomb. Among the ruins a few childish wraiths still played to keep up the pretense that they were alive, betraying by their feverish voices and hectic cheeks the thinness of the masquerade. Cocktail parties, a lost hollow survival from the days of carnival, echoed to the plaints of the wounded: "Shoot me for the love of God, somebody shoot me!" and the groans of and wails of the dying: "Did you see that United States Steel is down three more points?" My barber was back at work in the shop; again the head waiters bowed people to their tables, if there were people to be bowed. From the ruins, lonely and inexplicable as a sphinx, rose the Empire State Building and, just as it had been a tradition of mine to climb to the Plaza Roof to take leave of the beautiful city, extending as far as the eye could reach, so now I went to the roof of the last most magnificent of towers. Then I understood–everything was explained: I had discovered the crowning error of the city, its Pandora's box. Full of vaunting pride the New Yorker had climbed here and seen with dismay what he had never suspected, that the city was not the endless succession of canyons that he had supposed but that it had limits–from the tallest structure he saw for the first time that it faded out into the country on all sides, into an expanse of green and blue that alone was limitless. And with the awful realization that New York was a city after all and not a universe, the whole shining edifice that he had reared in his imagination came crashing to the ground. (Fitzgerald, "My Lost City")

6. TOWARD TOTALITY
planning for perfection

155

He flies through the clouds, peering out at those formations of air and water piling up far above his head. In a gap between the formations, an old medieval city comes into view. The plane lands; he rides in an open car through the old city and arrives at a vast field surrounded by giant columns where masses of men in uniform stand in grids reaching as far as he can see. It becomes night. The pageantry continues; any sense of reality disappears as klieg lights shoot around an immense open-air stadium and up into the sky from which he came, turning the space into a cathedral of light. Human beings and all that they have created merge into almost nothing. Only the graphic emblems of his power stand out.

This master of this universe was Adolf Hitler, and the scenes are from the 1934 gathering of the Nazi party in Nuremberg. Filmed by Leni Riefenstahl, the 1935 documentary *Triumph of the Will* reveled in a new kind of space. It was one in which both human beings and nature had been completely tamed. What remained was order, shaped into pure geometry.

Emptiness became the emblem of something beyond humanity. This void was the realization of the logical tendencies of technology, mass production, and the social movements that had produced it. The void was the result of a total war on reality.

Fascism as a political movement had a space. The space of the Third Reich wiped out any remnant of historical allegiances to a particular country or place (at least for a while). It was the space of the concentration camp and of the battleground, where humanity was literally destroyed. Before that, however, it had been the space of modernism: the space of the autobahn that tied the centers of production in Germany together, the space of the new "people's car" that rode on those new ribbons of asphalt, and the space of the parade grounds and stadia Riefenstahl was able to reveal in all their white void in *Triumph of the Will* and in her 1937 documentary on the 1936 Berlin Olympic Games, *Olympia*.

Behind this void lay a century of emptying out the city and the interior to make way for the logic of the machine and the mass movements of goods and people. It was the culmination of a war on pre-existing reality fought by manufacturers, but also by designers who believed that it was their calling to destroy the old world in favor of a new one. It was the logic of Vienna's Ringstrasse, the White City of Chicago, the Futurist rush away from the past and into war, the "explosion of the tenth of the second" caused by the camera, and the dream of inhabiting a new world all brought to an end point. In this void, then, an international movement arose, one which, in the decades between 1930 and 1960, built repetitive blocks of abstract volumes that served as mass and massive housing, office blocks, and even whole cities. Its achievement was the emptiness at the heart of the modernist victory—an emptiness that would also be its end.

155. Albert Speer, Cathedral of Light, Nuremberg Rallies, 1935.

156. Leni Riefenstahl, *Triumph of the Will*, 1935.

The creator of this void was planning. Industrial processes had made the actual assembly and use of things subservient to the organization of their production and consumption through the maximization of resources in a completely abstract and mathematical manner. The assembly line and the modern corporate organization were linked to distribution networks that soon dominated both the economy and the space of the modern city. Factories grew into vast complexes, office buildings dominated the city with their ever-higher piles of grids, and infrastructural systems took up more and more of the landscape. The centralized state disappeared into a bureaucracy at a vast scale. The German philosopher and Nazi supporter Martin Heidegger noted that, instead of people making things of their own free will, or nature freely growing to produce things, both people and nature were subject to the aggressive extraction of their energy by technology. Our world, he said, is ruled by "setting upon" and "challenging forth":

> That challenging happens in that the energy concealed in nature is unlocked, what is unlocked is transformed, what is transformed is stored up, what is stored up is, in turn, distributed, and what is distributed is switched about ever anew. ... Regulating and securing ... become the chief characteristics of the challenging revealing. (Heidegger, "The Question Concerning Technology")

Like iron ore in the ground or wheat supply, human beings become "standing reserve," valuable only in how they can contribute to technological development. Reality as we know it is only a place holder, an abstract and mute potential for action. The world is already modern even if it does not appear to be so.

To organize and control standing reserve, you needed planning, and to make planning understandable, you needed icons, symbols, or anchors. Scientists and bureaucrats could provide planning, while advertisers came up with the signs and symbols that would give people some-

157, 158. Otto Neurath, Pictograms, 1928.

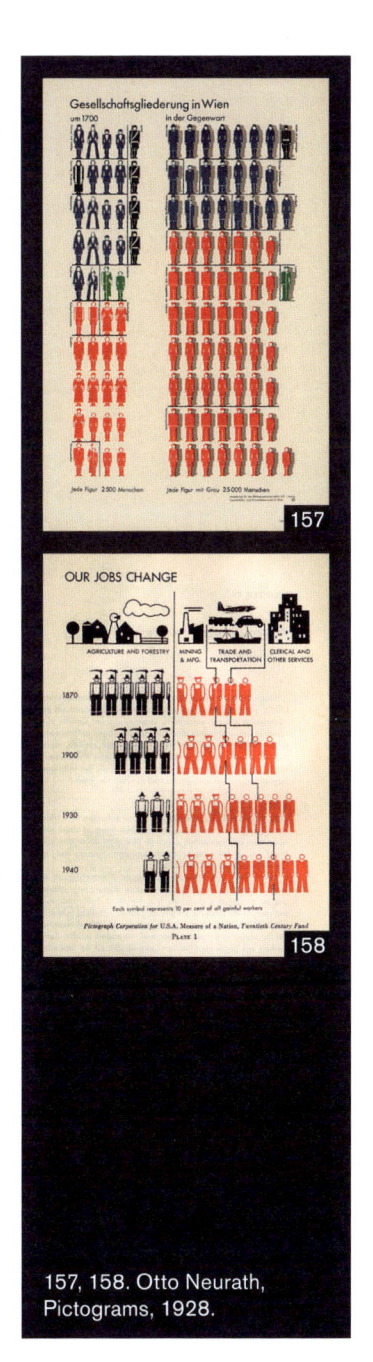

thing to hold on to. In 1928, the Viennese Otto Neurath developed the "language picture" or pictogram, as part of a systematic effort to collect, analyze, and, as succinctly as possible, visualize information. The serried ranks of workers and machines he depicted in his graphic statistics presaged the actual organization of such forces by the Nazis. But Neurath also collaborated with the Dutch urban designer Cornelis van Eesteren when the latter became city planner for Amsterdam in 1927. Van Eesteren saw planning not as an aesthetic, let alone a gestural effort. Instead, he set about measuring everything he could about the city: traffic patterns, wind speeds, land costs, the speed of movement. He then had a large team analyze this data and represent it in such a way that his General Plan of Amsterdam of 1935 seemed like an inevitability, and Neurath was a central part of that effort.

What disappeared in the midst of such efforts was architecture in a traditional sense. The making and shaping of the spaces in which these increasingly abstract activities took place became more and more regularized, planned out as scientific exercises, and anonymous in appearance. Physical frames that stood in the way were reduced to the absolute necessary to keep out the weather or others. Surfaces were made as smooth as possible. Ideally, architecture would just be a zoning and conditioning of space, or the pure light of the Nuremberg rally.

Against this threat of disappearance, architects took an ambivalent stance. On the one hand, they reveled in becoming scientists and manipulators of forms beyond formal properties. The most powerful of all architects in this period was Hitler's private designer, Albert Speer, who became the German minister in charge of allocating and moving all resources during the Second World War. In less extreme cases as well, the architect became part of a bureaucratic team, such as the one

159

that designed Rockefeller Center. On the other hand, architects and designers resisted the disappearance of traditional architecture, attempting to outdo the makers of symbols by creating forms that were abstract, yet so massive that they could stand as anchors in the sea of assembly lines and roads filled with fast-moving cars. They wanted to make great emblems of the state. In 1937, Speer started planning a New Berlin, which would replace the hodgepodge of the old city. Grand axes would cut through the city in the manner of Haussmann, but at a scale unprecedented in Western civilization. They would connect not the palaces for middle-class culture, but the centers for the institutions of the state that would create a thousand-year state of stasis. At the city's core would be a huge place for gathering, a staging point for party rallies that was essentially a void. Its dome would be so large that the designers expected it would create its own weather system. Architecture could resist its own disappearance, but it would have to be so big as to defy normal definitions of its task. It would have to be so immense and so monumental as to be almost incomprehensible; it would be a blank sign set against an empty space.

In the Soviet Union, planning also took over from experimentation once the Communist Party consolidated its power after the New Economic Policy of 1921 and Stalin's takeover in 1924. The logical and rational arrangement of goods, services, people, and places in order to create an ideal environment was more important to the Soviets than images or forms that were revolutionary in appearance or that appeared to change spatial relations.

Thus, when the collective planning agency came to envision the future of Moscow in 1935, they proposed a giant ring running around the whole city. It was a vast version of both the old city walls and the Viennese Ringstrasse; like this grand allée, it was to be a

159. Albert Speer, Welthauptstadt Germania, 1937.

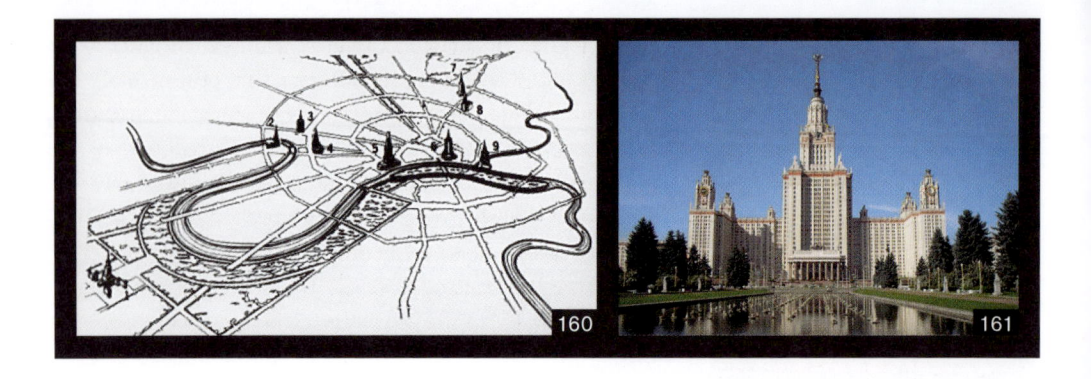

continuous boulevard with no beginning or end. Along it, cellular high-rises resembling office blocks, clad with the thinnest veneer of a classical architecture, were to rise as homes not for the middle class but for the workers. The focal points would be seven skyscrapers that would rival anything the Americans were building. These would not be pure expressions of vertical escape into the sky, however, but solid pyramids that would anchor the movement around their bases. They would contain the institutions of the state, such as the university or ministries, but they would also be the homes of the most important bureaucrats. The resulting "Seven Sisters" fixed the landscape of the Soviet state in space. Underneath them, a new network of subways connected the whole city. It went as deep underground as the skyscrapers rose up, necessitating escalators that were vertiginous. The subway stops and platforms were clad in marble and granite, thus monumentalizing and framing the frantic movement within these caves. At the very bottom, the ceilings turned into linked domes covered with tile. In their oculi, painters created false views of the world above: the Seven Sisters rising up into the clouds, athletes jumping into nothing, airplanes soaring overhead. The perfect world was a painted illusion deep underground.

Totalitarianism everywhere depended on new, rational spaces that would subject humans to their abstract laws. In Italy, where Mussolini came to power in 1922, modernism was at first the state style as well. Its leading proponents were Adalberto Libera and Giuseppe Terragni. In 1928, Mussolini started to drain the Pontine Marshes just to the south of Rome, in a Faustian effort to control nature and prove the state's power. In the newly reclaimed land, Mussolini decreed the founding of a number of new towns. Libera designed the largest of these, Sabaudia, in 1936. Built around a formal square of white stucco buildings whose facades sported grids and columns in front of closed masses, the town was a completely rational assembly of carefully zoned functions. Like a colony in a foreign country, it was essentially a bedroom community where people working in the fields or in the industry the Fascists hoped to establish could be stored.

160, Sketch of Seven Sisters, Moscow, Artist Unkonwn, 1947-1953.

161. Lev Vladimirovich Rudnev, Main Building of Moscow State University, Moscow, 1947-1953.

162. Adalberto Libera, Sabaudia, 1934.

Libera and several other architects inserted a number of large structures in the heart of Rome, including ministries and theaters. They were all massive blocks that had both modernist and neo-classical aspects. Though they had arches and columns, the detailing often would make you realize that the correct relationship between those elements, such as capitals or friezes, were missing. Instead, the architects emphasized their geometries at all times. The great train stations, including Florence's Santa Maria Novella of 1933 and the Roman one of a decade later, were objects of indeterminable scale sitting in front of large plazas. They were not so much representations of speed as they were just facts. The Rome station presented a slab that looked to be much higher than it was, and on the inside enclosed a vast hall with no apparent function other than to impress and control the crowds—in short, it was yet another huge void. These were magnificent containers, static monuments clad in a modernist veneer of white marble and devoid of any detailing.

In 1942, Mussolini intended to stage his own fair, the EUR, on the outskirts of town. It was meant to celebrate Fascist unity and achievements, though by then the Second World War was fully underway. Designed by Marcello Piacentini and a host of other Fascist architects, its centerpiece was a mysterious cube. Presenting a continuous screen of arched colonnades, the structure had a completely incomprehensible and almost surreal scale and function. It marked the mystery and the abstract force of the state, standing clearly at the head of the central square but giving no sense of what it was. It became the very emblem of absolute and untouchable power, somehow outside of time as well as outside of space.

The most radical of all the Fascist architects was Giuseppe Terragni. In 1936, he completed his masterpiece, the Casa del Fascio, the local headquarters of the Fascist Party in

Como. It was a white cube, more perfect than most other modernist architects had been able to build at that scale, and served as the main focal point for the square in which it stood, acting as a backdrop for mass meetings. An open grid, which took up two-thirds of the front facade, was perfectly balanced by the white expanse of the remaining third. There was no clear entrance, only this stucco apparition in the middle of the city. Instead of framing the Duce or whatever local dignitary stood on its balcony with columns, however, Terragni contained him with an open grid, reminding the public of the rational new world the Fascists believed they were building. The structure's exterior was remarkably free of ornamentation, and gained its power only from the fact that it stood in such stark contrast to the jumble of older construction around it.

On the inside, the grid continued, framing a grand central court whose ceiling consisted of glass tiles that suffused the very white space with soft light. You reached this empty space after passing through a low colonnade (or at least a geometric version thereof, for again the grid stood in for columns and beams) and then found yourself surrounded by a building in which the rationalizing tendencies had been taken to their furthest extremes by the fact that Terragni let that same intersection of horizontal and vertical elements reverberate all the way through every corridor and office, every window and every doorframe. It illustrated what later critics would point out long after the Second World War: that the "almost nothing" of modernism, in its denial of human memory, sense, and scale, could easily tend toward a kind of empty absolute that implied the victory of a searing white nihilism.

In surveying this field of grand, abstract, and anti-human buildings and spaces, I can't help but recall how Marinetti ended his "Futurist Manifesto":

> They will find us at last one winter's night in the depths of the country in a sad hangar echoing with the notes of the monotonous rain, crouched near our trembling airplanes, warming our hands at the wretched fire which our books of

165.

163. Adalberto Libera, Sabaudia, 1934.

164. Giuseppe Terragni, Casa del Fascio, Como, 1932-36.

165. Marcello Piciatentini, Esposizione Universale di Roma, 1942.

today will make when they flame gaily beneath the glittering flight of their pictures.

They will crowd around us, panting with anguish and disappointment, and exasperated by our proud indefatigable courage, will hurl themselves forward to kill us, with all the more hatred as their hearts will be drunk with love and admiration for us. And strong healthy Injustice will shine radiantly from their eyes. For art can only be violence, cruelty, injustice. (Marinetti, "Manifeste du Futur-

166   167

isme")

There was, however, an alternative to this (self-) annihilation. In the United States, architects found a way forward for architecture that could answer the call for planning and logic, would recognize the power of the state, and could create usable and somewhat adaptable spaces. Actually, they found two paths. One led toward the construction of infrastructure projects that celebrated the communal force of humanity; the second produced the generic, rational, and yet monumental structures for the large corporations that became the true world rulers after the Second World War.

In many ways, the American drive toward state initiation, design, and control of large infrastructure projects such as roads, dams, parks, and beaches, as well as the housing that went with these construction sites, paralleled what went on in the totalitarian states. Mussolini's draining of the marshes, Hitler's construction of the "autobahn" system starting in 1933, and the huge reclamation and dam projects the Communists undertook during this period, all tried to found a national sense of purpose and identity in the physical landscape. In the United States, the Depression of 1929 and onward and the election of Franklin Delano Roosevelt in 1932 led to the initiation of public works projects all over the country. The Works Progress Administration (WPA) engaged out-of-work artists, designers, and artisans in designing, building, and decorating community projects ranging from bridges to local swimming pools to park shelters. In most cases, these projects were fairly small—a pavilion here, a gate to a park there—but in other cases, they included highways in which every overpass and every entrance ramp became an occasion for stone carving that usually took its cue from either local flora and fauna or historical events.

One of the most beautifully integrated constructions the WPA oversaw was Timberline Lodge, outside of Portland, Oregon. Built high up on the flanks of Mount Hood, it adapted a public form of the Shingle Style that railroad companies had earlier used in the design of resort hotels along their lines through or to national parks. Designed in 1936 by W. I. Turner, an architect then working for the U.S. Forest Service, Timberline Lodge was a low-slung, expansive structure that answered the mountain's peak with its own spreading, centralized form. What was more remarkable than the architecture, however, was the extensive program of decoration you could find everywhere in the lodge. Wood beams and even newel posts all ended with carved versions of local squirrels or trees. Rugs based on motifs supposedly found in the work of local Native American tribes (though they sometimes had a more Southwestern style) adorned all the rooms, as did bedspreads with similar motifs. Local artists went out into the surrounding woods and drew the local flowers, producing images that both hung in the rooms and provided a complete catalog of the region's flora.

For, just as Neurath and van Eesteren wanted to rationalize information and representation, so the WPA was not only bent on beautifying communal projects while giving artists work; it also wanted to create a record of each place and what each community already had. WPA Guides documented the monuments of landscapes and historical highlights in towns and cities all across the country. The WPA also celebrated the power of communal action, producing a series of posters that showed the glories of the new world. Assimilating the jaunty sense of motion and the sweep of elegant ocean liners or trains that artists such as Cassandre had glorified in the headier days before the crash, as well as the abstracted, sans-serif, and streamlined letters, the angles, and the pin-wheeling compositions of the modernists, artists such as Lester Beall produced posters proclaiming the agency's achievements with great visual power.

The largest projects in which the U.S. government engaged, however, remained the public works programs. The most famous of these was the Tennessee Valley Authority

166. Section of the Autobahn, 1936-1939.

167, 168. William Irving Turner, Timberline Lodge, Timberline, 1935.

169 | 170

(TVA) that, with almost dictatorial power, reshaped an entire section of the American South. Erecting dams and catchment basins all along the Tennessee River and its tributaries, it used the electricity it gained from harnessing the water both to bring light to tens of thousands of homes and to attract major industry to this impoverished part of the country. Rather than merely building huge projects, however, the TVA reshaped an entire landscape, turning what were isolated valleys into either recreational lakes or productive factory towns connected by gently curved roads that offered picturesque views of the dams and their facades. The TVA also replanted and restored denuded hillsides to prevent erosion. In so doing, they regularized the landscape and filled it with high-tension wires, factories, and other monuments to civilization while appropriating and abstracting nature and its forms.

The greatest monument to this human-made landscape was not along the Tennessee River, but along the Colorado. Starting in 1930, the Bureau of Reclamation, another New Deal (as Roosevelt's collection of make-work programs were called) agency, began damming the only major river of the American Southwest in a gorge near Las Vegas, Nevada. The resulting Hoover Dam, finished in 1936, was for a long time the tallest and largest in the world. It created an immense lake behind it, in which the stark contrast between the deep blue water and the barren, reddish hills were like a modernist abstraction of the traditional romantic landscape of hills and lakes. The dam produced such a massive amount of electricity and water that it allowed for the growth of what were then small outposts such as Las Vegas and Phoenix into metropolises with millions of inhabitants each.

The massive dam's design, overseen by Gordon Kaufmann, captured the essence of both the scale and the nature of the endeavor. Kaufmann smoothed the dam into one continuous, sloped surface pinned down by vertical elements that started as buttresses and rose up as turrets, as if he were building the inside of a giant cathedral. Two intake towers stood in the middle of the lake as star-shaped emblems of man's power to tame nature. The actual power generation and administration buildings clung to ledges or hovered at the base of the dam, providing a visual clue of the geometric essence inherent in both the rocks and the dam itself. Sculptures by Oskar Hansen made the achievements of human beings in taming nature and creating electricity explicit. Inside the generating facility, which was open to the public, Kaufmann worked with artists and designers to create a streamlined version of an industrial environment. The generators were encased in a smooth metal housing you could admire from high up on bridges, while the surfaces were covered with terrazzo, smooth concrete, and metal that ended in the layers of curves and scrolls that the public had learned by then denoted luxurious speed and modern power. The Hoover Dam gave testimony of the power that modern humans had to redesign the landscape.

Yet, it was not the only such structure. In America alone, the Golden Gate Bridge, which opened in 1937 with a design by Joseph Strauss, along with countless other bridges across the country, used design to meld structural elements together into streamlined forms that reached across great voids or stretched up into the sky to support the long spans. In San Francisco, Strauss and his designers pulled the main span's design down to human level with lampposts that seemed to delaminate as they rose up to support the actual light. They extended the bridge out into the city with approaches that snaked along, through and over the landscape, drawing San Francisco out of its natural setting to the point where you could both leave and survey that inhabited rock. Against the nihilistic minimalism of the totalitarian regimes in Europe, America, and (to a certain extent) the Soviet Union, the Golden Gate Bridge posed the heroic forms of pure geometry, elongated, extended, and abstracted

169. Gordon Kaufmann, Hoover Dam, Nevada, 1931-1935.

170. Joseph Strauss, Golden Gate Bridge, San Francisco 1937.

nature, streamlined shapes, and the pure act of construction as tying humans to each other and nature.

The WPA-era design also entered into every community with the much smaller projects that politicians used to either solve social problems or distract people from them. Most notable in this respect were the countless works that Robert Moses undertook in the New York area. They ranged from massive public housing projects to the parkways that snake out of the city to Long Island, upstate New York, and Connecticut, the bridges that take the roads there, and the beaches and beach pavilions travelers find at the end of their journey of escape. Working with the almost absolute power that was entrusted to some public officials in this era, Moses managed to reshape the landscape of New York, from the large scale of where people lived and how they moved to the small scale of swimming pools and neighborhood parks that created a sense of community within the city.

With the advent of the Second World War, both the large and the small-scale public works projects came to a complete halt. When they resumed after the war, as in President Eisenhower's national interstate program, formalized in the Federal-Aid Highway Act of 1956, design was no longer part of the agenda. The post-war roads, dams, and bridges were usually built as cheaply and as quickly as possible. They rammed through the landscape rather than enhancing your view and your sense of overcoming the world around you. The state now felt no need to show the public what modern technology could do; it just built so that the engine of transformation could do its work. The era before the Second World War was the last moment when design still worked to create a sense of collectively belonging in a new place. After that, these tasks became separated. Each task—making you aware of where you were, what your community or society might be, and where you were going—demanded a different way of working, and all three of these modes of expression had increasingly less opportunity to state their case in a manner that allowed people to experience their achievements.

171, 172. Robert Moses, Orchard Beach, New York, 1936.

During the Second World War, great strides in production occurred. The warring states learned how to produce goods at an astonishing speed. They applied techniques of assembly but also of distribution, workflow, and management which were experimental or daring until then, but which became the basis for the explosion of consumer goods and the power of international corporations after the war. The things they produced, whether armaments or buildings, were remarkable not in appearance, but in the way they worked. In a way, design took a step back before the modernists' efforts to make objects and spaces look new, toward the earlier period when designers were

173

174

concerned with showing what objects were—or just with assembling them as rationally as possible. The Jeep, a sturdy, compact, and minimal version of the Model T, was a perfect example of this attitude, as was the German automotive venture, the Volkswagen. Pioneered by Ferdinand Porsche, the latter was meant to be car available to the people (*Volk*). While the car's bulbous shape still had echoes of streamlining, it also recalled the collage of gears and wheels encased in metal that had been the hallmark of industrial objects during the era when Behrens had sought to style AEG's products. The Kalashnikov rifle, first built in 1943, was designed to be clunky so that it could be made easily, but also so that there would be play between the elements, allowing them to withstand use and abuse, and so that it could be easily cleaned. As the AK-47 (the version produced in 1947), it became the most successful and democratic implement of death ever made. In architecture, the emphasis was also on speed, mass production, and modularity. The emblem of Second World War construction was the Quonset hut, a pure arch made out of sheet metal that was light, easy to put up and take down, and capable of being constructed anywhere. It was both a fragment of a pure geometry and an example of mass production. It was not, however, the kind of environment in which people wanted to live.

The first great emblem of the post-war era, and one that tried to build on the modernist dreams of a more rational, open, fluid, and flexible world, was the United Nations Building. Its design brought together elements of Rockefeller Center and the League of Nations—the streamlined image of exuberance with the collage of interlocking machinery churning out a modern world. It did so because its design was the result of a true team effort—itself emblematic of a new, more systematic way of working—that brought together Wallace Harrison, who had been the creative force behind Rockefeller Center, with Le Corbusier, the architect of the winning entry in the League of Nations competition, as well as with leading architects from the Soviet Union and many other countries.

The result is not pure; it is a collage of different elements, arranged in a manner that shows a process of compromise. Yet, each element of the United Nations Building conveys a message about the modern world. Its largest structure is the Secretariat Building, a business building, and the home for a new bureaucracy. Instead of being a block or a tower or a compromise between the two, it is a thin slab over 500 feet tall. Clad on its thin sides with white marble, it presents to both the city and the river a long facade of greenish glass covered with a metal scrim or sunscreen (what Le Corbusier called a "brise soleil"). The building's shape is pure, but has little of the solidity of previous office towers. It combines a sense of openness with a gridded mask that seems to speak of an incomprehensible complexity.

Next to the Secretariat sits the General Assembly Building. Instead of a dome or an arch, as had been common for the central spaces of democracy in the United States for more than a century, it presents an upward-turned and splayed curve as the image of the coming together of the whole globe. The shape is not centralized (though a vestigial dome sits, at the insistence of the more tradition-minded Americans, in its center) and not stable. It indicates that civic purpose is something you could now gesture at, rather than placing it confidently in the landscape. Inside the Assembly structure, the main hall is a warped version of a rotunda, its sloped front wall looming over the curved tiers of seats.

Weaving together these fragmentary geometries, which are like the more undressed bits and pieces of the confident building blocks of the modern world that had been erected before the Second World War, is a series of lower buildings and interior spaces that themselves form a collage of different elements. This collage effect is due partially to the fact that they were each designed

173. Willys MB Jeep, 1942.
174. Mijail Kalashnikov, Kalashnikov AK-47 Rifle, 1943-1947.

by architects from different countries and decorated with gifts from yet other states, but also to their attempt to integrate a disparate, semi-public, and still uncertain organization. As a result, halls range from low and extensive, covered in marble and stainless steel, to soaring lobbies where delegates sit under soft lighting, surrounded by fabric. Civic elements—including murals, an elaborately curving staircase intersected by a ramp supported by an arch that looks as if it belonged at the approach to a bridge, and even a pendulum indicating scientific equilibrium and measure—do not so much focus these spaces, as they become the gears or knuckles around which the whole operation turns. The United Nations Building is a true assembly of bits and pieces, none of them fixed to either each other or to the site, floating at the edge of the city and at the edge of any kind of coherence. What makes it work is the fact that it was built, despite widespread skepticism, and that it presents a more or less coherent vision of what the modern world could look like. That world would consist of fragments of geometric shapes housing modular spaces while also allowing for moments of expressive form, put together in a loose, perhaps even rambling manner, in which circulation elements become the most visible elements.

The United Nations Building, as well as such structures as the UNESCO Building, built a few years later to a design by Marcel Breuer in Paris, presented a model that was most directly influenced by a type that appeared in countries all around the world: the businessman's hotel. Hilton Hotels in particular, from Kinshasa to Amsterdam and from Chicago to Paris, inserted themselves into old cities as long, thin slabs, which was the most logical way to build a large number of hotel rooms, each of which needed privacy and a window, around a double-loaded corridor. The slabs floated over a collection of lobbies, restaurants, and meeting rooms where the local and international elite could gather to revel in the chances the modern world offered them while inhabiting, if even for a meal or a night, that very fragment of modernity.

175, 176. Le Corbusier, United Nations Building, New York, 1948-1952.

177, 178, 179. Marcel Breuer (with Pier Luigi Nervi & Bernard Zehrfuss), UNESCO Building, Paris, 1953.

But such hotels were isolated—if often highly symbolic and important—instances of a high modernism. Most of what carried forward the dream of modernism after the Second World War consisted of office and housing blocks that continued the logic of high-rise construction

205

and combined it with a thin version (in both a literal and visual sense) of the modernist cubes and rectangles of the prewar period. Skidmore, Owings, and Merrill, the firm that came to be identified with this kind of corporate modernism, designed the most emblematic of these, Lever House in New York, which was constructed in 1952. That firm perfected the sheathing of many variations on boxes, slabs, and other rectangular volumes with a "curtain wall" of glass. They did not develop the technology, nor were they stylistic innovators, but few firms produced corporate structures that were more perfect in proportion and detailing. Though Lever House was a modest structure of just over twenty stories, it made as radical a difference in the New York City grid as did Rockefeller Center because it responded to the setback requirements by bundling itself into a thin slab, clad in a greenish glass, hovering at the back of the lot over a two-story plinth, itself raised off the street, that surrounded an open courtyard. The building gave back a huge amount of space to the surrounding city, but that very same emptiness also made it more visible as an icon for a company that wanted to present itself as the epitome of clean, modern living.

Lever House brought some of the sense of free composition that modernist architects had developed before the Second World War into the heart of Manhattan, and tamed it into a slick-skinned, simple structure representing the essence of how tall office buildings worked, both as structures and as spatial configurations. That skin was like the perfect businessman's suit, or like the slick advertisements that were then being produced in the nearby towers on Madison Avenue, including ads for the Lever Company. Architecture had not disappeared; it had just become enough to clad a world newly unified by capitalism and bureaucracies.

But the very epitome of the new type of skyscraper arose six years later, when Ludwig Mies van der Rohe collaborated with the propagandist Philip Johnson in the design of the Seagram Building. At thirty-eight stories, it was a taller building, but also a simpler one:

it was a pure rectangle rising from the back of the site, with an empty plaza taking up most of the rest of the lot, its white marble contrasting with the building's dark bronze-toned skin. Mies van der Rohe wanted to express the fact that such buildings were made of steel, but fire codes did not allow him to, as they prescribed fireproofing on all structural members. So the architect pasted I-beams on the facade, representing the structure with ornament in the way nineteenth-century architects might have done. He then made the lobby completely open and empty, as well as almost double height, letting the elevator and service cores, again clad in blinding white stone, come down within this void. Inside the office floors, the grid continued through the division and subdivision of every office, but he carried it out in bronze with wood and stucco infill panels, so that it had none of the insistent lack of materiality of the Casa del Fascio. Everything about the Seagram Building was perfectly proportioned, nothing actually showed how anything worked or what it was made out of, and all the spaces were part of a larger, abstract order. Architecture gave order, place, and rhythm to whatever activity took place within it. The Seagram Building was an answer to the increasing complexity of modern life, one that tried to sweep away as many of the contradictory impulses, not to mention social and economic tensions, inherent in that world, in favor of a frame that provided clarity, rest, and logic in a monumental presence. You might almost say that the Seagram Building was the American corporations' answer to the absolute order of the fascist regimes.

The grid and the slabs that the grid ruled could contain anything. In Chicago, Mies van der Rohe designed a group of skyscrapers along Lake Michigan, including 860 Lake Shore Drive, completed in 1951, which was a metal tube lifted up and out of the urban context to contain

180. Skidmore, Owings and Merrill (SOM), Lever House, New York, 1950-1952.

181. Ludwig Mies van der Rohe, Seagram Building. New York City, 1958.

182

simple apartments. He even applied the same system to a public housing project just a few miles to the south. At the same time, he was working on the campus of the Illinois Institute of Technology, whose major focal point, Crown Hall (not coincidentally housing the architecture school that Mies van der Rohe directed), was completed in 1956. The school disported itself through the grid with the freedom of Rockefeller Center, the logic of isolated academic structures developed in the American campus tradition, and the look of factory buildings whose brick and glass facades were gridded off with steel members. One critic famously commented that the chapel, a modest structure that sat in a corner of the campus, looked like part of IIT's physical plant, while its boiler, which rose above the low-slung buildings around it, looked like a church.

The influence of such designs was immense. By housing any building in a structure made up of rectangular elements, whether made of steel or concrete, cladding them as much as possible with glass that let you see what was going on inside, and placing them freely within the landscape, separate from any surrounding structures, you could define the institution or inhabitants as being part of a new world. You could claim that the building was as logical as any company or new social organization; you could say that it was transparent and open; and you could rationalize that it was making the most of the constrictions of the new logic of rational organization. Skidmore, Owings, and Merrill, Ludwig Mies van der Rohe, and their countless competitors and students soon spread the glass-encased slab around the globe. These structures were anonymous and often interchangeable (Skidmore, Owings, and Merrill became famous for having "standard details" that often included whole floor plans), but at their best they were elegantly proportioned, flexible, and indeed very new in their appearance. That they were also very destructive of any

182. Ludwig Mies van der Rohe, 860 Lake Shore Drive, Chicago, 1948-1951.

sense of urban fabric, human scale, or local identity mattered little in the optimistic post-war era. These were issues that did not become evident until many of them had been built and occupied.

The best of the new gridded structures, such as Mies van der Rohe's Dominion Center, constructed in Toronto between 1965 and 1974; the elegant 1959 Crown Zellerbach Building in San Francisco, by Skidmore, Owings, and Merrill; and the SAS Hotel in Copenhagen, designed by Arne Jacobsen and finished in 1962, still stand as emblems of modernism. Their many lesser imitators, however, often have not outlived, either in fact or appropriateness, the brief moment when the world seemed to be ruled by simple but large corporate structures that were going to finally solve all problems. Ironically, among the most forbidding of all of these were the four slabs Wallace Harrison's firms designed across Sixth Avenue from Rockefeller Center. Their completely undifferentiated facades rose from barren, wind-swept plazas that stood as mute testimony to what the architects and their clients had lost after planning the complex interweaving of form and space, material and decoration, and different geometries in the original development.

The worst result of the drive toward the gridded high-rise as the all-purpose container was the construction of housing that neither had any relationship to an existing community nor created one of its own. Most such housing was clad in brick, whether the high-rises for the wealthy designed by Emery Roth and Sons in New York City or the cookie-cutter social housing projects plunked down all over the Western world. Such housing consisted either of slabs with double-loaded corridors, or of X-plans with centralized elevator cores. These blocks were replicated by as many units as the bureaucrats said were needed, and usually appeared in an open space that was a denuded version of Le Corbusier's dream of a regained nature. They had no ornament, and there was little indication of any scale. They were essentially boxes to store people. In Eastern Europe, a German system of concrete called *Plattenbau* reduced the structures even further into mere stacks of closed, inflexible, and mute containers.

The European variation on the gridded office (or apartment) block took the form of massive new building projects in the middle of devastated old cities. Auguste Perret, who had been a pioneer in using poured-in-place concrete before the war, rebuilt Le Havre, starting almost as soon as the war was over, with heavy, concrete towers and low-rise plinths, all ordered by strong frames. In East Berlin, the Communist regime bulldozed what was left of most of the old city to construct such showpieces as housing projects along the Karl Marx Allée, and covered them with vestiges of a neo-classical architecture.

The best of these plans, however, was the so-called Lijnbaan in Rotterdam, the city that had been such a hotbed for modernism before the war. In 1954, the firm of Van den Broek and Bakema replaced the city's core, which had been wiped out by aerial bombardment at the start of the war, with a pedestrian shopping street lined with glass-fronted stores and with apartments above this continuous line of retail. Behind the clean, rhythmic facades, service courtyards brought goods and people into the heart of the project, while beyond that, base lines of apartment blocks rose on one side and, later on, office buildings rose on the other side. The apartment buildings were set within green courtyards and stood in a strict north-south line paralleling the shopping street. All the elements of the city were still there, but they had been pulled apart, clarified, cleaned up, and ordered so that they could function in a more logical and more beautiful manner.

Beyond buildings, the grid also invaded every aspect of daily life. The so-called Ulm School of graphic design, founded in that German city in 1953, pioneered the notion that a page, poster, or book could be analyzed and divided into a series of proportional relationships that would organize text and imagery in the most efficient

183. Arne Jacobsen, SAS Hotel, Copenhagen, 1955-1960.

184. Emery Roth and Sons, 355 Lexington Avenue, New York, 1955.

185. Auguste Perret, L'Hotel de Ville, Le Havre, 1957-1958.

186. Jo van den Broek & Jacob B. Bakema, Lijnbaan, Rotterdam, 1953.

manner, while also creating visual balance and legibility. Using such no-nonsense typefaces as Helvetica and Univers, these designers created highly refined, clean, and seemingly empty images in which design seemed to disappear completely into a system in which everything could be typed and represented.

In the United States, European refugees such as Ladislav Sutnar and Herbert Bayer helped bring modernist principles to mainstream graphic design and into the ways in which major corporations presented themselves. While their work was often still evocative, using abstract blocks and diagonals to excite the page, their followers reduced content to blocks, disposed as simply as possible, and then used photographs to evoke the reality of whatever they were selling in as straightforward a manner as possible. This spareness was especially true in the work of the "California School" of modernists such as Alvin Lustig. What emerged between the grid and the photograph was the logo. Though pioneered by Behrens for AEG and Edward Johnston for the London Underground, the notion of representing a whole company with a single image reached its greatest power in the United States after the Second World War. The logo reduced a complex corporate or governmental structure into an abstract geometry that yet retained some echoes of reality, such as the eye that represented CBS's camera looking at the world or the viewer looking at television. Paul Rand in 1956 created the logo for IBM, whose computers were then promising a perfect cybernetic world, and in 1960 created one for Westinghouse, the prototypical industrial conglomerate. In 1964, Ivan Chermayeff designed the Mobil logo as a pure composition of blue, red, and white. Everywhere complex organizations were being reduced to singular statements.

The state, however, still ruled in most of the world. The most important and most problematic experiment in corporate modernism was built starting in 1956 in the middle of Brazil. Laid out by Lucio Costa along with landscape architect Roberto Burle Marx, and with its major buildings designed by one of the young collaborators on the UN project, Oscar Niemeyer,

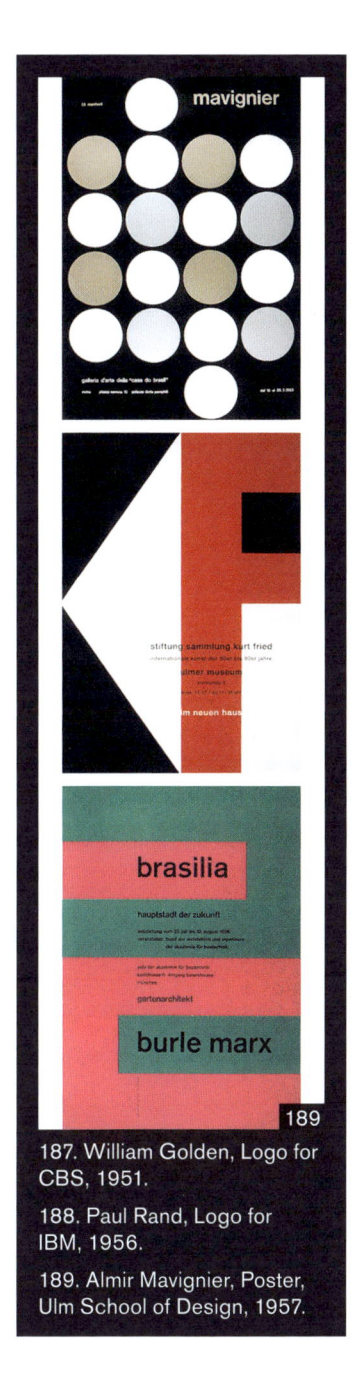

Brasilia was to be the country's new capital, thus re-establishing the nation beyond the reach of tradition and the confusing, competing interests that controlled its large coastal cities. Commissioned by a reformist president, Juscelino Kubitschek, the city was to cover more than two thousand square miles. Its plan was meant to resemble a cross with curved arms—not for religious reasons, but to mark possession of the place. The major axis that held the curved wings, of a scale that completely dwarfed the Mall in Washington, D.C., and any other such civic plaza, served as the city's major public space. Beyond that, Costa divided the city into a super-grid defined by major highways. In the first part to be built, each of these "sectors" was designated for a different group of citizens, and each was subdivided into smaller bands where housing developments or office buildings were to be built. The planners kept all the functions strictly separate, creating a tropical version of Le Corbusier's Plan Voisin, with high-rises surrounded by vast amounts of open space.

Niemeyer's buildings became the icons of the new Brazil, as well as of a state-planned architecture. The secretariat, where the bureaucracy ran the country, is a doubled version of the UN Secretariat, with a narrow space between the two slabs. The Congress Hall is a large bowl hovering over a plinth. A cathedral is a basket of concrete ribs ringing one central space, while countless churches and chapels spread throughout the city sport curving, arched, and swooping roofs over spaces encrusted with tile. Monuments dot the civic plazas, including a massive concrete beam cantilevering out on both ends from a central support to commemorate the building of Brasilia itself.

Nowhere else did a country this large build a new capital at such a scale and speed. By now, Brasilia is a city with over two million inhabitants. Its great monuments bake

187. William Golden, Logo for CBS, 1951.
188. Paul Rand, Logo for IBM, 1956.
189. Almir Mavignier, Poster, Ulm School of Design, 1957.

190

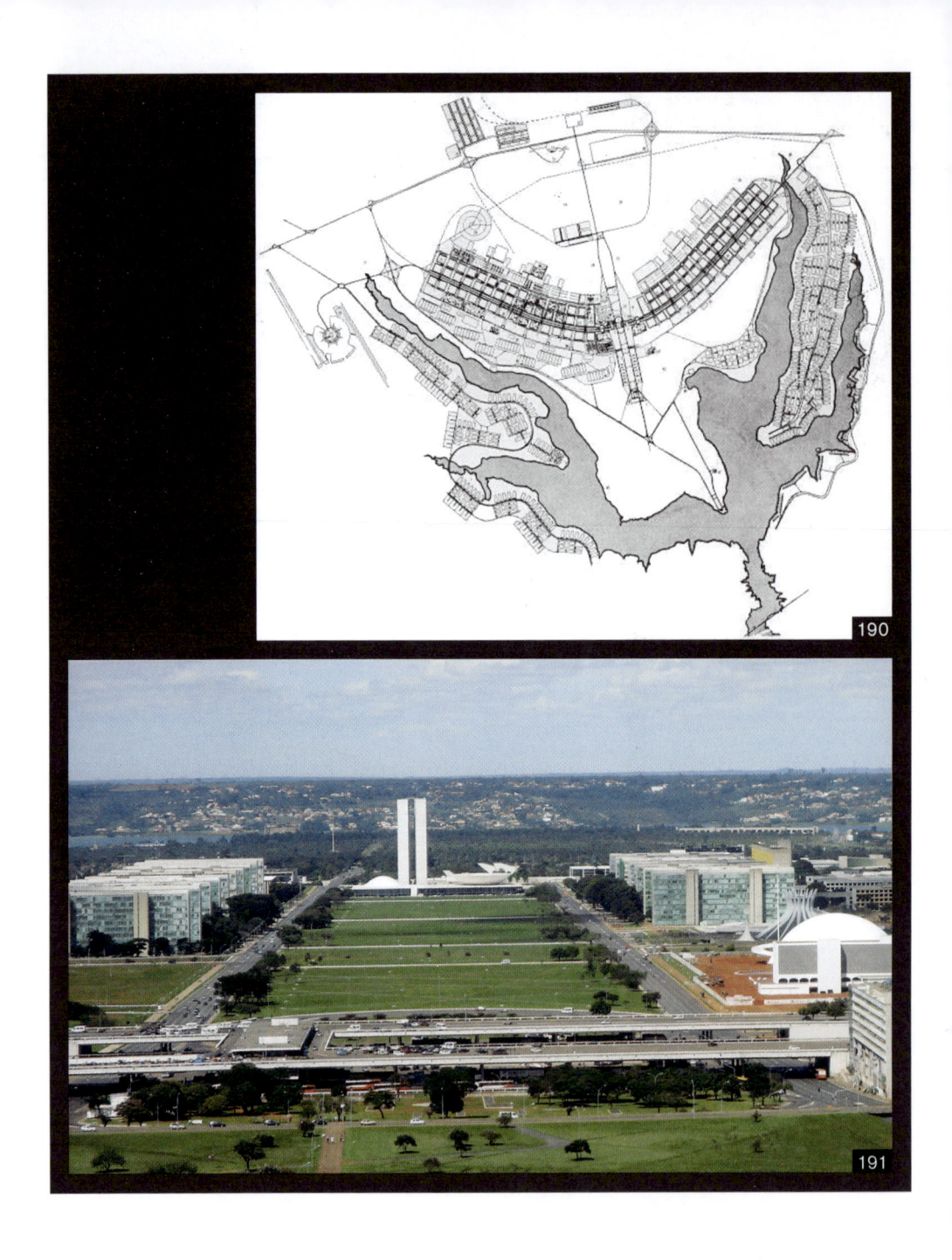

191

under the sun, somewhat dilapidated, but still clear in form. They reduce the whole country to the pure shapes that modernist architects thought were the essence of all things, and contain vast amounts of people and power. What distinguishes these building blocks of a modernist total environment are not only the carefully modulated, but strongly delineated spaces in which Burle Marx placed them, but also the flourishes Niemeyer added. Roofs serve both to shade the buildings and to distinguish the different ministries and agencies through their shapes. They are often part of Brasilia's public space, with great ramps and stairs allowing inhabitants to rise up to survey the realm of government. Identity and movement modulate the stark signs of power to make them part of an urban composition.

Unfortunately, the scale and simplicity of the architecture and planning are such that the buildings remain isolated and alien. The city that has grown up around them has burst the bounds of dividing highways and has occupied the open space between the high-rises with the things people need in a city: small, affordable, and flexible housing, shops, and other facilities that serve everyday life. Vast parts of Brasilia consist of shantytowns, and even in the middle-class areas, the clarity of the modernist geometry is difficult to find. Reality has taken over, and modernism has become subsumed in the complexity of everyday life.

Four years after the dedication of Brasilia, Kubitschek's successor was overthrown. His dream of a more just democracy disappeared under the boots of a military regime. Niemeyer, Costa, and Burle Marx continued to build, but the dream of a total architecture that would embody a new world had proven too radical and too unfeasible. The question now became, How could modernism be something you could live with and in?

190. Lucio Costa, Brasilia Pilot Masterplan, 1960.

191. Oscar Niemeyer, Esplanada dos Ministérios, Brasília, 2006.

7. THE HUMAN FORM ENDURES
contingent modernism

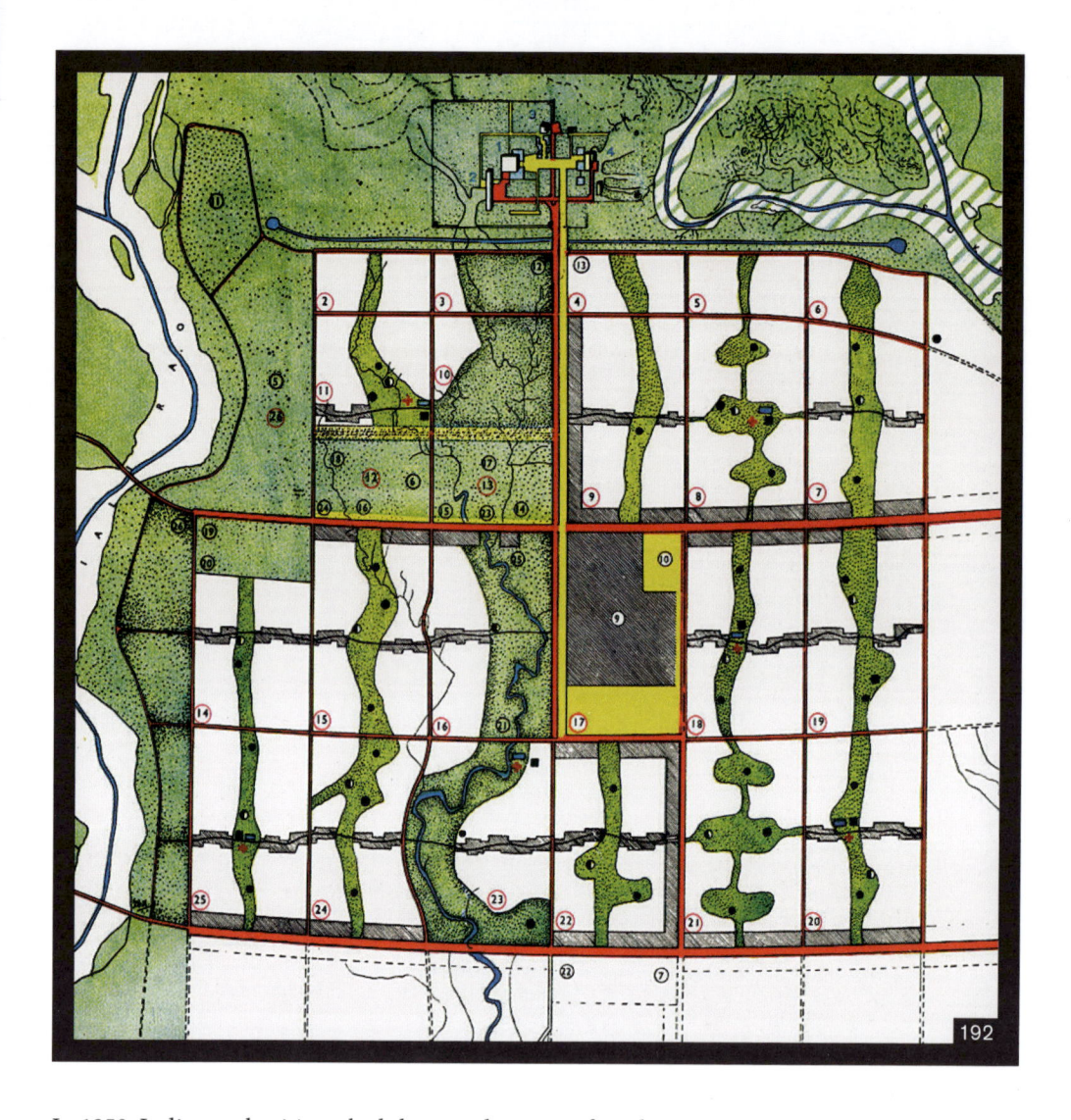

In 1950, Indian authorities asked the grand master of modernist geometries, Le Corbusier, to take over the design of a city of the same scale and just as far removed from Western Europe as Brasilia. Chandigarh was to be the new capital of the Indian part of the Punjab. Originally designed by Albert Mayer and Matthew Nowicki, it became Le Corbusier's first chance to put his ideas about urban planning into effect. The city, sitting on a semi-arid high plain like Brasilia, was to have 150,000 inhabitants in its first phase and would mark Indian control

192. Le Corbusier, Chandigarh Plan, 1951.

193. Le Corbusier at Chandigarh, Photographer Unknown.

over what had become, after the division between India and Pakistan two years earlier, disputed territory. Like his pupil Niemeyer and the urban planner Costa, Le Corbusier laid Chandigarh out in a grid, dividing it into sectors. His geometry, however, was more intricate: he differentiated between seven levels of circulation, from the highway connecting the new town to the rest of the world to the lane leading to a house, and wove the resulting circulation elements through each other. Within each block, he also planned for both public and retail facilities. In some ways, Chandigarh was less radical in its approach than Brasilia and certainly more realistic in its responses to the real needs of urban settings and their inhabitants than some of the grander prewar and wartime schemes for new cities, attempting as it did to replicate some of the settlement patterns that had been used for colonies since Roman times.

At the city's core, Le Corbusier envisioned a vast plaza, again like that of Brasilia. Fronting it were the provincial Assembly, a building intended for the central government bureaucracy, and the tallest structure, the High Court. For a central monument to focus this grouping, Le Corbusier chose not a piece of geometry or an object commemorating the construction of this place. Instead, at the end of plaza he placed a giant, open hand made of reinforced concrete gesturing toward the sky. Though the sculpture was of an immense scale and the hand itself was so abstracted as to be difficult to understand, its meaning was clear: it represented humanity establishing itself on the land and opening itself up to that landscape.

In designing the buildings, Le Corbusier also brought the human figure and, he hoped, the complexity of human life, back into architecture. In 1948, he had developed a system of proportion he called the "Modulor." It was based on a male human figure standing with its feet

![194]

slightly splayed and one arm lifted up. Le Corbusier believed that, by measuring the relative length of the overall body, arms, legs, torso, and head, you could develop mathematical principles that would not only help to visually control construction of any scale, but also make sure that, no matter how large a building became, it would always have a direct and empathetic relationship with the body of the person observing and inhabiting that structure.

Starting in the years before the Second World War, Le Corbusier had moved away from the white "machines of living" that he had helped popularize. His designs became heavier, the concrete out of which he made his buildings became more evident and started to mold and modulate the basic geometry of cube, rectangle, and circle. The buildings no longer floated on thin columns but sat on the ground, and they were heavy and often dark. The Maisons Jaoul, built outside of Paris in 1955, summed up how far Le Corbusier had come: it is an assembly of brick blocks with concrete slabs, some of them with vaulted roofs. The building seems to sink into the ground, and light comes through small windows and slits. It is more like a modern version of an ancient cave than a pristine invention of a machine age.

The buildings at Chandigarh have the same heaviness. The Assembly Building is a large block hiding behind a deep concrete screen. To enter it, you have to pass through a tall, cool arcade whose roof is a shallow U-shape gesturing out toward the central plaza. Inside, the major gathering spaces sit as isolated circles within a dark "hypostyle" hall whose sea of columns holds up the roof. This is a place of mystery or repose, not of energy and enlightenment. Nothing reveals itself, nothing invites or excites; everything is fixed, shaped, and shaded.

Chandigarh represented the return of a sense of place inhabited by human beings back into the realm of modernist architecture. Though it still followed the rational principles of urban planning Le Corbusier had helped formulate before the Second World War, as a built reality

194. Le Corbusier, Palace of Assembly, Chandigarh, 1951-1965.

195. Le Corbusier, Palace of Assembly interior, Chandigarh, 1951-1965.

196. Le Corbusier, Chapel of Notre Dame du Haut, Ronchamp, 1954.

it moved beyond those rules of separation. It stated how architecture could modulate and mold our lives through the application of modern technology and in response to modern life, but could also, in doing so, create something other, something more mysterious, and, architects such as Le Corbusier hoped, more satisfying.

Le Corbusier's postwar masterpiece, Notre Dame du Haut, is an embodiment of that search for something more eternal and mysterious. This pilgrimage church in Ronchamp was built between 1950 and 1955 on what had been an ancient holy site. Le Corbusier placed a vaguely square object on this hilltop, but it was by no means a box. Its four walls cant in, sheltering underneath a concrete roof that curves up and away from them. Small slit windows at random intervals pierce the walls. A semi-oval cylinder rises up into a bell tower next to the chapel. Inside, you find yourself again in a modernist version of a cave: a dark space with thick walls through which light barely passes, the ceiling hovering over you and the ground sloping away. Nothing lines up; forms slide by each other, and the fragmentary forms contain but do not enclose you. Architecture is a pure play of forms in light, but an enigmatic one in which it is difficult to name what each shape might be, how it was made, or what it does. At Ronchamp, Le Corbusier moved through the reduction of architecture to form, and into a realm where you could question what form was and what your relationship to such fundamentally unknowable phenomena might be.

This humanist strain in modernist architecture had its roots in the period before the Second World War and in areas beyond the main power centers of architecture. It responded to local conditions and materials, as well as to the theories of writers such as Sir John Summerson and Lewis Mumford, who asked architects to consider how they could answer to the human being and his or her memories and expectations, fears and hopes. Memory, place, scale, texture, and color helped us find a place in the world, these theoreticians argued, and the assault of technology had only made it all the more necessary that we be able to do so.

The most accomplished architect to modulate his designs in response to such concerns (though not to theoretical impulses) was the Finn Alvar Aalto. Though Aalto's early works, such as the 1927 Viipuri Library (in what is now Russia), were modernist in their thin, predominantly white forms, in their designs he already exhibited an interest in theatricality and the exploration of the expression of function that shaped his later buildings. The Viipuri Library is a split-level design. You come in through a low, long lobby, walk up a half-flight of stairs, and then find yourself in a tall space lit from above. Books line the walls around you, and a circulation desk is right in front, in the middle of space. You can then go up another half level on broad steps that stretch from wall to wall to a reading room with a window out to the park. Slotted underneath this space you find a further surprise: the assembly room, where an undulating wood ceiling and wood walls modulate sound, making you feel as if you were in a cocoon. Everything about this design heightens your sense of where you are and what should happen in that space.

After the Second World War, Aalto designed more libraries, community centers, and other civic facilities, first in his native Finland and then in other countries. In the Seinajoki Library, for instance, constructed in 1958, Aalto contrasted the compact rectangles that contain the book stacks with a fan-shaped reading room. The orthogonal part of the building served to anchor the building to the site and to its functional components, as well as being the place where you slipped into the building between the shifting geometry of the bars. The fan, which became a common theme in his work, opened itself up to the light and the landscape.

In the Säynätsalo Town Hall, completed in 1952, the brick-clad buildings rise up a slight hill around a grassy courtyard. At the top, the tallest structure contains the Council Chamber, its roof held up with a fan of wood

197. Alvar Aalto, Viipuri Library, Viipuri, 1933-1935.

beams caressed by clerestory light. Moving through the building, you are always aware of where you are in relation to the other spaces and the landscape. The rise and fall of ceiling heights, the constriction and opening up of spaces, and the change of materials from stucco to brick to wood to glass all choreograph, rather than merely arrange, the building into something that draws you into a direct relationship with all its parts. It does so, moreover, because Aalto designed every door handle, every railing, and every other piece of hardware so it would respond to the human touch, curving and cupping wrapped metal and wood to meet the hand. He designed lighting that molded the light into a soft, reflective glow, and populated his buildings with plywood furniture that responded to the curve of the human body in repose.

The combination of site- and function-specific form, honestly used materials, and a sense of dramatic enscenement of the central civic functions of our society became, through Aalto's work, one of the central arguments for why we still needed architecture in a modern era. We needed architecture because it could make places—at least at a civic scale—in a landscape that was increasingly monotonous. Instead of the sites we knew from long use and habit that were assembled out of mass-produced materials, and that were designed, built, and owned by forces out of our control, these structures proposed forms you could truly inhabit, that you could feel, and that seemed real and specific.

Aalto built several projects in Germany and the United States that helped spread his influence. His Finnish Pavilion for the 1939 World's Fair in New York highlighted the wood for which his country was famous in every aspect of the building, and presented photographs on a three-story-tall waving wall of that material that canted in toward the viewer. His Baker House dormitories at the Massachusetts Institute of Technology, completed in 1948, offered an alternative to the slabs of housing then beginning to rise all around the world. Above a collection of common rooms at different levels and of different shapes, each reached through carefully planned stairs and anterooms, and each suffused with natural light, the dorm rooms form one continuous, brick-clad wave that answer the curve of the Charles River along which the building is situated, while breaking up what would otherwise be a rather long and unrelenting line of rooms.

With Aalto's work it became clear that form and shape had a role not just in fragments for civic gathering, but also in buildings as a whole. It also became evident that there was a generation of architects who were thinking about how to deform and inhabit modernism. These developments took at least three different directions. In one mode, architects tried to specify and make more complex the very systems and grids modernism had developed, as Le Corbusier had done at Chandigarh. Prominent among the designers choosing this direction were such architects as Jaap Bakema, of the firm of Van den Broek and Bakema in the Netherlands, and Alison and Peter Smithson in England. The Smithsons engaged in unrelenting studies of how they could create public housing that would have the right scale and configuration for different inhabitants, and yet build it in a rational and even modular manner. A second path led architects to experiment at a small scale with new materials to create domestic environments and specific interior locations that would be more responsive to their inhabitants. Here the architects grouped around *Arts & Architecture* magazine in California played a prominent role, though Europe developed its own domestic variations. In the third mode, architects such as Louis Kahn explored how architecture could be used to re-imbue the central institutions of our society with meaning.

In the first mode, architects carried on the work started before the Second World War by the Congres Internationale d'Architecture Moderne, or CIAM. Spearheaded by Le Corbusier, this shifting group of

198, 199, 200, 201, 202.
Alvar Aalto, Säynätsalo Town Hall, Säynätsal, 1933-1935.

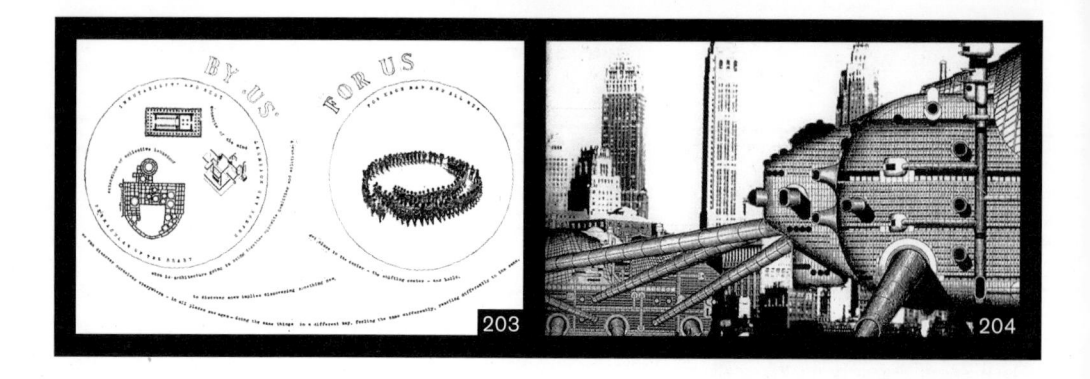

modernist architects sought to codify a pseudo-scientific way in which architecture and urbanism should work. In 1928 they had proclaimed that "the destiny of architecture is to express the orientation of the age," and that to do so it must align itself with the "economic and sociological plane" through abstract planning and the use of mass production. By the time of the 1933 Athens Charter, a document they produced at the end of a meeting on a boat on their way to that city, they had turned to the actual contours of the city, proclaiming that it was made up of four elements: housing, work, recreation, and traffic. Each of these needed its own form and its own technology, but "the key functions … develop inside built volumes subject to three imperious necessities: sufficient space, sun and ventilation." Not only that, but in the city, housing came first, and it had a particular character:

> If the cell is the primordial biological element, the home, that is to say the shelter of a family, constitutes the social cell. The building of this home, after more than a century of subjection to the brutal games of speculation, must become a human undertaking. The home is the initial nucleus of town planning. It protects man's growth, shelters the joys and sorrows of his daily life. (Preparatory Committee [CIRPAC] of the Athens Charter of the CIAM, "The Charter of Athens")

To plan for such a "cell," architects needed to be able to balance the tendency toward the rule of abstract, systematic organization and construction with the need to make units that were specific and commodious. For the next twenty years, the members of CIAM spent their meetings fighting about how this could be done, until finally the team preparing what was to be their tenth congress, in 1955, split off to form their own organization. Actually, not wanting to fall into the same problems they felt had turned CIAM into a bureaucracy with a dogma—a kind of meta-state authority in international modernism—they refused to set up any kind of formal organization. They called themselves Team 10, and their meetings consisted of long ar-

203. Aldo van Eyck - Team 10, *The Otterlo Circle*, 1959.

204. Ron Herron, *Walking City*, 1964.

guments among friends who became enemies, reconciled, and then broke apart again.

Not much that the Team 10 members actually built (which was relatively little) is worth remembering. Their forms were massive and still rather alien to both people's lives and their settings. In many ways, Team 10 marked the end of architects' attempts to develop a central theory and practice of modernism—an endeavor that had never really succeeded. What seemed to work was the adoption of selective principles and the adaptations of new technologies in a manner that was conscious of a place and time and tried to open up a modernist space, as happened in Finland, India, and Los Angeles.

Team X did have a tremendous influence on their students, and some of the best and brightest went on to be just as productively unproductive. Peter Cook, Michael Webb, and several other young architects working in London in the early 1960s put out a magazine called *Archigram*, a collaborative effort that became a catchphrase for the group. I remember as a small boy opening up the Sunday London *Times* and seeing one of their visions, a herd of spheres "walking" across the Atlantic Ocean to moor in New York, splashed all over the front page. They imagined architecture and space suits merging into "suitaloons" that would let you survive even in the nastiest ecological mess, and they proposed structures that would automatically keep constructing themselves as mergers of cranes and enclosures.

Like their mentors, this generation built almost nothing, though they had a tremendous influence, in turn, on a new group of young architects who were as enamored of cars, airplanes, and rockets as they were of steel and concrete: Richard Rogers, Norman Foster, and other "Lords of High Tech" later took Archigram's visions and built them in steel and glass Erector Sets that owed a great deal to Team X's interest in structural expression and modular spaces.

The one place where modernism was most free to experiment in a manner similarly open to the landscape, but (seemingly) free of the weight of traditions, was in Southern California. In this place, with a generally mild climate inhabited by people who were almost all brand-new immigrants, a place that was moreover open to experimentation in all kinds of social and economic endeavors, and that was tuned, through the presence of the entertainment industry, to the importance of imagery, a new kind of modernism began flourishing after the Second World War. Its house organ was *Arts & Architecture*, a magazine founded and edited by critic John Entenza. In 1945, Entenza launched the "Case Study" program, in which he sought to use some of the technologies that had been developed during the war to create affordable housing for the tens of thousands of immigrants who were streaming into the area every year. The program encouraged what critic Esther McCoy soon called the "second-generation modernists" to use prefabricated panels, steel frames, plastics, and other mass-produced components to create cheap homes.

None of the multi-unit schemes Entenza tried to get started were ever completed (beyond a few twin houses), but over two dozen Case Study houses were constructed by the end of the 1960s. Though various in their appearance, they all took to their logical extremes the combination of an open scaffolding around flowing living spaces, encased by a strong and blank set of walls, that Rudolph Schindler and Richard Neutra had helped develop before the war. Open and light, these houses invited the landscape in while isolating themselves from whatever urban aspects were still attached to their sites. They were small and low, but expansive. Their forms were marked by grids, but the relations between columns and beams, and between windows and opaque panels set within that structure, as well as the doors of storage units and the other accouterments of the domestic environment, were everywhere fragmentary and loose, often consisting of various systems sliding by each other.

The most famous Case Study house was Pierre Koenig's #22, built in 1960 on a bluff overlooking Los Angeles. Like many structures in the program, the house consists of a solid block housing services and bedrooms, set at a right angle to a mainly glass volume that cantilevers out over the hill. In a famous photograph by Julius Shulman, whose images helped popularize the program far beyond its limited scope, two women sit in cocktail dresses perched at the far corner of the living room while the city's grid spreads out beneath them into nighttime infinity. Koenig (and Shulman) captured the artifice of architecture in its audacious movement beyond solid land as well as the dissolution of that natural landscape into a grid of lights and steel and glass created by technology. You could inhabit his cell of high design in the vast new human landscape. You are part of the technological grid, instead of hiding away from it in a private sphere, but you also float above that world in a world that, through the magic of technology, is all your own.

In 1949, the couple Charles and Ray Eames had completed their own house in the Case Study program. Facing a meadow to the front and backing up to a cliff, the house presents itself as a pure grid of steel that was snapped into place in a few days. The designers' aim was to create the house completely from prefabricated materials. When all the parts arrived, they redesigned the house on-site to make it more respectful of its surroundings. They split the studio off from the living box, creating a sheltered courtyard between the structures. Inside, a double-height living room takes up half the rectangular volume, with bedrooms stacked on top of the kitchen and service areas in the other half.

205. Pierre Koenig, Stahl House, Case Study House n°22, Los Angeles, 1960.

206

What makes the house remarkable is its simplicity. The snap-on composite panels, which are mainly white but include some red and blue pieces, mix with glass to enclose the interior areas. Wood ceilings and floors are the only other architectural elements. The Eames House is a condensation of bits and pieces produced elsewhere into the simplest form imaginable. The skeleton frees itself and subsumes the wall, opening the house up to nature (except to the rear, where a concrete retaining wall holds back the hillside). The grid had become not a figure in itself, but a true frame for living, through which the activities of life could flow. It established a relationship between the inhabitants and nature, and brought technology home to make a house. There is no more than that to this house.

Actually, there was something more, for the Eameses were not just architects, but designers of furniture and interiors, exhibition stagers, and innovative filmmakers. During the Second World War, they had started to experiment with bent plywood, and in 1949 produced their first chair using that material, the LCW. The Eameses adapted the tradition developed by Michael Thonet, Mart Stam, and Alvar Aalto to the human body, engaging in countless experiments to make their chairs more responsive to the user. After standardizing what they felt was the perfect support for back and bottom, they produced countless variations on the basic base, ranging from plywood laminates to spindly metal. They then started using plastic, creating chairs that not only could be in any color, but could also be strung together into multiples. They experimented with extending the same principles to armchairs and to the design of mass-produced benches that became staples in airports around the world. To this line of seating elements, the Eameses added a storage system in 1950 that took the principles of a metal grid with infill panels which they had developed for their house to the scale of cabinets and office desks. The thin rods that supported the often brightly colored boxes gave you the sense that your changing needs could find a place within this "kit of parts" that you could reassemble in any way you wanted.

Though the Eameses' designs remained more expensive than they would have liked, and though a true kit of parts that was affordable to the masses was not developed until companies such as Ikea began producing goods at a large scale two decades later, the Eameses were part of a global explosion in what came to be called "good design." In the United States, the Herman Miller furniture company, which produced the Eameses' designs, worked with designer George Nelson to domesticate the materials and processes of mass production at a scale of which the

206. A. Charles and Ray Eames, Eames House, Case Study House n°8, Pacific Palisades, 1949.

Bauhaus teachers and students could only have dreamed. In addition to encouraging Herman Miller to work with a large group of talented designers, Nelson also contributed designs that in their look as well as their materials attempted to represent the modern age in a playful, colorful, and friendly manner. His "atomic clock" of 1957, for instance, made the mysteries of science that had produced the horrors of Nagasaki and Hiroshima into a star-shaped dial with colored balls denoting the hours. Meanwhile, textile designer Alexander Girard borrowed images, patterns, and textures from non-Western cultures, including especially Mexico (also a favorite of the Eameses), to bring color and an intense rhythm into the more and more standardized forms of American homes and offices.

Goods such as these were available at a new class of stores, the most notable of which in the United States was Design Research in Boston (co-founded by Walter Gropius), as well as through the so-called "shelter magazines" that promoted "good design." From *Good Housekeeping*, *House & Garden*, and *Better Homes and Gardens* through California's progressive *Sunset Magazine*, they all sold the notion of an environment consisting of mass-produced goods made out of modern materials that could create living and dining rooms, kitchens, dens, and bedrooms that were harmonious, inviting to the human touch, and yet affordable, easy to clean, and easy to change. Instead of presenting social rituals, these magazines suggested, furniture and furnishings should mark and enable the rituals of eating, sleeping, cooking, studying, and that activity new to the middle-class repertory, relaxing. The frame for this new world of modern domesticity was not only the experimental houses of the Case Study program, but also the split-level ranch house, developed in the late 1940s by architect Cliff May and popularized in *Sunset Magazine*. Here the living area became a loftlike multipurpose room, as airy as any the modernists had built into their white villas, but as low-slung and open to the American landscape as Frank Lloyd Wright's Prairie School houses. The bedrooms were stacked on top of service areas and retreats (called the "family room," den, or "rec center") in compact, cellular components.

In the "good design" suburban home, many of the dreams of modernism came together. A rational, open space, fed and constructed by technology, could exist within abstract enclosures and geometric forms. It could respond to the realities of modern existence, but it could also frame the human body directly, rather than through the rituals of social convention. It could create a complete new world for the middle class, separate from the confines of the traditional city. And it could do all of this at a scale of unit production, both of the houses and their goods, that was unprecedented. Modernism was indeed triumphant.

In Europe, the experiments in both architecture and design were confined to isolated homes and expensive products. The most notable of the latter were the furniture and design produced in Scandinavia. In fact, "Scandinavian design" became synonymous with "good design" and with the aspirations of the middle class. The Ant chair, designed by Arne Jacobsen in 1955 (inspired, as he himself said, by the work of the Eameses), became a cheap, flexible element in homes, but also in schools, offices, and restaurants. Jacobsen and his compatriots, such as Finn Juhl, Hans Wegner, and Verner Panton, used plywood and plastic laminates to create completely fluid forms. Poul Henningsen's 1958 Artichoke lamp softened the glow of the light bulb with countless white petals. In Finland, a revival of glass craft led to the production of continuously curved forms created by companies such as Artek. They brought Aalto's fan shapes to the realm of the tabletop. In that same country, Marimekko adapted peasant motifs, abstracted them, and produced fabrics that you could use for wall hangings and walls as well as dresses.

All these elements fused together into what came to be seen—in magazines and films and that new medium, television—as the modern middle-class interior. The families

207. George Nelson, Wooden Atomic Clock, 1947.

208. Alexander Girard, Folk Art Textile Designs.

209. Arne Jacobsen, Ant Chair, 1952.

210. Alvar Aalto & Aino Marsio, Vase, 1937.

211   212

in sitcoms such as *Leave It to Beaver* and *The Dick van Dyke Show* and in films such as Jacques Tati's 1956 *Mon Oncle* lived in open cubes or split-level homes with strong horizontal lines. These homes sported wall-to-wall carpeting, wooden sideboards with no ornamentation, and chairs and sofas that were simplified versions of the ones Danish designers such as Arne Jacobsen and Hans Wegner had created, while a Navajo rug, a Chinese painting, or a Mexican pot provided an occasional splash of color. This mixture of generic, unornamented forms, an emphasis on extension and horizontality, and the incorporation of exotic elements from the "primitive" cultures then being opened up to mass travel and publicity was not usually the result of the efforts of either great designers of individual products or interior designers. It as often as not came out of the hunting and gathering that housewives did in department stores, guided by what they saw in the mass media.

In the United States, the emergence of a dominant taste was part of the rise of a consumer culture that had started before the Second World War but did not become widespread until then. America had won the war and was now reaping the fruits of its victory in the making of what by the mid-1960s became the "Great Society," where everyone was to be well-fed, productive, and especially surrounded by all the creature comforts one could imagine. It was with the wonders of the American kitchen—its slightly rounded, almost completely unornamented, and above all else large forms dominating a landscape of linoleum, aluminum, and other human-made surfaces—that Richard Nixon in 1959 famously sought to prove to Nikita Khrushchev that democracy and capitalism together created a superior socioeconomic system.

If you looked closely at these refrigerators and stoves, as well as at the quasi-modern furniture in most suburban homes, they were on the whole not particularly well-designed. While industrial designers such as Norman Bel Geddes, Raymond Loewy, and Walter Dorwin Teague expanded their practice, and George Nelson attracted his stable of designers to

Herman Miller, most companies merely copied the work of these masters. They adjusted the designs so that they were easier to make, using cheaper materials and adding an occasional ornamental flourish to make the pieces communicate their modernity.

Jet Age and Space Age design soon added a new layer of elements to the household, including cigar-shaped versions of the more traditional and gentler bull-nose curve and literal pictures of aircraft. The simple geometries that had been central to modernism since the 1910s made way for elongated, curving, and convoluted lines, becoming a kind of modernist rococo. These references to the future soon mixed with elements that designers took from those rugs and pots from all over the world and that housewives were picking up at stores or bringing back from their trips. Alexander Girard, another member of George Nelson's circle, specialized in fabrics. As mentioned earlier, he looked especially at South and Central American models and integrated them into lines of textiles meant to cover furniture as well as walls. He even moved beyond the home, designing for airlines and for the show-stopping restaurant La Fonda del Sol in New York, which in 1961 made Mexican styles look chic and elegant in all their colorful exuberance.

Other designers brought a sense of the organic into the household. Russel Wright and the Hungarian émigré Eva Zeisel picked up on a vibrant tradition of modern "art pottery" developed by firms such as Bauer and later Heath Ceramics in San Francisco. They made softly undulating dinner services and coffee sets, using colors that delighted in their unnatural qualities. Soft in hue as well as in form, these shapes slid into the broad, low forms of the American home with ease. In a more extreme manner, artist Isamu Noguchi designed palette-shaped coffee tables (1944) and even a masklike radio (1937). His shapes

211. Jacques Tati, *Mon Oncle*, 1968.

212. Nikita Khrushchev and U.S. Vice-President Richard Nixon during their tour of the American Exhibition in Moscow, 1959.

213 | 214

took elements from modern artists' dissection of human and mineral forms, combined them with an abstraction of surface and support that was proper to modernist furniture, and then styled them into pieces that were continuously curved assemblages. Even more extreme was work by George Nakashima, who combined strict orthogonal geometries, which he held up with thin and clearly expressed structural members, with slabs of wood he found, polished and finished, but left as fragments of the natural world.

Taken together, these mechanical and organic forms, when added to the derived modernism of the mass-produced furniture and suburban homes, enlivened a space that was both open and characteristic in its horizontal reach and split level, but also, in the efficiency and ease of use of its implements, democratic, or at least available to many. That new open world was finally and securely domesticated. Modernism had become part of the daily life of millions and had become comfortable—mainly because it was not just functional, but also contained echoes of the familiar forms of historical styles, the human body, and nature, as well as evoking the promised world of the future.

What would the architectural equivalent of this modern interior be? Already in 1943, critic Sigfried Giedion, writing with architect José Luis Sert and artist Fernand Léger, had called for a "modern monumentality." Civic structures, they argued, should be "expressions of the highest cultural needs of man … expressing collective power." Noting that modernist architecture had led to a "devaluation of the monument," they believed that it would be necessary, in the postwar era, to carefully place, collectively design, and assert the importance of "mileposts" and "focal points" for a new society (Giedion, Sert, and Léger, "Nine Points on Monumentality"). They believed that designers could achieve their aims by working with artists to create convincing forms, designing mobile or temporary monuments, and using light and plain colored planes.

Modernist architecture after the Second World War, however, seemed to have difficulty with this notion. Having stripped architecture of columns and pediments, architects realized that abstract geometric planes did not have an equal resonance, whether because they lacked any relation to the proportions of the human body or because they were not part of an age-old tradition that brought with it the weight of history. They turned instead to the constructive framework of the building as the place that might re-imbue the central institutions of society with a communal image and might create a sense of place larger than the individual human being, while not dissolving into scientific abstraction or bureaucratic cells.

For architect Louis Kahn, this effort became his life's work. Though he had already built some public housing and a community center, the first design he completed that gained any fame or had any impact on other architects came late in his life: the 1951 design of the Yale Art Gallery in New Haven, Connecticut. For the Yale Art Gallery, Kahn went back to the box. Rather than trying to dissolve it or make it more expressive, he turned it into a simple, cubic volume that contained open spaces in four floors. He achieved these loftlike galleries by using the latest advance in structural engineering, a "space-frame" or triangular framework of triangular elements called a tetrahedron. He then further abstracted the cube on the outside by making one side a brick wall on which thin concrete stripes denoted the floors, while on the other side the building presented a gridded glass-and-steel facade. That was about all Kahn seemed to do, though in reality the choices of where you entered (sliding in past the brick wall) and how you moved through the building worked to make you always aware of the simple fact of the building's construction. What made the architecture work was the clarity of the frame and the space it enclosed, the balance between solid and void, and the

213. Russel Wright, American Modern Dinnerware, 1937.

214. Isamu Noguchi, Coffee Table, 1959.

215

perfect proportion of each element. With this building, Kahn began to reassert architecture as the placing, framing, and filling out of a new kind of space.

In subsequent years, Kahn developed what critics Sarah Williams Goldhagen and Rejean Legault, in their 2001 book of that title, have called an "anxious modernism" that somehow produced, out of the pulling apart and the beefing up of the standard elements of modernism, a supremely self-confident set of structures. Kahn's idea was to go back to basics in order to go forward. He had a romantic idea that, if you could return to such simple questions as how and where people gather, how you hold a book in a library, or even how a kitchen abuts a living room, and then control the compositions that come from the framing of such acts with the purest and simplest geometries possible, you would connect these moments to an essential truth about how you lived and acted in the world. Kahn believed in the division between spaces that were "served" or communal, important or ritualistic, and "servant" elements such as staircases and the housing of lesser functions. The former spaces should be open, but clearly framed, large, and defined by geometry, whereas the "servant" elements should be expressive and closed objects that supported these shapes.

It is in Kahn's work that I believe modernism reached its final, and perhaps most tragic expression. Having awoken to the danger of the loss of humanity and place through the corrosive influences of planning and technology, he transformed what had been in many ways the most destructive symbol of that process, namely abstract space, and turned it into something beautiful. He did this by sheltering that space within a structure that was so overtly monumental that it made space into a kind of religious experience.

That certainly was how it felt for me when I first visited the Salk Institute in La Jolla, California. Its first phase opened in 1965, and was the only phase to be completed in Kahn's lifetime. You approached the institute then through a grove of trees along a meandering path (according to a design by Mexican architect Luis Barragan) and found yourself on an empty plaza paved in white travertine. A single channel of water runs down the middle of this empty space, disappearing out of sight where the cliff on which the Salk sits drops off toward the Pacific Ocean. On either side of you are concrete and glass towers that turn their faces toward the sea; they are four stories tall but only occupied every other floor by scholars' offices, which are marked by weathered teak siding. The actual laboratories sit in large blocks behind these offices, and beyond that, the stair towers buffer the complex from the open land to either side. The Salk Institute is a building that contains and facilitates science in blocks Kahn clad in carefully poured concrete whose pour marks he deliberately left to break up their expanse.

The Salk Institute centers on an open and empty space that has no function and looks out at infinity. To Kahn, this space was that which architecture provided beyond function and the organization of functions. Out of the use of complex geometries and simple materials assembled in strict rhythms of open and closed, served and servant, came space to create something he was later to call "The Room," a place of gathering, reflection, and repose by which one could know where one was. Standing in that courtyard, surrounded and framed by clear form, I felt liberated and in place at the same time.

In the Yale Center for British Art, completed in 1975, the Room became the central part of the space. This building is deceptively simple: it consists of a rectangular block Kahn divided into 20-by-20-foot bays, creating a structure that is visible as a grid on both the inside and the outside. The architect introduced the grid by carving four bays out of the base at one corner, letting you enter

215. Louis Kahn, Salk Institute, La Jolla, 1959-1965.

through them and past a column that states the geometry, and then letting the space explode up into a skylit courtyard. The galleries themselves follow the grid, and the concrete columns and beams give the Center a sense of being a highly refined version of a factory loft structure—except that the panels between the columns are covered in stretched Belgian linen framed with white oak. On the top floor, coved skylights wash natural sunlight down into the space past lenses and filters that make it less harmful for the art on display. The Yale Center for British Art's heart is the Room: a three-story tall, oak-paneled, and skylit space, occupied only by a cylindrical concrete staircase, where some of the collection's larger paintings are on display.

In both these buildings, Kahn tried to mine the complexity of geometry to create a diversity of spaces that were still identifiable as part of a larger whole. The clarity of served and servant blocks in the Salk and the clear, sensual concrete grid at the Yale Center for British Art both allowed you to understand how each building was made and what it was made of. A sense of belonging and sensuality then came not from adding flourishes or curves, but from Kahn's manipulating the elements in a theatrical manner so that you moved through them with a clear understanding of what each piece was and finally arrived at a point where Kahn's order both sheltered you and opened you up into a free space, a space that the architect sought on purpose not to define.

Nowhere was Kahn more explicit in his purpose than in the 1972 Phillips Exeter Academy Library in Hanover, New Hampshire. The building's organization is ingenious. Like the Yale building, it appears to be a simple block, in this case a brick-clad cube that abstracts the neo-Colonial (and in some cases Colonial) architecture around it. The building consists, however, of eight floors that Kahn carefully masked by making the windows double-height. On the inside, these tall spaces light double-height reading rooms where you can either read at a carrel by the window or sit in a larger, more public space over which the light washes. The stacks beyond this fill up the space to the building's full height. To make this all work in terms of structure and access, Kahn created a central atrium or Room. The arrangement appears eminently logical, though also driven by an intuitive approach to what a library is: it should be both part of the community and larger than it; it should be a place where books are piled up together, but where you can also read in a sunny place; and it should be a place of focus and grandeur. Kahn laid this all out for the user by having you wander through a brick arcade until you find the door, where you enter into a low vestibule and then rise up along a curved stair whose marble is polished to three degrees—rough for the structure, smoother for the treads, and smoothest where the hand touches it. Then you arrive in an atrium rising up the full height of the building. On all four sides the concrete structure forms perfect circles through which you can see the stacks behind wooden balconies. Above your head, a concrete X washed by light from clerestories ties it all together and marks the heart of the institution. From here you can go wandering into the stacks and toward learning, but it is this central space that makes you aware of the building's structure, function, and community, all in one act of architecture.

Kahn died suddenly and alone in a restroom in New York's Grand Central Station in 1974. He was on his way back from Dhaka in what is now Bangladesh, where he was designing a new capital complex. When it was finally finished in 1983, it was a place of great beauty and tragedy. Made of brick and concrete, it is a castle of democracy presenting cylindrical forms rising out of a lake amid impoverished surroundings. Circles and triangles carved into these huge and monumental round towers reveal the ramps and stairs, the places of gathering and meeting that make a democracy work. At the heart is another great Room, but this is actually the place of democracy at work, the parliament itself.

216. Louis Kahn, Phillips Exeter Academy Library, Exeter, 1965-1972.

217

However, by the time the building was finished, democracy was difficult to find in Bangladesh, and Kahn was dead. The building also had something tragic about it, resembling ruins, as many of Kahn's buildings did, as much as a finished structure. Kahn's projects were often bigger than they needed to be, and their geometries and structures were evident in such dramatic flourishes that the actual functions seemed overwhelmed, until you saw the care with which Kahn sought to make sure each had its own scale, light, and material that invited, rather than merely housing, use. Unlike Le Corbusier in Chandigarh, Kahn looked at the past consciously, trying to find models in history he could use to shape buildings that appeared archaic and thus more real. At the same time, these contemporary crumbling castles were suffused with an absolute geometry and a sense that there was a system underlying all you saw and touched. System and imagery came together in fragments that were at times overwhelming and at times inspiring, and together they sheltered that last opening, the Room, the space Kahn felt was at the heart of architecture—the place where, in a time of war and conflict, humans could make a society for themselves. Such heroic humanism, however, ultimately failed to stop the dissolution of common institutions as places of shared value. Only a few monuments could stand that much design, and only a few clients could afford to build them. The notion that we could

217. Louis Kahn, Bangladesh National Assembly Building, Dhaka, 1982.

218. Louis Kahn, *The Room*, 1971.

all agree on principles, values, and forms, and could find a common humanity in the place of the objects built out of them, proved elusive. Then nothing else was possible, and architects had to build out of despair.

8. WOODEN SHIPS
the modernism
of complexity
and contradiction

Stills: If you smile at me, I will understand
'Cause that is something everybody everywhere does
in the same language.
Crosby: I can see by your coat, my friend,
you're from the other side,
There's just one thing I got to know,
Can you tell me please, who won?
Stills: Say, can I have some of your purple berries?
Crosby: Yes, I've been eating them for six or seven weeks now,
haven't got sick once.
Stills: Probably keep us both alive.

Wooden ships on the water, very free and easy,
Easy, you know the way it's supposed to be,
Silver people on the shoreline, let us be,
Talkin' 'bout very free and easy...

Horror grips us as we watch you die,
All we can do is echo your anguished cries,
Stare as all human feelings die,
We are leaving—you don't need us.

Go, take your sister then, by the hand,
lead her away from this foreign land,
Far away, where we might laugh again,
We are leaving—you don't need us.

And it's a fair wind, blowin' warm,
Out of the south over my shoulder,
Guess I'll set a course and go...

—"Wooden Ships,"
by David Crosby, Stephen Stills, Paul Kantner.

In 1968, the system fell apart. After decades of governments and corporations expanding their reach to organize more and more aspects of reality, along the way analyzing, gridding, and rationalizing city, suburb, and countryside, bedroom, office, and playground, and after decades of designers trying to give shape to that modern space with designs that sought to represent, present, contain, or humanize the new reality, love and death conspired to fill that new void with both terror and beauty. In rural New York State, hundreds of thousands gathered in a vast open space to tune in to groups such as Crosby, Stills, Nash, and Young, and drop out, while in Vietnam some of their brothers were dropping like flies as the bureaucracy and technology of the United States were pulled apart by the combined forces of the jungle, age-old traditions, and a spaceless guerilla war. Meanwhile, in Paris, a year before the Woodstock festival and right after the Tet Offensive, history repeated itself as students tore up the Haussmann boulevards in defiance of the state. This was, however, history taking its revenge as a truly self-conscious farce: the students wanted not power but its opposite—an amorphous, sensual state of enjoyment. "Beneath the paving stones, the beach," was their motto. History was back; and the state, along with God, was pronounced dead. And so were, by many students and teachers alike, architecture, design, and their desire to create a new space for the modern human.

What were designers to do? Many of them dropped out and tuned in, abandoning their professions—a process

219

made easier by a series of economic setbacks that culminated with the recession of 1973, when many of the last of the large-scale projects started in the 1950s and 1960s ground to a halt. Others began looking beyond the canons of modernism to find answers to a society in crisis. There was a sense that the dream of building a modern world had failed, and that it was time to build, as the popular song quoted above had it, "wooden ships" with which you could escape the violence and moral and economic bankruptcy of modernity.

Six years before, along the California coast, a group of architects had begun designing such "wooden ships" on land. These were in actuality a prototype for a new collection of spaces gathered together in the landscape in a manner that seemed natural, rather than imposed. The buildings made sense according to the rituals of daily life in a design governed more by the desire to delight and perhaps even amuse than to impress and order. Looking at how locals had been making houses for decades along the rugged coast, while also mining their extensive knowledge of architectural history, Charles Moore, Donlyn Lyndon, William Turnbull, and Richard Whitaker (collectively known as MLTW), together with landscape architect Lawrence Halprin, designed a community called Sea Ranch that was meant to be a vacation retreat, three hours north of San Francisco. Though it was a real estate project instigated by a development firm that owned nine miles of the coast, Sea Ranch was to become a place where you could enjoy nature and come together with friends and family—a kind of middle-class weekend commune.

For the sixteen years that I lived in California, I tried to get up to Sea Ranch as often as possible. We would rent one of the houses, secure in the knowledge that the vision was shared enough (and encoded in covenants) that we would always be in an environment that felt as if its geometries were unfolding out of the landscapes. The best part, however, was outside. Halprin had envisioned the landscape as preserved and further articulated by the houses, rather than as the kind of tabula rasa most modernists saw in the "old" landscape. He grouped the sites for the future homes along "hedgerows" running parallel to each other and at right angles to the ocean, turning the existing meadows into "rooms" that could become the outdoor equivalents of Louis Kahn's great indoor spaces. When MLTW designed the first structure, Condominium One, in 1965, they clustered the condo units around a courtyard sheltered from the ocean breezes, and then massed the whole building so that it rose up with the meadow away from the cliff, pinning it down to the site with vertical elements that housed lofts and clerestories. Inside the unit that Charles Moore designed for himself, the wood posts and beams, as well as vertical wood siding, remained visible around a space that rambled around various nooks, crannies, and balconies. Moore said he thought of it as a big barn, filled with compact spaces for eating, cooking, or sleeping which he likened to the saddlebags in which cowboys used to carry their essential belongings on the trail. Here was a living space that was not ordered and rational, not white and abstract, but honest, warm, complex, and comfortable. Though modernist notions such as honesty of materials and compaction of technology were present, they hid under forms, shapes, and spaces that were familiar and thus comforting, inviting inhabitants to invent uses for them and complete them with their own furniture and implements.

Moore designed a number of houses for himself in the course of a career of almost half a century that ranged

219. Charles W. Moore, Donlyn Lyndon, William Turnbull, Jr. & Richard Whitaker (MLTW), Sea Ranch, Condominium One, 1965.

220

from California to Connecticut, back to California, and then finally to Texas. In all cases, the homes focused on a ritualistic center, most clearly visible in his first home, in Orinda, California, which he completed five years before Condominium One. The house was a little temple with a pyramidical roof resting on four posts. It was what British critic Sir John Summerson in a 1948 essay, "Heavenly Mansions," had called the "aedicula": a basic form that marked the place where the Pope sat (the baldacchino), where Jewish weddings took place, and where children hid when they turned a table into a hiding place. Summerson believed that this elemental architecture could connect the holy and the most basic human instinct for shelter and place-making.

Making a home for yourself in an increasingly complex and confusing modern world became a central task of architecture—and of the increasing number of designers who made, as a popular book and exhibition organized by Bernard Rudofsky at the Museum of Modern Art in 1964 put it, "Architecture without Architects." Drawing on ancient techniques and using available materials, people could move back to the country beyond the suburbs. They could buy farms and renovate them or build new structures that looked just like the old ones. All over Europe and the United States, and later in countries such as South Africa and Australia, rural communities became the site for such new/old constructions that made people feel more at home. There was even a bible for this group of people: Stewart Brand's *Whole Earth Catalog*, published between 1968 and 1971, which showed them how to make and outfit their own homes.

Part of this movement was also a rediscovery of craft, with people teaching themselves how to turn wood or pots, carve or decorate, sew, and even build. Inspired by objects that they could visit in their free time (something

220. Charles W. Moore, Donlyn Lyndon, William Turnbull, Jr. & Richard Whitaker (MLTW), Sea Ranch, Condominium One, 1965.

221. Bernard Rudofsky, *Architecture Without Architects*, Exhibition at The Museum of Modern Art, New York, 1964.

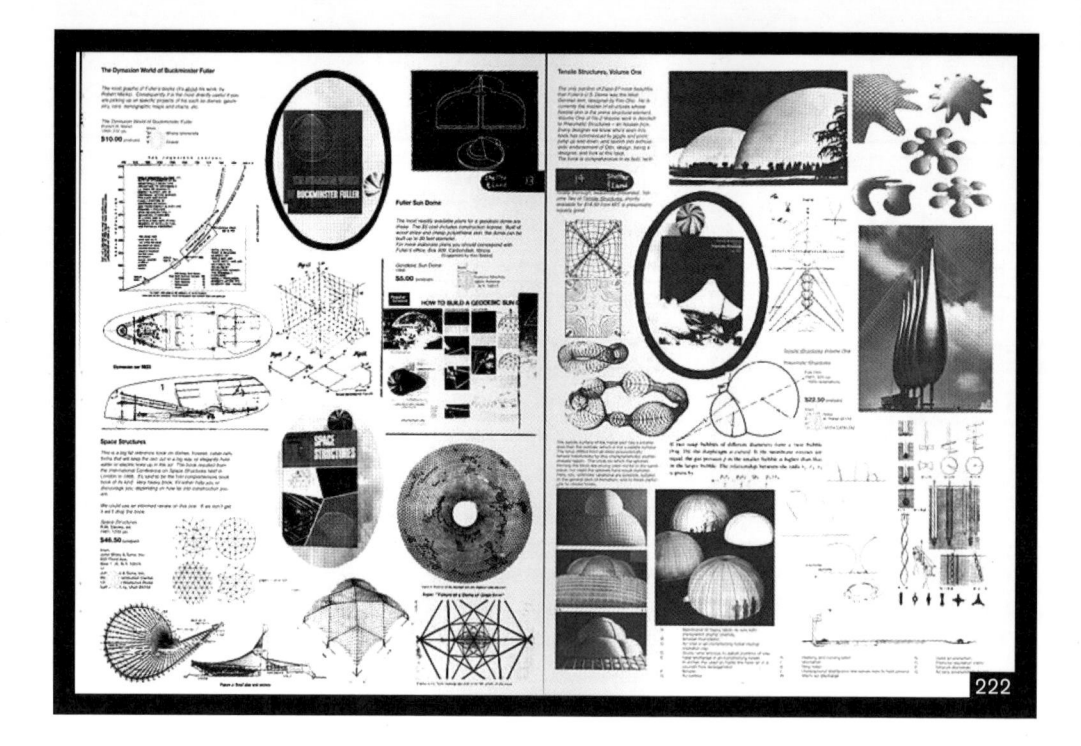

much more bountiful in the 1960s than it ever had been) or on vacations to exotic places, they began incorporating the spare inventions of the Shakers, the cosmic patterns of New England quilts, the jazzy colors of Eastern European peasant clothes, and the swirls and mandalas of India in the objects they wore and used. While high modernism had been made popular by its portrayal in film, magazines, and later television, the craft revival used the medium of popular music to reach all over the globe. In San Francisco and New York, graphic designers such as Victor Mososco, Lee Conklin, and Wes Wilson designed posters for performances of groups such as The Doors, Jefferson Airplane, and the Grateful Dead that borrowed heavily from late-nineteenth-century art nouveau designers like Aubrey Beardsley, and then swirled those swooping, drooping lines around Indian and Chinese symbols. Album cover art brought these images to millions. Clothes worn by rock stars used the foulard patterns that the British had brought from India to England two centuries before in combination with rougher elements and forms from Afghanistan and Nepal.

At concerts such as the Monterey Pop Festival in 1967 and Woodstock two years later, organizers claimed they were presenting not just music, but craft and alternative ways of living

222. Stewart Brand, *Whole Earth Catalog*, 1969.

223. Victor Moscoso, The Doors Poster, 1967.

224. Woodstock Music and Art Festival in Bethel, New York, August 1969, Photographer Unknown.

and worshiping as well, in elaborate craft fairs that soon proliferated all around the Western world. When the Club of Rome Report of 1972 and the oil crisis of 1973 made it clear that there were limits to untrammeled development, this interest in the reuse of the forms and motifs of other cultures and of the past merged with the interest in literal reuse, leading to a passion for antiques, second-hand clothing, and historic buildings. There was a growing sense among both "hippies" and more mainstream consumers that the past was better (and cheaper) than the present or the uncertain future.

Most of this "retro" design just happened. Its engine was more often than not a rejection of any notion of style or design (however sincere that dismissal may or may not have been), and many of its proponents prided themselves on being self-taught. To many people, modernism was part of the problem—not just as a style but also as part of the process of planning every aspect of daily life, from the rituals of cooking in the Frankfurt kitchen to the arrangement of social space for the state. It was complicit in the production of alien environments, and was no longer an alternative to revolution, as Le Corbusier had believed, but part of its repression. The architect or designer as a professional was, by his or her very designation, suspect. The alternative ideal was something vague—perhaps the new peasant society Mao seemed to be building in China, or the communities in the jungles where Che Guevara was fighting American-trained armies, or the mystical nebulae seen in drug-induced trips, or the open nature and old farms of the countryside—but it was not architecture.

In 1973, critic Manfredo Tafuri wrote the most succinct elegy to modernism. Translated in 1976 as *Architecture and Utopia*, it accused architects of "bad faith": they had worked for the centralizing state and for ruthless powers, pretending all along that they could produce the most perfect, free, and open space possible. Capitalism had used them because they substituted the dream of heaven on earth for the pie in the sky religion promised, and thus deferred compensation for the workers. "To ward off anguish by understanding and absorbing its causes would seem to be one of the principal ethical exigencies of bourgeois art," he began his treatise. "It matters little if the conflicts, contradictions, and lacerations that generate this anguish are temporarily reconciled by means of a complex mechanism, or, if, through contemplative sublimation, catharsis is achieved" (Tafuri, *Architecture and Utopia*). Thus, architects either wrested utopia from the logic of social, economic, and technological conditions, or offered a vision beyond that. With these categories, Tafuri summed up and dismissed all forms of modernism as a reflexive reaction. By the 1930s, he said, these utopias turned into fascist total spaces, consumer products took over the dream, and architecture itself turned into planning. All that remained, said Tafuri, was nothingness—the void, the sign of complete failure and abstraction: "No 'salvation' is any longer to be found within it: neither wandering restlessly in labyrinths of images so multivalent they end in muteness, nor enclosed in the stubborn silence of geometry content in its own perfection" (*Architecture and Utopia*). The answer to this predicament, he argued, was to be found not in architecture, but in radical politics.

Architects did become part of popular movements, though often as no more than consultants. Ironically, their role in such movements was, more often than not, to stop their colleagues from building and to preserve structures that predated the modern era. Historic preservation became a major issue in both the United States and Europe. The days of tearing down whole neighborhoods to build rational new districts came to an end as architects made common cause with community pressure groups and activists to preserve historic structures. From New York to San Francisco and from Copenhagen to Paris, they stopped projects for major freeways, high-rise developments, and "slum clearance" dead in their tracks. Inspired by Jane Jacobs, a critic who in her 1961 *Death and Life of Great American Cities* extolled the virtues of the traditional street, the porch, and everything else that helped promote relations between individuals through the marking and framing of ambiguous social spaces, these architects began arguing that the city was better without modern interventions. The major achievements of much of the architecture of the last quarter of the twentieth century were in the preservation of existing structures and neighborhoods, rather than in the building of new forms. Its monuments include Greenwich Village in New York, the Castro in San Francisco, the Canal Zone in Amsterdam, and countless other historic city centers around the Western world.

Following what was essentially a popular movement, architects found in eighteenth- and nineteenth-century structures those accoutrements that they believed could ameliorate the soullessness of the modern city. Porches could serve as stages from which to watch the passing parade and thus create a sense of community. Bay windows could break down the monotony of row houses. Bright colors accents on carved woodwork could give viewers a sense of care and catch the eye with their patterns and hues, thus cutting into the fast-paced, outcome-oriented atmosphere of the city. Gables would make houses look like homes; windows that were taller than they were broad could relate to the human body; and small, purpose-built rooms could convey a sense of variety to the interior. At a larger scale, stone or stone-clad structures could add a sense of history and solidity to office buildings or apartment blocks; arches could welcome entry; and towers, turrets, and spires would mark significant locations in neighborhoods. All the elements that modernism had swept aside piece by piece in a century of corrosive abstraction were now seen as exactly those elements that could create interest, liveliness, continuity, and even community in the built environment.

225. Houses in the Castro Neighborhood, San Francisco.

226

227

The preservation movement was spearheaded both by individuals moving back into historic structures, originally in part because it was all they could afford, and by neighborhood action groups resisting urban redevelopment. In New York, the tearing down of the neo-classical Pennsylvania Station in 1963 and the attempt to demolish Grand Central Station in 1967 galvanized the movement, while in San Francisco activism arose in reaction to the 1964 attempt to build a highway right through the city and its largest park. In Amsterdam, the clearing of a large swatch of land through the city's historic core to construct an underground subway led to pitched battles between police and activists. Eventually it caused the reconstruction of one of the neighborhoods in a historicist style mimicking the original street patterns and, to a certain extent, the shapes and detailing of the nineteenth-century buildings that were torn down.

In furnishing homes, reusing chairs or tables you might find at a thrift store suddenly became as acceptable as historicist styles, which had always dominated most interiors in terms of sheer numbers. "Antiquing," or hunting for great finds, became an acceptable way to furnish a home. While the mass market continued to consist of traditional forms based mainly on seventeenth- and eighteenth-century prototypes, more discerning furnishers of homes became intrigued by late-nineteenth-century furniture. Because of the craft orientation of the late 1960s, Arts and Craft furniture and decoration, from William Morris wallpaper patterns to Gustav Stickley "craftsman" furniture, became especially popular.

Yet, few designers chose to adapt or adopt these modes of design. Serious furniture designers retreated instead into the making of one-off pieces, often emphasizing the beauty of natural materials, as in the work of Dakota Jackson. Those who chose a larger market adapted a more scientific approach to accommodating and celebrating the human body: ergonomics. First coined in 1857 by Wojciech Jastrzębowski, this quasi-science became a way of shaping first furniture, and then all kinds of objects, to the human body. Office chair manufacturers adopted these ideas, while designers such as Bill Stumpf began to create shapes whose sinuous lines traced the human back and bottom, while their steel frames still celebrated the mechanical world of business.

Everywhere soft lines began to appear. Even automobiles became more rounded and more streamlined than the whiplashes and curves common in the cars of the 1940s and 1950s. The prototype of this movement was the Citroen DS, first produced in 1955 to a design by Flaminio Bertoni. This "goddess" (*la Déesse*) of cars was as smooth as the American cars were angular. It was low to the ground when you entered, but lifted up when you started the ignition, thus accommodating itself to the act of entering and then driving. Later French and Italian cars exaggerated these curvilinear lines even further, while also trying to capitalize on the renewed popularity of such quaint products (at least to Americans) as the Volkswagen beetle or the Citroen Deux-Chevaux. All of these cars were highly animate and even playful in their use of articulated headlights, bulbous forms, and even such interface-inviting features as the Deux-Chevaux's canvas roof, which you had to roll up by hand.

Graphic designers moved beyond the reuse of historical forms or the fluid shapes of the work commissioned by rock bands toward an embrace of a harder, and at the same time more colorful and historicizing, palette. In Eastern Europe, designers such as Roman Cieślewicz and Jan Lenica created bright announcements for films and theater pieces that had a deliberate innocence and roughness, picking up on the area's long fascination with what was seen as a still-vibrant peasant heritage. In Japan, while Ikko Tanaka tried to keep a more modernist discipline to his work, at the same time using fragmentary forms and bright colors, Tadanori Yokoo and Takenobu Igarashi combined traditional Japanese

226. Bill Stumpf, Ergon 3, 1976.
227. Flaminio Bertoni, Citroen DS, 1955.
228. Ikko Tanaka, Tanaka Sharaku.
229. Anthon Beeke, Naked Ladies Alphabet, 1969.

woodcut imagery, especially drawn from the *ukiyo* or "floating world" of the late nineteenth century, with Western typefaces and gridded compositions. In the United States, Milton Glaser famously turned Bob Dylan's hair into a tangle of rainbows on a 1967 album cover. Other graphic designers, such as Dan Friedman, used fragments, both of images and of typography, combined into collages. In the Netherlands, Anthon Beeke delighted in shocking audiences with images of nudity, as in his 1980 poster for *Troilus and Cressida*, which showed a horse's private parts in close-up, while letting a classical modernist grid control his highly affective imagery. Collectives such as Wild Plakken and Hard Werken were more expressive and fragmentary in their imagery, though they also continued to order their designs with the invisible lines of modernist organizational principles.

Many designers were looking for a way to use the fragments of the past that were now available to them, while believing that there were, or should be, no more imposed rules, and that design should accommodate the human presence. They all worked in a society in which information and imagery were moving at ever faster paces, as globalization, computerization, and the standardization of production made it possible to access ever more objects, images, and spaces. Authority was something to be distrusted and even fought against, while satisfaction in daily life was more interesting than either a political or a designed utopia. In this sense, perhaps Mao's short-lived statement of liberality made sense: "Let a thousand flowers bloom."

In 1966, architect Robert Venturi published a slim volume called *Complexity and Contradiction in Architecture* that became a handbook for architecture's survival and resurgence. In it, he proclaimed:

> I like complexity and contradiction in architecture. … I speak of a complex and contradictory architecture based on the richness and ambiguity of modern

experience. ... Architects can no longer afford to be intimidated by the puritanically moral language of orthodox modern architecture. I like elements which are hybrid rather than "pure," compromising rather than "clean," distorted rather than "straightforward," ambiguous rather than "articulated," perverse as well as impersonal, boring as well as "interesting," conventional rather than "designed," accommodating rather than excluding, redundant rather than simple, vestigial as well as innovating, inconsistent and equivocal rather than direct and clear. I am for messy vitality over obvious unity, I include the non sequitur and proclaim the duality.
(Venturi, *Complexity and Contradiction in Architecture*)

In answer to Ludwig Mies van der Rohe's famous statement that "Less is more," Venturi concluded, "More is not less." Or, as Charles Moore often put it even more succinctly in his lectures, "Less is a bore."

Venturi illustrated his points both with historical examples, which betrayed a strong preference for baroque and rococo elements most modernists would have thought in bad taste, and with his own work, which he modeled directly on these premodern buildings. He thus sought to erase the break modernism had proclaimed with the past, preferring to return architecture to an unbroken tradition of the manipulation of plan, elevation, form, and detailing to create buildings that would be familiar, represent their functions, invite human participation, and delight the senses. At the core of his working method was a deep humanism he grounded in the reading of anti-modern literary theory. He did not reject the modern world, but did not quite embrace it,

230. Robert Venturi, Vanna House, Chestnut Hill, 1963.

either. Quoting August Heckscher, Venturi wrote that he sought a "unity which maintains, but only just maintains, a control over the clashing elements which compose it. Chaos is very near; its nearness, but its avoidance, gives… force" (*Complexity and Contradiction*). Revolution could indeed be avoided by architecture.

In his own work, Venturi, soon in conjunction with his wife, Denise Scott Brown, sought to make his point, as Le Corbusier had done, with buildings that appeared simple but were complex. The most famous of these was the home he designed for his mother in a Philadelphia suburb in 1961 and built in 1964. The Vanna House looks like a child's drawing: a gabled roof, an off-center chimney, and an oversized window denote shelter, warmth, and sociability. Denoting is exactly what Venturi sought to do: instead of representing the actual function, construction, or layout of the house, or presenting an ideal set of relations between the various elements, he chose to make a graphic representation of paper-thin elements. For the house's facade is everything, and its body extrudes back from that image of domesticity with no modulation. Inside, a staircase winds around the chimney, rooms are shoehorned together, and the whole becomes a carefully crafted assembly of very tight spaces. Venturi was a master at a new kind of game in architecture: how to design floor plans as ingenious puzzles. Combined with the strong images he drew on his buildings' outsides, these tricks of the trade reduced the task of architecture to saying what the buildings were about and skillfully assembling their pieces as efficiently as possible, and then slicing through both image and plan with cuts that surprised and delighted. In the Vanna House there is an indentation right in the facade's center that is also the place where you enter. In other designs, diagonals slash through plans to liberate the boxy rooms toward views and lights.

Charles Moore also pursued this technique, and both had learned it, at least in part, by looking at the Shingle Style houses that critic Vincent Scully had unearthed and popularized in the 1960s. Venturi, Moore, and their fellow designers went searching for what they felt was a truly American architecture. It would be ingenious, and would use inherited traditions, but freely. Their model was Thomas Jefferson, rather than Le Corbusier (though they were more influenced by modernist architects than they cared to admit), while their purpose was to make buildings that would fit into a landscape that they felt had been best served by the structures built when America was undergoing its first major expansion. The rambling homes, the grand stone edifices of rural courthouses in the style known as Richardsonian Romanesque that married granite blocks with courses of red sandstone and exaggerated features such as arched entrances and towers, and the proud assertion of individual structures in the Jeffersonian grid, became their ideals. With MLTW and various other firms, Moore produced countless homes whose plans were variations on octagons or hexagons and clashes between 45- and 60-degree angles, but whose spaces were defined by riots of sloping roofs, unexpected nooks, and light grazing in from angled windows or clerestories. Venturi proposed small municipal structures, few of which were ever built, as signposts for civic importance that squeezed bureaucratic realities into intricate geometries. Together with Scully, Moore also

231. Robert Venturi, Vanna House, Chestnut Hill, 1963.

232. Charles Moore, Bonham House, 1961-1962.

233 | 234
235 | 236

educated a whole new generation of architects at elite institutions such as Yale, Princeton, and the University of Pennsylvania. This group came to be known as the "grays" because of their preference for untreated, vertical wood siding, but also because of their interest in the complexities Venturi had outlined. Their work presented the first coherent American alternative to the white world of the modernists since the Second World War. It forsook forward-looking utopia for a backward-looking nostalgia.

The Grays had not just invented their work out of nowhere, as they, in keeping with modernist doctrine, often claimed. They were deeply indebted to premodernist models, as well as to regionalist and humanist architects such as Alvar Aalto and Louis Kahn (for whom Venturi had worked), and to the countless, more anonymous designers who sought to domesticate modernism. This was true in the United States as well as in Europe, where the Team 10 group presented a more natural bridge to what soon came to be called postmodernism. Designers such as Giancarlo De Carlo and Aldo van Eyck began abstracting their historic prototypes, and shared some of the same interests in a flattening of facades and the intricacies of plan as fascinated their American colleagues. While De Carlo researched historic building types in Italy and put them to use in the design of such projects as the Urbino university campus, planned starting in the late 1970s, Aldo van Eyck designed a house for unwed mothers in Amsterdam (1978) whose colorful steel facade was meant to evoke and fit in with the existing historic buildings while creating defined but fragmentary social spaces on the inside.

While many architects and designers tried to adapt themselves to a new role and to the proclamation of the death of their disciplines, others tried to create architecture out of this confusion. British architect James Stirling had recourse to historical forms in his design of the Leicester University Engineering Laboratories of 1959 to 1961. The building is a collage of elements. First, Stirling designed a large and open engineering laboratory that recalls the industrial heritage of Leicester, but is lit with rotated and extruded square bands of skylights. Stirling then housed the offices and classrooms in a glass-clad tower whose thin panes and mullions recall the constructivist dreams of the early twentieth century. He made this reference even clearer by cantilevering the main lecture hall off the tower's base in a direct reference to Melnikov's 1928 Rusakov Workers' Club. Air vents next to the entrance ramp recall the early modernists' fondness for nautical imagery and reinforce the sense that the plinth resembles a piece of an ocean liner. None of the references are direct, and Stirling kept the look of the complex unified by reducing the materials to red brick,

233, 234. Giancarlo De Carlo, University College, Urbino, 1958-1976.

235, 236. Aldo van Eyck, Hubertus House, House for Unwed Mothers. Amsterdam, 1978.

237. James Stirling, Leicester Engineering Laboratories, Leicester, 1959.

tile, metal, and glass, but he used the historic prototypes to make the building more complex and familiar at the same time. It was as if he were making an instant piece of history, but one that also included modernism, rather than rejecting it.

Stirling's next designs used fewer direct historic references, but instead broke the rectilinear aspects of the box and the grid down into gestures, such as the fans of glass that sheltered the 1964 Cambridge University History Faculty Library or that opened up to the view in the 1971 Queens College Dormitory in Oxford. He also introduced playful elements into the way he presented his designs, drawing the plan of the 1971 Olivetti Training Center in Milton Keynes as a crashing plane by emphasizing the winding path that led to the two winglike classrooms. Stirling was interested not in the vernacular but in the complexity and contradiction Venturi had found in the great masterpieces of architecture. When he began to rediscover nineteenth-century Beaux-Arts architecture, he delighted in the geometric complexities of its plan organization rather than in its stylistic accoutrements. In this appreciation, he was joined by many architects whose eyes were opened to the possibilities of building design as taught at the Académie des Beaux-Arts in Paris in the eighteenth and nineteenth centuries, when it was the subject of a 1976 exhibition at the very temple of modernism, the Museum of Modern Art in New York.

In the late 1970s, after a long period of not seeing any of his buildings constructed, Stirling designed a series of three art museums for German cities. They were all collages of fragmentary geometry shoehorned into and at times mimicking historic street patterns. Only one of them, the Staatsgalerie in Stuttgart, was finally constructed in 1984. From the street, it does not even appear as a building, but rather as terraces cut through by ramps and leading to an undulating glass fragment of a facade framed with bright-green painted steel members. To experience the site, you do not have to enter the building: the architect designed a route up the terraces and

238. James Stirling (with Michael Wilford), Neue Staatsgallerie. Stuttgart, 1977-1984.

through a central, round courtyard, and then up into the residential neighborhood above the museum. Inside, the public spaces are free-flowing sequences of lofts shot through with bright colors and what appear to be overly heavy columns. The galleries are rectangles with central openings and skylights. Modernist forms with whimsical elements and exaggerated versions of neo-classical forms coexist in a structure that looks purposefully unfinished and disappears into the existing urban fabric. The final touch Stirling added consists of little jokes, such as what look like a half-sunken arch and stone blocks strewn around the courtyard, which in fact act as vents for the parking garage underneath and double as benches on which to sit.

For Stirling and many of his colleagues, the

239

fragmentation of modernist elements, the use of historic quotations, the integration of buildings into existing conditions, and the use of light-hearted motifs all served one central purpose: to undercut exactly that monumentality that Louis Kahn had tried so hard to preserve. They believed that the only way architecture was going to survive was if it appeared to be easy to use, as friendly and as much fun as consumer goods. It had to deny the fact that it was commissioned by any power that went beyond an individual's control, and instead look like a happenstance gathering of forms and spaces you could explore. In this way, architecture could weave itself back into the fabric of everyday life.

To the Italian Aldo Rossi, however, it was exactly monumentality that had to be saved. Rossi was concerned above all else with the city as the site of memory. The city's churches, palaces, libraries, and other monuments were interesting to him not so much for the specifics of their design, as for the fact that they had been designed in a manner that was meant to keep them in our memory—that is, to memorialize certain people, institutions, or deeds, and frame them in an enduring manner. As a whole, the city embodied the totality of such efforts at persistence and thus was a tribute to a collective, as opposed to an individual, culture layered over time. It also had the power to catch and hold each of our individual memories, as the variety of experiences to be had in a dense urban setting or in highly potent architecture would remain in our mind. At the core of either personal or collective memory were certain forms, dimly perceived, that you could find embodied in any number of phenomena. Rossi's own sketches showed collages of statues of saints, coffee pots, the Milan cathedral, Coke bottles, and beach cabanas, and he then composed his own architecture out of such remembered forms.

Similar to Stirling after his first period of success, Rossi became known first and foremost as a theoretician and teacher, especially through the publication of his *Architecture of the City* (1966) and *Scientific Autobiography* (1980). His own work was at times somewhat less convincing. His most powerful early design was the school at Fagnano Olona (1977). It consists of the simplest of elements, mainly long rectangles covered in stucco-clad brick and pierced by square windows with cross mullions. The school's centerpiece is a round auditorium outfitted with tiers of wooden benches. Rossi had the factory-like chimney for the school's boiler photographed from behind one of the cross-mullioned windows, emphasizing the conflation of an absolute geometry with an element that to some recalled a concentration camp. Every element in the school, from the gabled pergolas connecting the classroom wings to the relentless symmetry of the whole complex, serves to reduce the building to its elemental and at the same time most evocative forms, as if Rossi was taking architecture back beyond its historic roots to its basic building blocks. If the images were disturbing, that was all the more appropriate, as the past haunted him and should haunt all of his, Rossi believed. Only from that disturbance could new forms emerge.

Such a sense of a productive archaism meant to act as a new beginning was especially apparent in what became his most influential design, the Modena cemetery. Though its final version was, by the time it was finally started in 1978, not nearly as powerful as the drawings Rossi had produced for the original 1972 competition for the commission, its oft-reproduced forms resonated throughout the architecture world. The cemetery's central structure is an open cube with square openings and no roof. Around that structure, which acts as a columbarium, Rossi arranged the remainder of the cemetery in layers of white walls. A chimney again haunts the project with memories of a less natural form of death. The Modena design evoked something so abstract and absolute, but at the same time so redolent of the forms inherent in the architecture familiar to the inhabitants of the area, that it managed to collapse time between the most ancient and the most

239. Aldo Rossi, Fagnana Olana School, Varese, 1972-1976.

240

240. Aldo Rossi, Modena Cemetery, 1971.

modern experience into a timeless monumentality. Rossi was at his most successful in the kinds of projects that were by their very nature wrought with memory and dedicated to a social purpose. When he tried to apply the same principles to housing developments and, later on, to shopping malls and office buildings, his recipe of brick and stucco blocks, square windows, and basic geometries proved incapable of imbuing these quotidian structures with the kind of memory and meaning he wished to leave in the city. His methodology thus showed both the potential and the limits of the uses and reinterpretation of the past. Architects could draw on the history of form, which had been abandoned in the modernist rush to look only toward the future through the lens of technology and geometry. They could still maintain and embody the rational production of an artificial, human-made space that lay at the self-conscious core of modernism. Instead of producing utopias, designers could build monuments to utopia, or fragments of it, that kept hope, dreams, and memories alive in what was becoming an environment shaped increasingly not by architecture, but by economic and functional demands that were leeching design out of the human-made environment.

In the United States, architect Michael Graves followed a path similar to Rossi's, though with considerably more success, at least in economic terms. When he started his career, he was part of a group that came to be known, after a 1972 publication of their work, as the "New York Five." The five—Richard Meier, John Hejduk, Peter Eisenman, Charles Gwathmey, and Graves—were all architects who were interested in recapturing the formal, if not the ideological, innovations of prewar modernism, and in particular the work of Le Corbusier. What they discovered in the work of the early modernists was similar to what Stirling and others had discovered in the Beaux-Arts plan: an expressive formal structure. They found a world made up

241

of an articulated structure, pierced by equally clearly formed circulation systems such as stairs and ramps, and then enlivened by elements such as bull-nosed rooms, "piano curve" windows, and layers of ribbon windows. Le Corbusier's "five points" had turned into a menu of shapes that could directly address the human body as it found itself framed, moving through, and mirrored in the white-painted cages of abstracted forms.

Starting with his 1976 design for the Crooks House in Fort Wayne, Indiana, and following with the Plocek House, built in rural New Jersey four years later, Graves began to distinguish his work from that of his colleagues by eroding the grid, fragmenting the forms, and introducing colors into his buildings. Soon classical elements, highly abstracted and flattened, followed. Graves's early masterpiece was without a doubt the 1983 library at San Juan Capistrano. It consists of a sequence of rooms that are outlined with columns and contained by walls that step forward and shape the rooms into different geometric figures. The lines of columns continue to the outside, where they form pergolas defining approaches and courtyards. Windows frame views of the outside, while serving as formal focal points within each room. Graves coded the various elements with paint, believing that lower elements should be red, referring to the earth, while higher pieces should mimic the blue of the sky. He also recalled Italian villas in a manner that seemed appropriate to a suburban Los Angeles landscape whose formal monuments had been designed first by the Spanish to recall their Mediterranean homeland and then by the Anglos in imitation of the Spaniards' first nostalgia for their home country.

While architects continually confronted the limits of their attempts to bring history and human occupation back into modernism, furniture and industrial designers had fewer such problems. In 1981, Italian designer Ettore Sottsass founded the furniture design group Memphis, which shocked the furniture world by showing such pieces as the Carlton bookshelves and the Casablanca buffet. These were loose accumulations of planes stacked one on top of the other, each colored differently and made coherent through the application of a busy texture. Together they evoked African sculptures or the totems of the Pacific Northwest. They were also pared-down versions of the kind of traditional, formal pieces that might have adorned a nineteenth-century salon. Like Venturi, Sottsass delighted in the possibility of multiple readings and associations. The interiors Memphis produced in subsequent years took the ideas of the furniture to an environmental realm, filling restaurants and private apartments with riots of color and fragments of geometry, until finally, in the mid 1990s, Sottsass began producing houses from Singapore to Colorado that resembled a child's stacked-up toy building blocks. Summerson's reduction of architecture to a game played by a child under a table was becoming a large-scale type.

Just as they had in previous eras of modernism, architects dominated furniture design. Michael Graves and Robert Venturi both produced versions of classic furniture pieces ranging from the Chippendale chair, which Venturi reduced to a plywood cut-out, to the club chair, which Graves turned into an overstuffed fragment of a theater marquee. In all these elements, the past was seen as an attic to be raided for the bits and pieces out of which a contemporary space could be created.

Finally, furniture and architecture merged. On January 8, 1979, Philip Johnson appeared on the cover of *Time* magazine holding a model of his latest design, for the headquarters of AT&T in New York. Johnson had made a name for himself as a classic modernist designer, collaborating with Ludwig Mies van der Rohe on the Seagram Building and then producing several decades' worth of both corporate and private commissions that tried to stay close to the abstract geometries and minimal monumentality of late, corporate-oriented modernism.

241. Michael Graves, San Juan Capistrano Library, San Juan Capistrano, 1981-1983.

242. Ettore Sottsass. Memphis Design. Carlton Bookshelves, 1981.

243. Philip Johnson on the cover of *Time* Magazine, January 8, 1979, Artist Unknown.

244

Over time, however, Johnson began adding ornament and making gestures that were proto-postmodernist. Then he went completely over to the other side, producing a design for AT&T that looked like a giant Chippendale breakfront extruded to the size of a skyscraper. The merest hints of columns rose up from a base that was an open, arched arcade and culminated in a top that was entirely pediment. With this one design, Johnson managed to sum up the transformation of modernism, through the application of a cloak that referred to historical styles, into a building block that yet remained without any particular scale, material, or purpose. Postmodernism and modernism had become integrated.

What was remarkable was the complete collapse within and around the office buildings and other structures that were containers of modernist space. The sense that architecture and urban planning could open up a new space that would be rational, abstract, and free was completely gone. Instead, only fragments of buildings were strung together with the elements of a past world, from columns and pediments to armoires and easy chairs. The new postmodernism proclaimed itself as a pragmatic reversal of modernist idealism that had swept the world clean not just of the remainders of the past, but of all sense of human habitation and any recognizable sense of place.

By 1980, however, postmodernism had become its own style and doctrine. It was given its more or less official name by critic Charles Jencks, who in 1977 had published what became its bible, *The Language of Post-Modern Architecture*. In it, Jencks claimed that modern architecture was "bankrupt" because it had failed to create places people would like or even love. He exhorted architects to "speak" in the "language of the vernacular," reducing architecture to a form of communication. How things were made, why they were made, who owned them, or what went on inside them was of secondary importance, Jencks implied, as what mattered was the ability of a house to say it was a house in a way that its potential user (or recipient, in semiotic speak) would recognize it as such. It was all a matter of appearances, and in a democratic society you should appear to be part of a multicultural, international society dominated by mass media, with which you had to compete. Just as television and other such media had collapsed space, so architecture must now reduce itself to consumable and placeless bites that would, ironically (and irony was a good thing in the rhetoric of postmodern architecture), create the illusion of a place. Make an apartment building efficiently, but then give it a gable and porches, and it would be a home, Jencks claimed.

The summation of postmodernism and its most public appearance occurred in 1980, when Italian architect and theoretician Paolo Portoghesi directed the first Architecture Biennale in Venice. It was a pendant to the century-old Art Biennale, in which countries presented their artists' best work around a central theme and exhibition set by a curator. Portoghesi planned a *Strada Novissima*, or New Street, in what had once been the city's arsenal. Here, he asked the leading postmodernist architects to erect a fantasy facade in each bay. There was no space in the resulting columns, grids of windows, and washes of color; there was only the presentation of what each architect felt was the essence of his work. Architecture had become pure advertising.

In 1984, when they were commissioned to create designs for the Los Angeles Olympic Games of that year, architect Jon Jerde and graphic designer Deborah Sussman did away even with the background buildings. Due to budget cuts and the far-flung nature of the Games in the sprawl of the Los Angeles region, they found that they had very little chance to create the kinds of monuments that had made some of the other Olympics so memorable. Instead, they came up with a logo, color scheme, and series of building blocks they could use to mark the approaches, entrances, and most salient aspects of already existing facilities. Using candy-colored versions of reds, blues, greens, and yellows, they created an aedicula and a porch to guard the entrance to the Olympic village. They used sonotubes (cardboard tubes used as forms to pour concrete) to line the entry to the main stadium. The

244. Paolo Portoghesi, Strada Novissima, Venice, 1980.

245

246

247

245, 246, 247. Jon Jerde, Deborah Sussman, LADOC Design Team, Temporary Structures for the Los Angeles Olympic Games, 1984.

whole "system" was a kit of parts they laid out in a handbook, rather than actually creating working drawings for all the venues. What mattered ultimately was the way that it looked on television, which is how many more millions experienced the Games than came to Los Angeles. Seen in the small frame of the television screen, the 1984 Olympics indeed appeared as if they were taking place in a small but global village—a fairytale land of peace and bright colors where everybody could find a hint of some form they could relate to their own national colors or native constructions.

The 1984 Olympics may have been postmodernism's most successful moment. For a few weeks, a festival of bright forms unfurled itself across one of the world's largest cities and made it seem like a coherent and wonderful place to most of the world's population. It drew on a lively scene in architecture and design that at the time included Charles Moore and many of those influenced by him, as well as the most promising designer of the period, Frank Gehry. At the same time, Los Angeles itself was beginning to develop a strange kind of coherence that seemed postmodern, but that would in the end not need the washes of color and the fragments of a classical canon that movement wanted to spread throughout the world. Like many other cities, Los Angeles was becoming a vast assemblage of forms and images that appeared, changed, and disappeared without end. Los Angeles was becoming the epitome of sprawl, that concatenation of human dwellings without a seeming center that spread from the Pacific Ocean over the first mountain range and into the high deserts. It had no defined spaces, only the continual flow of the freeway and the boulevards, the pans and the swoops of the films made there, and the flow of immigrants that were spurring its growth. Columns and even fragmentary geometry could not express or control this kind of new world. It would take a different approach to make sense of this continually moving reality.

9. AFTER MODERNISM
experimental design

248

I have always loved modernism. Perhaps it was because I grew up in the Netherlands and had my first powerful experience with architecture when visiting the Schroeder house. Perhaps it was because my parents were prototypical academics who filled our house with "good design" they purchased from Design Research and similar stores. Whatever the reason, even seven years of education in the neo-Gothic idyll of Yale University couldn't cure me of the sense that I felt at home in modernism. My timing was a bit off, though. When I became a more or less serious scholar of architecture, that modernism had fallen apart into antagonistic camps. One side sought to revive the most abstract, ahuman forms of modernism, while the other rejected it completely. I felt caught between a realization that the imposition of technologically based form had proved to be disastrous and a sense that you could not hide from the reality of modernity, nor was it pleasant to do so.

Then, while I was in my first year of graduate studies, Frank Gehry showed up. He proposed, in the 1985 monograph about his work, that "A building under construction is much more beautiful than when it is finished" (foreword to Arnell and Bickford, *Frank Gehry*). With that phrase, which he had first coined in the late 1970s, the Los Angeles–based architect defined a radical change of approach to architecture and design. It signaled acceptance of the world as it is and an attempt to reveal and reorganize that reality. If Tafuri had believed that architecture was over, and postmodernist architects had reduced it to a play of facades, Gehry and many other designers around the world reinvigorated modernism in the last few decades of the twentieth century, precisely by rejecting the notion that they had to make a modern world. The world was already modern, it was just up to the designer to gather, assemble, and articulate that modernity. The victory over the past had been won, the old reality had been wiped out, middle-class values governed the world, and the fragments of the vanquished world had been reincorporated into that new world. Now all of it was available for reuse and reinterpretation, and that act, rather than the completion of whatever one designed, was the primary task of the architect.

248. Frank Gehry, Spiller House, Venice, 1980.

The corollary to this task was the notion that there was not a particularly defined field in which to operate. Cities were dissolving into sprawl. Buildings were defined by codes—whether these were life safety, building, or financial codes, as well as the codes of communication the postmodernists had codified on their facades—and so there was little work for the architect to do. Any space you might inhabit in the modern world was contingent: by 1990, according to the U.S. Census Bureau, the average American moved once every three years and that figure was accelerating. You had to furnish homes with the understanding that such a place was only temporary. The space in which you operated had become even more difficult to define, as computer and communication technologies collapsed space and time in a manner even Walter Benjamin could not have imagined. We lived among fragments in a fluid and continuous space, and design was about both recognizing and finding your way through that space, and then making yourself at home in it.

Frank Gehry translated his beliefs into forms that seemed unfinished, open, and rough, but because they were made out of the fragments of the modern world, they were also recognizable. He became most well-known for leaving exposed the wooden "stud" walls out of which most houses in the United States have been made since the introduction of the balloon frame. Instead of covering the building's exterior or separating rooms from each other, the walls became scrims through which you could see what was happening in the other space. Gehry experimented with this way of creating ambiguous spatial boundaries in the Davis House of 1972 and the Spiller House of 1980, as well as in his own house, a project he started in 1978. Space as well as views flowed between inside and out. Similarly, Gehry used chain-link fence as screens and as definers of space, most notably in his

Cabrillo Marine Aquarium of 1979. On his own house, the fence mimicked the outline of the gable of the existing house onto which he had added, while he stripped part of the exterior siding off to reveal the existing stud walls.

The Gehry House is a collection of fragments referring both to the history of modernist art and to the existing setting in which the architect worked. The kitchen addition preserves the existing asphalt driveway as a floor and mirrors the small panes of the old house's windows in new kitchen cabinets. The adjacent dining area looks out at the surrounding landscape through a window whose angular forms turn the transparency of modernist glass into a piece of sculpture, while another window looks like a piece of an El Lissitzky composition that has landed in suburban Los Angeles.

The Gehry House brought out the promise of the Shingle Style's free flow of spaces, invigorating it with postmodernist quotations that came not from ancient art history, but from modernist inventions of the previous century. It also looked, or so Gehry himself claimed when I asked him about it in 1983, as if "I just went to the local salvage yards and gathered some stuff together." The result was an architecture that is familiar and yet strange, open and yet defined by the fragments of form that were all architects had left at the end of the twentieth century.

Modernism always comes out of the reality of modernity in a given place, and so it was with Gehry's work. While he was engaged in his experiments, critics in Los Angeles such as Ed Soja and his most talented student, Mike Davis, were pointing out that the old obsession with creating a coherent form was the expression of a desire for a coherent system of control that was exactly the heir to the logic of capitalism in its most oppressive form. To them, there was little difference between the dream of a new kind of historical familiarity and the desires and designs of fascist regimes. Soja, in his seminal *Postmodern Geographies: The Reassertion of*

Space in Critical Social Theory of 1989, argued instead for an acceptance of the city's "multinodal" reality and for the production of fragments that could easily be reformed and reused as a form of social and political criticism. Soja and Davis were taking literally Manfredo Tafuri's desire to return to politics, but through a criticism of the city.

Soja drew on the work of philosophers such as Henri Lefebvre (especially his *The Production of Space*) to outline a call for resistance to exactly the kind of structures the modernists had produced in the preceding century. Soja, after Lefebvre, called them "spaces of representation," which included everything from architecture and design to laws and traditional literature (Lefebvre, *The Production of Space*). He proposed opposing them with "representational spaces," a slippery and indefinable form of resistance that would keep changing as it wormed its way, guerilla-style, through the complex urban organism of Los Angeles.

Though both Soja and Davis were highly critical of the work of Frank Gehry (and any other architect), I believe that Gehry did produce a form that embodied the kind of slippery space they sought: the fish. He first made it as a lamp, and then used that form to shape parts of buildings and eventually such structures as the 1987 Kobe Fishdance Restaurant and most of the parts of the Bilbao Guggenheim of 1997. To Gehry, the fish was an emblem of perfection, but also, as he liked to say in his lectures, a "slimy, slippery thing" that could never quite be defined. He also claimed he had been inspired by the carp he had played with as a child in the family bathtub every week before they were used for dinner. Highly personal and enigmatic (which Soja believed "representational space" had to be), it was also an absurdly recognizable form that changed into a modernist, fluid abstraction when it became part of a building. One way to make architecture that resisted capitalism or retreat appeared to be to create

249. Frank Gehry, Gehry House, Los Angeles, 1991.
250. Frank Gehry, Fish Lamp, 1983.

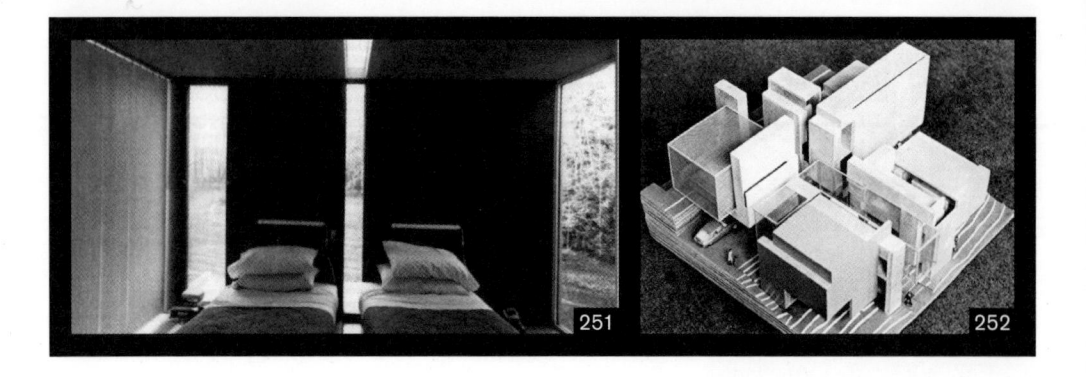

create personal, yet evocative enigmas. Gehry was not the only "bad boy" to reinvigorate architecture. If Gehry started taking buildings apart and leaving them like that, as early as the late 1960s the architect Peter Eisenman ripped what he saw as the closed and mute structures of built form apart to investigate its internal contradictions. Starting with House I and proceeding year by year, house by house, for more than a decade, Eisenman explored what he called, in his 1974 essay "Conceptual Architecture II: Double Deep Structure I," "deep structure." Basing his work on the ideas of mainly French philosophers such as Ferdinand de Saussure, he began designing multiple and contradictory grids that he superimposed. The idea was that under every seemingly rational resolution of form there was, if you just changed scale or perspective, a multiplicity of other forms and resolutions. The more you knew, the more you knew that you didn't know. Fueled by psychoanalytic angst and the sense that resolution was not possible in the modern world, Eisenman began designing structures of ever-greater complexity.

In House VI, designed in 1972 as a retreat in rural Connecticut, a void cut through the marital bed, and stairs led to nowhere. By the time he designed House X in 1980, Eisenman believed that the final point of the house was a model of it as it appeared in orthographic projection, to be buried in the finished structure's swimming pool. The house was not built, but Eisenman continued to metaphorically excavate. His designs of the 1980s, by then heavily influenced by his reading of the philosopher Jacques Derrida, consisted of archaeological digs in which he recreated structures that had been present on the site, like an armory that rose, chimera-like, through the twisted grid and uncertain spaces of his 1989 Wexner Center for the Arts in Columbus, Ohio. The buildings were not the point—the digging and investigation or, as Derrida would put it, the misreading was. Creating a finished text or building was suspect, as it meant you had given in to the modernist dream of creating a perfect product, story, and system of space. The gathering and tracing of fragments, combining them and teasing out their contradictions so that their relationship could never be resolved, was the most productive act in which any maker in any field could engage.

Eisenman taught his mode of architecture at the school he had founded in New York, the Institute for Architecture and Urban Studies. It became a hotbed of experimentation, encouraging students to create designs that could not—and perhaps should not—be built. A new axis appeared between this school and a much older establishment, the Architectural Association in London. Both New York and London were places where it was not easy to build during the late 1970s and early 1980s, especially if you did not want to just repeat established forms. Both cities, however, had a lively literary and artistic scene. As London had sunk into economic malaise, the punk movement had arisen, building on the remnants of the "swinging sixties" to create a vibrant movement in music, fashion, and art. Punk, developed in both cities, was an art of rejection and shock, a making based on breaking. Punks wore clothes that they had torn and repaired with safety pins, and preferred no-rent squats to apartments even if they could find the latter. The rejection of everything that was meant to be good taste and normal behavior became their act and their art. At the Architectural Association, as at the Institute in New York, there was no need to serve clients or finish projects. Under the inspired leadership of Alvin Boyarsky, the AA, as the school was known, collected some of the world's most talented teachers and students to work through the idea that architecture was not the production of buildings but a form of experimentation in and on the built environment.

Three of the teachers who frequented the schools in both New York and London became especially influential. Daniel Libeskind, who was in London only briefly, brought a mystical approach to the AA that concentrated on the moral impossibility of building in an era that he felt was so corrupt. To Libeskind, every attempt to build

251. Peter Eisenman, House VI, Cornwall, 1975.

252. Peter Eisenman, House X, Bloomfield Hills, 1979.

253

had led to violence and terror. Instead, he engaged in the making of drawings based on arcane musical and mathematical principles and on his musings on the poetics of structures. In 1987, he became fascinated with the notion that architecture was the continual production of new relations, as in a machine, and he built a contraption that would evoke the early devices for time measurement produced in the Renaissance. After the model burned, he made architecture out of the event by designing an art installation, *Line of Fire*, a zigzag line evoking the fire. When he entered a competition to design a museum that would tell the history of the Jews in Berlin, he used the same form as the building's organizing shape. Architecture was, after all, not a question of inventing new forms or making things based on function or place, but just a reorganization and re-examination of reality in a manner in which the personal and the social fused. Libeskind built a model for the project covered with pages from a pre-World War II telephone book listing the names of all the Jews who had been lost in the Holocaust. With this highly expressive form, he won the competition. The final building is so radical that it has no front door and no facade. It also does not have spaces that are easy to use. Instead, it is a labyrinth of concrete walls, architecture stripped down to its bare bones. The rooms do not function, but in their emptiness they evoke what was lost and what is absent. This absence, also touted by Eisenman, but turned by Libeskind into a metaphor for the destruction of the German Jews, became for these architects the emblem of their architecture: it was a rereading of the empty, abstract space of modernism, now not as a positive force, but as a lack—something through which you sensed the place that the constructed space had replaced, and through which you sensed the impossibility of utopian construction. Buildings had to evoke absence in order to be present.

Unfortunately, Libeskind soon gave up his research in favor of a career designing more functional buildings whose forms tried to be as spectacular as Gehry's later works. The same trajectory held true for his two colleagues at the AA, Bernard Tschumi and Zaha

253. Daniel Libeskind, Line of Fire, Venice Biennale, 1985.

254, 255. Daniel Libeskind, Jewish Museum, Berlin, 1989-1996.

Hadid. Tschumi's breakthrough came when he won the 1983 competition for Paris's largest new park, the Parc de la Villette, which opened in 1987. His guiding principle was the psychological principle of transference: just as patients need to see their therapists as the embodiment of everything they were afraid of, so Tschumi designed a set of bright red pavilions that were emblems of rational systems of control. Strewn around the park in a strict grid, the pavilions have no function in and of themselves, but became locations for restaurants and other public facilities. Their real function was to be reminders of what Tschumi wanted to be absent in the park, but which would always be there—namely, a sense of predetermined order. Users could wander along what he in a description of the project labeled, in the competition boards, a "cinematographic promenade" past fragments of gardens designed by others, or by historic market buildings Tschumi had preserved. The park was a collage of memory, design, different settings, and scenes, all strung together by an element that the designer hoped would use the same logic as that of film and mass media.

Though Tschumi's later designs have not been as successful as the Parc de la Villette, his influence as a teacher, first at the AA and then as dean at the Columbia School of Architecture starting in 1988, was immense. He coined the phrase "event structures" to designate what were not so much finished buildings as loose containers for activities in which the function of architecture was to act as a catalyst for events that might not otherwise take place. Sometimes his tools were as simple as placing student mailboxes on a slanted floor at the heart of his Lerner Student Services Building at Columbia, finished in 1999, so that picking up your mail would become a social occasion. Sometimes he reactivated existing buildings in unusual ways, as when he

256

strung studios along the roof of an old mill building in Le Fresnoy as part of a new media center that opened in 1997. In all cases, the emphasis on such moments, not the building's ultimate shape, was the point of the architecture.

For Zaha Hadid, however, shapes were the point, though they did not assemble themselves into traditional buildings either. As a student at the AA, Hadid shook up the world of architecture with such early works as her thesis project, a proposal which borrowed heavily from Russian constructivist imagery in seeming to scatter fragments across a map of London. In 1982, she won an international competition for a new apartment building and club at the top of the Peak in Hong Kong. Her proposal was a reinterpretation of that mountain's rocks, which in her evocative painting turned into shards of geometries floating off the slopes, cantilevering into tentative containers for the program elements, and dissecting the high-rise apartment and office blocks above into something halfway between the human-made and the geological.

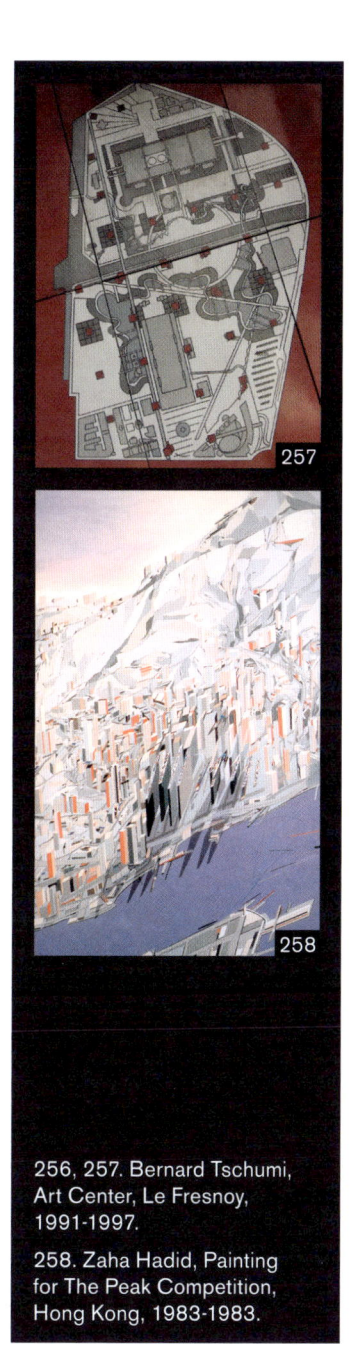

256, 257. Bernard Tschumi, Art Center, Le Fresnoy, 1991-1997.

258. Zaha Hadid, Painting for The Peak Competition, Hong Kong, 1983-1983.

In subsequent works, her architecture became an unfolding of the planes of the city or the landscape, twisted and turned into sharp, elongated, and cut-off building blocks for buildings that rose at acute angles, with large prows and ramps swooping around them. Utterly unbuildable, they changed the way many of her students (and young architects around the world) thought of the possibilities of architecture. Hadid made them believe that they could defy gravity as well as convention. Yet, when she came to construct actual buildings, such as the 1993 Vitra Fire Station in Weil-am-Rhein, Germany, or such later structures as the 2003 Center for Contemporary Art in Cincinnati, Ohio, they were only shadows of this exuberance. She did manage to recapture much of it in the 2005 design of the BMW Factory offices and social spaces built outside of Leipzig, Germany.

By then, Libeskind, Tschumi, and Hadid, together with such former revolutionaries as Coop Himmelblau ("Cooperative of the Blue of Heaven") in Berlin—which started its practice with the statement "Architecture Must Burn"—had large, established practices and were designing major buildings all around the world. Often startling in their appearance, these structures were part of the resurgence of architecture as the making of attractive, iconic emblems of capitalist achievement, but they had little of the evocative power of the architects' early designs. Having started with rejection—the notion that architecture should not be built—and the evocation of absence, these designers had begun to create affirmations of the role architecture plays today, not just in the building industry but also in the culture industry. Beyond merely framing institutions, architecture creates evocative images by which any institution, public or private, can define itself.

To this day, the AA and several other architecture schools continue the tradition of seeing architecture

259

260

261

as a form of experimentation, and designers ranging from Lebbeus Woods in New York to Wes Jones in Los Angeles to Raoul Bunschoten in Rotterdam, as well as countless younger architects who may or may not become practitioners, create designs that cannot be built. These schools also support the dominance of the current aesthetics of fragmentation, expressive form and tortured structure, now ever more liberated by advances in computer-aided design. The buildings always suffer, however, from the fact that their design impulses come from the idea that one should not build.

While they were experimenting, a group of students and friends who had lived in London during the 1960s and 1970s figured out a way to actually make buildings that, at least at first, looked experimental. When Renzo Piano and Richard Rogers won the competition to design a new city library and national museum for Paris in 1971, which later came to be called the Centre Pompidou in honor of the president who instigated the project, they imagined dissolving the building into a kit of parts. The art would be able to move up and down the space of the gallery (both horizontally and vertically) using pulleys, and people would move along the front facade on giant escalators. The building would be covered with electronic advertisements and the mechanical systems that are usually hidden from public view.

The Pompidou as built still has some of those elements, and shocked people when it first appeared, but the final version is much calmer; it lacks the electronic expressions and much of the mechanical movement. Subsequent buildings by Rogers, Piano, Norman Foster, and other proponents of "High Tech" architecture became increasingly more refined, subdued, and elegant—though Rogers's Lloyd's of London Building of

259, 260. Lebbeus Woods, *Underground Berlin*, 1988.

261. Zaha Hadid, Lois & Richard, Rosenthal Center for Contemporary Art, Cincinnati, 2003.

262, 263. Richard Rogers, Lloyd's of London Building, London, 1986.

264

1986 stands out as an expressive masterpiece. By now this is the default or standard mode of designing office buildings: a little bit of structural and mechanical expression, a slick skin, and modular spaces enliven boxes for business. These "Lords of High Tech" now run some of the larger design offices in the world.
Such contradictions between experimentation and the need to get something made (or to make money) pose less of a problem to graphic and industrial designers. The world of graphic design in particular has been liberated by the advent of new computer and communications technologies, as well as by the fragmentation of everything from traditional media forms (television into cable into Internet channels, magazines into zines and blogs) to our attention spans. Yet, even in this field, the initial explosion of creativity that came out of the dark times of the 1970s has by now given way to the instant appropriation of any form of experimentation in slick advertisements.

Los Angeles and London were, again, together with New York, the places where most experimentation first took place. In Los Angeles, designers such as April Greiman began using type fragments of disparate kinds in underground magazines and student publications. The magazine *Wet* became a locus for such assemblages of contradictory graphic forms collaged into highly expressive page layouts. They were the typographic equivalents of Gehry's and others' architectural collages of the same period, bringing together the sensuality and fragmentary nature of L.A.'s culture into something that made sense in a modern world.

Much earlier than in architecture, the computer energized graphic design. Greiman scanned and digitized her own naked body for a 1986 issue of *Design Quarterly*, and font designers began playing with the computer's ability to stretch, splay, and otherwise distort what until then had been quite literally a limited vocabulary. Beyond such abilities, the computer also allowed designers to move large bodies of information around with a freedom that they could barely have imagined previously. The magazine *Émigré*, published in the Bay Area by

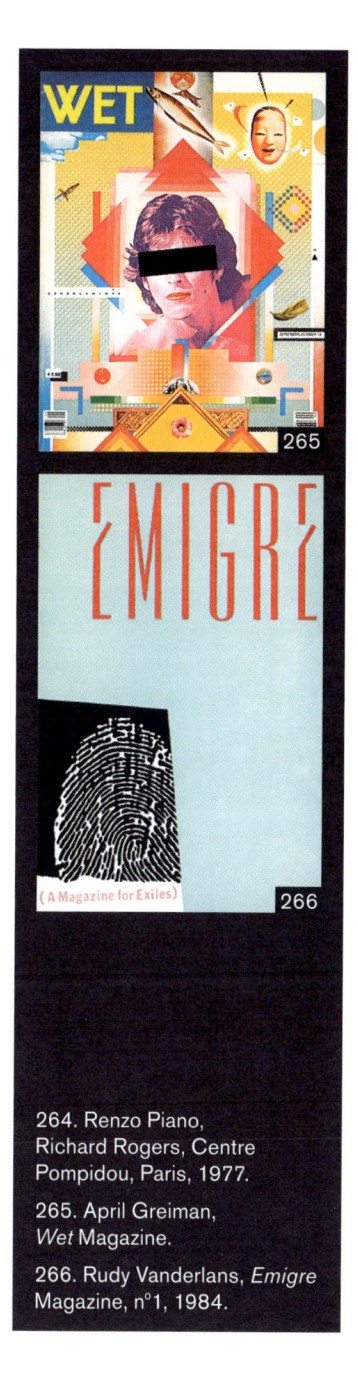

Rudy Vanderlans starting in 1984, was at the forefront in such experimentation. Working with some of the best young designers, Vanderlans turned each issue into a site of implied three-dimensional space in which type at different scales conveyed a variety of meanings. The organization of these elements resurrected the achievements of suprematist and Bauhaus designers. To these designers, the page was just the site of intersection of much larger geometric patterns.

Émigré and the Southern California scene, dominated by the film and music business, generated endless possibilities for the likes of David Carson, a self-taught and self-proclaimed bad-boy designer who started out working for underground surfing and skating magazines and developed a rip-tear-paste aesthetic that the computer could translate into slickly varnished collages. In London, designers began ripping and tearing apart forms as they found them, starting with the flyers for concerts. Their efforts were later collected in Bryan Turcotte's appropriately titled 1999 book *Fucked Up + Photocopied*.

In 1994, the magazine *Wired* appeared, chronicling the contours of the new world being opened up by computer and communications technologies. Its first spreads were taken up by visual essays that various designers carried out in vivid colors using fragments of scanned images taken from film, television, and wherever the designers could find them, layered with sparse, but provocative text. In the hands of some of the best of these designers, such as Erik Adigard, the pages were cosmic in scale and aspiration, saturated in color and direct in their messages. Adigard and the other *Wired* designers expanded into working on books and websites, attempting to catch the exploding multitude of images being thrown off by both old and new media in ever more fervid, but also ever more direct and abstracted shapes.

264. Renzo Piano, Richard Rogers, Centre Pompidou, Paris, 1977.

265. April Greiman, *Wet* Magazine.

266. Rudy Vanderlans, *Emigre* Magazine, n°1, 1984.

While some designers became caught up in the endless possibilities offered by these new technologies, others used the very freedom these tools offered to create much more sparse and pared-down modes of composition. Lorraine Wild, one of the most influential teachers and designers in Los Angeles, drew her inspiration from the clean lines and reduced palette of mid-century modernists, keeping their discipline while opening up white space and unexpected relations by slipping, layering, and slightly distorting blocks of text and imagery. In London, the punk scene had produced possibilities for designers such as Peter Saville, who designed album covers and posters for the postpunk scene, but also allowed collectives such as Tomato to pare down their designs to combinations of seemingly random scribbles and a few isolated blocks of text.

All of these designers were unfolding their work in a field that was vastly expanded. While architecture remained wedded to buildings and urban design, even if its designers tried to escape from the tomb of construction to engage in critical experiments, graphic designers could move beyond the confines of the printed page and the poster to deploy their designs in a bewildering array of ephemeral media and in the projected world of film and television. This movement off the page had started when graphic designers such as Saul Bass created designs for movie title sequences, such as for *The Man with the Golden Arm* (1955) and *Vertigo* (1958), even though these mass media generally ignored the work of more thorough graphic designers for decades. By the 1980s, however, as the hegemony of mass market outlets controlled by monolithic corporations and catering to an amalgamation of tastes began to break down, designers could suddenly work for much more specialized audiences and could see their work produced much more easily. Outlets such as MTV hired young designers to create intros, transition films, and random images.

The core of all these designs was no longer text, imagery, and page and the relationship between these three, as it had been for centuries, but the ability to condense meaning into some hybrid of all three. The purest expression of this new condensation was the computer icon, introduced by Clement Mok and his team at Apple Computer in 1983. The simple array of what started as reductive images became a lexicon out of which an astonishing constellation of meanings and forms could be constructed. The simple forms of the arrow, the folder, and the trashcan all reduced a plethora of images and their associated references to simple, almost completely abstract forms. Thus, the logic of developing technology, as at previous moments in the modern era, led to the reduction of compositions of elements into an efficient and multivalent form.

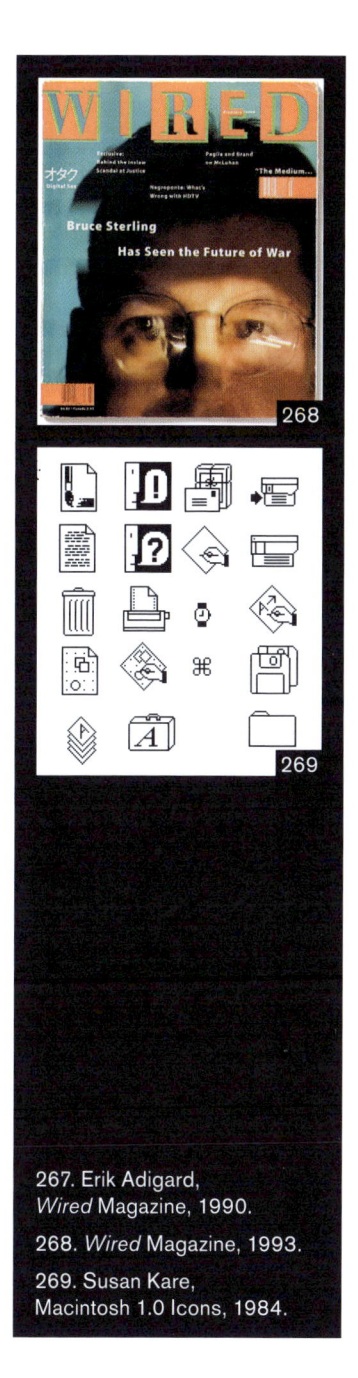

This became the paradoxical nature of graphic design, one that stood in contrast to the previous era of postmodernism. On the one hand, the computer made a seemingly endless variety of imagery possible, leading to an aesthetic centered on a free collage of type, images, and ancillary elements such as underlines and graphic fragments of type (commas, exclamation points, arrows). On the other hand, those elements themselves became increasingly reduced to simple and easy to recognize icons. This also led to a countervailing strategy, evident in the work of such high modernists as Lorraine Wild or in the large-scale, expressive posters of the Japanese designer Makoto Saito, of stripped-down compositions that gained their strength by letting these few isolated icons or fragments of type stand out.

The production of iconic form became a central strategy in industrial design as well. Postmodernism had been problematic in this field, for the simple reason that it depended on the breaking down of objects into appearances tailored for specific audiences ("speaking" a particular language or dialect) as well as on the addition of whimsical and nonfunctional elements.

267. Erik Adigard, *Wired* Magazine, 1990.

268. *Wired* Magazine, 1993.

269. Susan Kare, Macintosh 1.0 Icons, 1984.

270

When objects had to be mass-produced, this trait created problems of efficiency and often failed to appeal to a broad base of consumers. The designer who was most successfully able to bring some of the sheer fun and exuberance of postmodernism into a more reduced palette was French designer Philippe Starck. While he initially became known for a pared-down version of postmodernism in which he reused classic French furniture forms in cut-out and blown-up forms, as in the 1984 Café Costes opposite the Centre Pompidou, by the 1990s he was producing both objects and buildings that were much more abstract. In some cases, his mass-produced plastic furniture retained some memory of historic forms, as did the 1991 Bubu stool with its triangular legs and overall reference to a pouf, or occasional footstool, while at the same time being an assembly of pure geometric forms.

The most iconic object Starck produced during this period was the 1990 Juicy Salif juicer. Though not particularly practical, it became a popular object because of its playful merger of the basic conical form of its functional predecessors with insect-like legs, as well as because of its evocation of spacecraft or a more general jet-age design. Starck and other designers of the period realized that such everyday activities as cooking were no longer part of a world of production but were rituals of consumption. The object had to act as an icon in these rites. In this sort of design, the streamlining of forms that had started in the 1920s and that gradually removed all traces of how things were made or how they were used reached an apogee. Rather than merely being styled to hide its innards and its application, the object took on the status of a free, uncommissioned or functionless art object, standing for its own qualities and working because of its associations with historical forms or the human (or other animal's) body. The trick for designers became how they could make their objects simple and abstract enough that they could, on the one hand, be efficiently produced and, on the other hand, invite a host of different associations. The most common approach was to abstract classic and familiar forms, whether they were furniture or kitchen appliances, into iconic abstractions that caught the essence of what the object was meant to do, while adding whimsical bits that made them seem more animate. A vast array of consumer goods were redesigned in this manner starting in the late 1990s, ranging from the more expressive forms developed by Rubbermaid and KitchenAid in the United States to the evocation of classic modernist shapes by Braun in Germany. An added element was concern for how objects were used and how they fit into the human hand in a manner pioneered by Tucker Viemeister in his work for the OXO Good Grips line of kitchen implements.

In all these ways, industrial designers made their objects into a strange combination of technology, human form, and abstract object. It was as if what had been the various actors on the modernist stage—from machines, to their human users, to the abstract frameworks humans created by utilizing machines to contain their implements and their lives—were merging. Starck even took this approach into architecture, creating interiors for hotels such as the Paramount in New York in 1988 that had a surreal quality: you were not quite sure what was alive, what was a tool, and what was just art. In buildings such as the Asahi Beer Hall in Tokyo, completed in 1990, he fused all of these forms into a complete abstract object, part furniture, part building, and part sensuous sculpture.

Ironically, in the design of the actual agents of much of this change, the computer and communication technology, there was less chance to be expressive. Perhaps only the designers at Apple Computer managed to make the computer seem less like an alien box connected to an invisible world of wires and electrical pulses and more like a rounded and putty-colored consumer object that you could even put on the kitchen table. As the computer moved from an invisible location into the office and the household, designers began to mold it into ever more bulbous and expressive shapes.

270. Tucker Viemeister, Kitchen Tools for OXO Good Grips, 1990.

271. Philippe Starck, Juicy Salif, 1990.

272

The same was true of the telephone and soon the cellular telephone, which turned from instruments into molds of the human body, fitting themselves like negative images onto the side of the head. As the innards of these objects became ever smaller, the notion that they might disappear altogether or might become just projections or virtual displays did not seem so far-fetched. Under the guidance of Stefano Marzano, designers at Philips Consumer Electronics (as well as at such companies as Samsung in Korea) began experimenting with how future objects might become additions to mirrors displaying news or weather, integrated into clothing, or part of the table on which one ate or worked. Those objects that would remain would be expressive forms that could take their place along with the other objects a consumer would collect. You would have them not because of their usefulness, but as part of a collection of forms to frame and occupy the endlessly wired and flexible modernist environment, so that you could personalize it by means of that very assembly.

The notion that objects should either disappear or become icons, drinking in associations and giving back a sculptural presence, even spread through the automotive industry, where the car and the bus fused together into a completely abstract container called the van or, later, the MPV (Multiple Person Vehicle) or the more truck-related SUV (Sports Utility Vehicle). These objects, suffused with technologies, were meant to be completely anonymous. On the interior, more elements increasingly disappeared into nothing more than displays, while the dashboard and the seats became completely suffused with information and easy controls that otherwise did not have any independent form. The passenger car, when it remained, cloaked itself in historic forms, such as the reborn VW "Bug" or Tom Matano's Mazda Miata, which recalled a pared-down version of postwar racing cars. In the case of the Renault Twingo, designed by Patrick Le Quément in 1993, the car even took on animate characteristics, resembling a bug in an animated cartoon. The best designs, meanwhile, fused many of these elements into objects that were themselves iconic. While the BMW 3 series, developed by anonymous teams of designers throughout the 1980s and 1990s, became the perfect fusion of lines evoking speed, engineering, and ease of use, both the Infiniti J30, designed by Jerry Hirshberg in 1992, and the Audi TT, developed under the guidance of J. Mays in 2001, consciously caught the balance between container and the fluidity of motion in what were highly abstract and highly expressive objects.

Architects picked up on this reduction of objects to icons as well. Frank Gehry's work had already developed into animate forms that seemed to evoke everything from flowers to classical sculpture (he based his design of the Bilbao Guggenheim on a study of the rendering of cloaks in medieval carved wood statues). In the Netherlands, designer Ben van Berkel, working in a small studio with his wife, Caroline Bos, and later with the larger UN Studio, designed objects that were, as he put it, "both blob and box." From his earliest switching station in the town of Amersfoort in 1986, to the much later Mercedes-Benz Museum, completed in Stuttgart in 2006, van Berkel sought to meld interior spaces into a modernist continuum of space by using a process he called "deep planning." He then clad his buildings in shapes that reduced all of the forces acting on construction—from technical issues such as structure and safety concerns to social concerns such as building codes and context—into one seamless shape that would encompass all of them without seeming to respond to any one particular issue.

The most successful creators of iconic form were without doubt the Swiss designers Jacques Herzog and Pierre de Meuron. Trained by Aldo Rossi, but also instructed in the Swiss tradition of premiating engineering concerns, they designed taut structures that evoked a host of associations in their simplicity and almost archetypal form. In 1986, they reduced a house outside of Basel to a deformed abstraction that they poured in concrete, and made it look like a child's drawing of a house. It was also stretched and

272. Tom Matano, Mazda Miata, 1989.

273

274

simplified so that, in its detailing, it was an heir to the abstractions created by either Rossi or Louis Kahn.

Reaching beyond the evocation of historical forms to a much more basic set of shapes, Herzog and de Meuron managed to design buildings that had a clear form but seemed to change and develop as you moved around or through them. In some cases, the buildings literally changed, as moss or mold grew on them. In their designs for the Ricola Corporation outside of Basel, starting in 1987, they took the plant's various elements and stripped them to their essence before elaborating them into sculptural forms. While the office block became a shimmering vision of what a glass office building could be if it were not constrained by structure (hidden from sight, as in the industrial design objects of the day), the adjacent storage shed is a structure of horizontal wood slats stacked one on top of each other. It has no visible body and no function other than storage, becoming instead an iconic evocation of a way of building with wood reduced to a diagram of that tradition and assembled into a scaleless statement.

Herzog and de Meuron's most successful and visible designs were a pair of switching stations on either side of Basel's central railroad station, designed in 1994 and 1996. Wrapped in metal strips, these giant machines for regulating train traffic twist and turn as they rise up from their constricted sites. The cladding protects the sensitive machinery from electrical impulses, and the design evokes that sense of a cloak, as if these are heavily dressed human figures or animals with protective hides. At times, the metal bands, which change hue as they weather and as the sun hits them from different angles, are designed so that they open up like eyes to let the few operators inside look out or receive sunlight. Though the overall shape is thus completely logical, it does not explicitly state any of these generating forces. Instead,

273, 274. UN Studio, Mercedes Benz Museum, Stuttgart, 2007.

275. Jacques Herzog & Pierre de Meuron, Central Signal Box, Basel, 1998-1999.

it seems as if the designers have molded them as completely independent forms stating their presence in the city. Architecture has become a way of drinking in the complexity of the city, rather than adding to it. It has become a consumer of space, structure, association, and human expectations, giving only an enigmatic version of itself back. Herzog and de Meuron's switching stations are like the monolith in the 1968 science fiction film *2001: A Space Odyssey*, abstract transformers that stood in for and organized the space and culture around them.

The iconic movement in graphic and industrial design and architecture pointed to an end of things. Gathering force at the end of the millennium, this approach self-consciously accepted both the referential qualities of postmodernism and the abstractions of high modernism. It tried to sum up everything designers had learned about responding to and embodying technology in shapes that were both monuments—which is to say, agents of memory and the fixing of time—and implements responding to the human body, either as mirrors or as activators of space. Designers reduced the tragic gestures of Le Corbusier's late work, Louis Kahn's empty constructions, Stirling's collages, and Gehry's dance of stripped-down forms and slippery fish into their most basic shapes. Using computers, these designers realized that they could in fact meld all of these elements, if they wanted to, into singular shapes. The further history of design would seem to be one of carving ever denser and more evocative objects; and thus, the freedom of the new space opened up by the industrial and social revolutions of the nineteenth century seemed to be coming to an end.

That space has somehow survived, however, if in a convoluted manner. It was preserved most effectively in the Netherlands, a country that is itself a prototype for the space of modernism. Human hands created the seventy percent of the Netherlands' central area that is reclaimed land, a gridded expanse of meadows and irrigation ditches in which there is no original nature. Dutch architecture is an elaboration and filling in of this artificial space with dwellings, urban agglomerations, and other structures that have little of the monumental presence that major structures acquired in other countries—they would sink into the mud, in any case.

Dutch urban planning is a question of the continual rearranging of a limited amount of space, and has in fact been called, since the Second World War, "spatial arrangement" (*ruimtelijke ordening*). Brought into the country by the occupying Germans, this approach to collective space sees the whole country as artificial space that has to be continually developed to be ever more efficiently used, while providing a maximum amount of free space to as many different occupants as possible. Thus, the guiding principles in spatial arrangement are not axes or dense masses contrasted with open areas, but a three-dimensional grid that is either filled or open. In 1934, the planner Cornelis van Eesteren, who had earlier collaborated with Theo van Doesburg in the design of three-dimensional intersections of pure lines and planes that could house an artist, laid out the future plans of Amsterdam by collecting data on everything from soil conditions and wind directions to the movement of pedestrians and bicyclists through the existing city. Condensing this information into icons that he developed with the Swiss graphic designer Otto Neurath, van Eesteren produced a plan to translate the existing grid of meadows on the city's outskirts into new neighborhoods through the mechanism of data collection, turning the city into an optimized machine for urban activities.

During the late 1980s, designers developed a new twist on this tradition. Starting with the 1988 layout for an eastern extension of the city of Rotterdam, landscape architects began taking charge of planning. A group of them, including Frits Palmboom and Riek Bakker, argued that because the production of new forms no longer produces novelty and abstraction, we should understand all urban growth as a reorganization and intensification of existing

276. Jacques Herzog & Pierre de Meuron, Ricola Storage, Laufen, 1987.

277. Frits Palmboom & Riek Bakker, Prinsenland, Rotterdam, 1985.

conditions. Thus, they left in place most of the original demarcation of different fields and farms in the site for urban expansion, along with many existing roads and original structures. Rather than either wiping out or replicating the old, they kept it and wove the new through the existing structures. The result was a hybrid between the recognizable and the abstract, the familiar and the startling.

Over the years, landscape architects such as Palmboom, Dirk Sijmons, and Adriaan Geuze elaborated these ideas into neighborhoods throughout the Netherlands. At the same time, landscape architects in other cities were moving toward a similar practice of revealing and shaping existing conditions, rather than just imposing new forms on the land. In San Jose, California, George Hargreaves started in 1985 to resurrect the Guadalupe River, which had been turned into a concrete-lined drainage ditch. He developed a long line of walkways, amphitheaters, copses, and thin meadows, and recarved the river banks all the way from downtown (and by 1994) to the city's airport twelve miles away. The result is a line of connection, a space that is half-natural, half-human-made and all continuous. In Duisburg, Germany, starting in 1995, Peter Latz preserved the old Krups steel mill, turning its industrial forms into art centers, look-out platforms, and more than anything else, consumer versions of these emblems of production that let you explore the area's past. He left the landscape around them alone, in part to turn back into the forests that once grew on the site, and in part to become a series of defined gardens woven between coal storage bins and slurry lines with the help of a few fragments of classic garden architecture such as clipped hedges and flower beds.

It would seem that the corollary to the reduction of all form and space to an enigmatic icon was the extension of spatial manipulation and its integration into both planning and the landscape. In architecture, this integration took, for many architects, the figure of the spiral. Though the spiral became evident in Ben van Berkel's Mercedes-Benz Museum and in many of Zaha Hadid's buildings, it was the former filmmaker, architect, and urbanist Rem Koolhaas

278, 279. George Hargreaves, Guadalupe River Park, San Jose.

280. Peter Latz, Landschaftpark Duisburg-Nord, Dusiburg.

who first developed it. Trained at Eisenman's New York Institute for Architecture and Urban Studies, as well as at the AA in London, Koolhaas first made a name for himself with his 1979 book *Delirious New York*. There he claimed that the true legacy of modernism was a combination of iconic structures like the skyscraper, the freedom of possibilities offered by the New York street grid, and the empty, cavernous, and sensual space carved out under, above, or in the skyscrapers, a space that finally leaked out and turned into an integrated place of modernism in Rockefeller Center.

When he started practicing himself, Koolhaas at first assembled fragments of modernist icons, ranging from the panoptical prison embodied by the Arnhem jail to the glass and steel grids of office blocks, to the expressive ramps Le Corbusier sent curving through his buildings. In his 1993 design for the Kunsthal in Rotterdam, however, he condensed all of these elements into a compact form. The museum is a collage of a stone box, glass planes sliding underneath this seemingly heavy object, exposed structures that recall a High Tech striptease, and off-kilter versions of a black-painted steel canopy that seemed to derive from the work of Ludwig Mies van der Rohe. Though it appears to be postmodernist in its multiple references, Koolhaas abstracted these elements enough that they have an overall coherence. What really makes the whole hold together—or, rather, continuously fall apart—is the fact that he posed all of the references and elements as fragments responding to the split between a higher-level street on one of the city's main levees and what had been a low meadow between them. A sloped path that makes this relation clear pierces the building. Rooms then open up from a door in the middle of the path into a spiraling set of spaces that you enter at mid-movement. The first space is both an auditorium and a hallway, so that functional definitions implode and then develop through narrow passageways both up and down into larger exhibition galleries that lead back into each other.

Koolhaas developed this way of bleeding spaces into each other, as well as erasing functional divisions, in a number of buildings during the 1990s and the first decade of the twenty-first century. In the Dutch Embassy in Berlin, of 2004, the spiral leads all the way from the front door to the roof, cutting through all the offices and ceremonial spaces, while also permeating these areas and turning each one into a fragment that seems to have no shape or stability of its own. In the Seattle Library of the following year, the spiral is almost all public, condensing the surrounding urban environment into a series of loftlike reading rooms. In all cases, the buildings maintain a presence as a collage of different materials and images, all of which seem to be vaguely familiar fragments from either surrounding structures or from the urban culture in general. They are condensed into a form that is warped by the continual spatial development of what to Koolhaas was an unfolding of form and space that has no beginning or end, yet that eerily recalls an involuted version of the Ringstrasse.

To Koolhaas, architecture was no longer the autonomous production of form; it was the analysis and recombination of existing data and form into something that he believed was, through the medium of space, a critical rearrangement of existing social conditions. The only reason to make buildings was that they used a particular lexicon of structure, material, and space to build concrete, though highly contingent, alternatives to existing reality. These moments of coherence could then be icons, or symbolic operators, in a consumer society. If you could achieve a critique of modernity in another medium, then you should do so, as Koolhaas also did in his writing and consulting for entities from large publishing and fashion companies to the European Economic Union. What was central to modernism was not that highly abstract space of critical reorganization, nor its being fixed in form and structure, but the corrosive self-consciousness of which space was only the expression and for which buildings, objects, or images might be either the tomb or the mirror.

281, 282. Office for Metropolitan Architecture (OMA), Kunsthal, Rotterdam, 1993.

283. Office for Metropolitan Architecture (OMA), Dutch Embassy, Berlin, 2004.

10. RE-MODERNISM
design for sprawl

284

In 1993, the tens of thousands of manufacturers, designers, journalists, and design groupies who gathered each year for the Milan furniture fair, or Salone, were startled not by the appearance of a new product, as they were used to being, but by the appearance of a lot of old stuff. A collective of designers from the Netherlands that called itself Droog (or "dry," as in dry humor or minimal affect) presented objects consisting of cast-off materials they had given a new use. Rody Graumans showed a chandelier consisting of dozens of bare light bulbs, their exposed wires tied together at the lamp's top. Richard Hutten came with a collection of different archetypal seated elements he combined to create hybrids of benches and chairs, such as chairs consisting of a stool and a separate, U-shaped back, or a child's chair that was no more than a smaller version of one wooden armchair placed on top of the first. Hella Jongerius rethought traditional vase forms and sinks in rubber. In the most rhetorical element on display, Tejo Remy gathered together cast-off drawers, stacked them up helter-skelter, and tied them together with a cinched strap to form a chest of drawers. In each case, a traditional element reemerged in a new material, or was made out of recycled fragments of older furniture. The time of making new things, Droog said, was over. In the next millennium, the task of human beings would be to reuse and rethink, to reimagine and reconceptualize what already exists. At its best, design would be a gathering together that would reveal new possibilities within the world we thought we knew.

Over the next decade, Droog continued to experiment with such recombinations and reconceptualizations. Jongerius moved on to making vases that were half ceramic, half plastic bottles, as well as to remaking Delftware with new imagery. Designer Piet Hein Eek, though never part of the Droog organization, made a name for himself with tables and chests consisting of cast-off lumber laboriously reassembled and covered with layer after layer of varnish. Paul Hessels integrated implements such as knobs and tissue dispensers into the grid of the tiles you could install in your bathroom or kitchen. Peter van der Jagt designed a doorbell that consisted of two wine glasses suspended upside-down with an exposed hammer activated by an electromagnetic pulse that rang the two glasses in sequence. Lamps stacked up on top of each other to create a taller version of each individual element, furniture torn apart and reassembled, chairs consisting of stacks of rags, finished fragments of antique chairs mixed with new elements, furniture charred almost beyond recognition—the creativity of the Droog designers seemed endless, but was always disciplined by the notion that design is a playful gathering of existing materials, an unveiling of possibilities within existing technologies, or the expression of old forms in new ways.

One of the most poetic moments in Droog Design's history came in 1999, when the collective proposed a series of objects intended to help revive Oranienbaum, an old estate in Eastern Germany. The suggested items made use of local materials and skills. The most beautiful of them was a standard hay bailer retrofitted so that you could sweep the leaves off the estate in the autumn, collect them in the bin, and then have the specially shaped funnel spit out the compressed debris in the shape of a bench. During the course of the spring and summer, the bench would slowly fall apart again, so that it could become part of the next year's building materials.

In such lyrical, but also sensible and sensual suggestions, the Droog movement finally captured the self-consciousness of modernism fully. It had been clear since the failure of the large bureaucratic systems and their utopian forms in the middle of the twentieth century that modernism was not going to produce the perfect space that would dissolve all old relations, both physically and conceptually. Instead, modernism had retreated to its original position as a movement within an existing world and against existing modes of making things. Now, however, history

284. Hella Jongerius, Long Neck and Groove Bottles, 2000.

285. Rody Graumans, 85 Lamps, 1993.

286 287

repeated itself not as tragedy or farce, but as criticism and irony: modernism was now a way of stating a belief in a better world within the realities of the existing one. Design accepted the world around one as it was, but infused it with an alternative that was stated not outside of daily life, in the utopian or avant-garde mode, but within the realities of everyday existence. If that realization had first appeared in the guise of a rejection of modern forms and eventually in the coherent recapture of the past in postmodernism, it had, by the turn of the millennium, reached a level of maturity in that designers were no longer interested in fleeing or quoting from either the premodern or modern past, but were instead using the essential concepts of modernism while working with whatever material or in whatever situation was at hand.

Modernism became representational, in the sense of reflecting back the personal experiences of the maker while being so fragmentary, contingent, and unfinished that it refused mass production or assimilation. It was functional, but in a completely no-nonsense manner, taking the paramount importance of use and comfort for granted, rather than flaunting its workings. The mechanics or an object's structure were exposed, but again not in a rhetorical manner. The wires or the steel beams just hung out wherever they were necessary. Space was there to be opened up, but only through "unbuilding," leaving unfinished and deformed versions of otherwise functional structures.

There certainly were equivalents in architecture to Droog Design's experiments in furniture and industrial design. In the 1980s, architects in Los Angeles had started to reassemble cast-off materials to create buildings that were fragmentary and unfinished in their appearance. Thom Mayne, one of the leaders of what came to be known as the "dead tech" movement, once said, referring to architects such as Richard Rogers and Norman Foster, who were then making a reputation with machine-like buildings: "If the British High Tech guys are the ones with the white lab coats," he once told me, "we're the mechanics with greasy overalls working on the bottoms of cars." To Mayne and his one-time partner in the firm Morphosis, Michael Rotondi, architecture was a question of reassembling and articulating the beautiful mess of their native Los Angeles into forms that were not so much coherent as they were expressive of the inherent contradictions and instabilities of that environment. In Mississippi, the Rural Studio, under the direction of Samuel Mockbee, gave the same idea a social twist by asking student designers to employ everything from used tires to salvaged lumber to create new houses, community centers, and even a chapel for a very poor, rural community. In Australia, Peter Stutchbury designed post-hippie shacks that looked as if Frank Gehry's early houses had been made out of driftwood. And in South Africa, Urban Solutions and StudioMAS designed combinations of bus stations and open-air markets in which simple concrete skeletons turned into parking garages, frames for the stalls, and shelters, disappearing behind both planned and ad hoc decorations.

The design firm MVRDV, which started in Rotterdam in 1993, has taken these notions to an abstract extreme. Much of its work consists of an analysis of economic and social data, which they extrapolate into absurdly logical reorganizations of the physical environment. Thus, they used one project to imagine all of their native country, the Netherlands, as condensed into vertical layers, with one for agriculture, one for living, and one for waste disposal. They then extended their horizon to the whole world, imagining, in the 2005 project *KM3* that all human habitation could be condensed into dense towers spread across the planet and located in the places where they could most logically make use of local resources. What separated this kind of exercise from utopian thinking was that MVRDV envisioned the resulting structures not as universal grids but as collages made up of existing structures intensified, rationalized, and abstracted.

286. Rural Studio, Glass Chapel, Auburn, 2000.

287. MVRDV, KM3, Network, 2005.

288. Morphosis, 72 Market Street Restaurant, Venice, 1983.

In their built work, MVRDV followed this notion of super-rational reassembly by designing housing blocks, such as the 2003 Silodam in Amsterdam, which consists of twenty-seven different forms of apartments, each more or less a quotation of existing housing blocks in the area, stacked on top of each other. The 2002 Hagen Island housing development organizes fragments of row houses, clipped apart and shifted backward and forward in a gridded block. Each one is a simple cube with a pitched roof covered with a different material. The result is eerily like a traditional village of isolated but highly similar objects that seem of a piece, but which are abstractions of what a child might draw as a house form.

Though these exercises had precedents in the collages of artists such as Richard Hamilton and the early visionary drawings of Archigram and the Office for Metropolitan Architecture (Rem Koolhaas' firm) they were possible above all else because of the computer. With that tool, architects and designers not only could break all information apart and reassemble it into structures and fluid forms that design firms such as MVRDV could manipulate in complete freedom, but they could also represent these collages in completely convincing, three-dimensional images and even models. The designer no longer drew lines on a blank sheet of paper, but scanned in existing forms or plotted recombinations of basic properties.

Architects now see the computer as a device for collecting data as well as images and for then producing forms that more closely follow that information. This sometimes leads to fluid shapes, as when you feed the combination of wind, gravity, and other forces into the computing device and ask it to optimize a form, such as a tall skyscraper, that is subject to extreme versions of these forces. The computer can also let you mimic the flow of human beings or automobiles through space, carving buildings into the negative mold of human activity. In general, however, such "bloblike" shapes seem to work only in special conditions; as finished forms, they remove themselves so far from existing and remaining reality as to take on the familiar form of utopian purity. It is perhaps no coincidence that many of the computer-produced dreams resemble the exaggerated forms and landscaped extrusions imagined by designers from Sant'Elia to Horta in the era when the technologies of steel and concrete production were first enabling architects to imagine new worlds and new spaces.

Only by making technology, space, and their representation into the subject of design inserted into or commenting on the realm of daily life can a designer even hope to engage a self-conscious modernism instead of fleeing into the machine itself. The firm of Diller + Scofidio (now Diller Scofidio + Renfro) has been taking the reality of a world suffused and in many ways controlled by technology, as well as by social and economic patterns, as the basis for work that has, until recently, not led to the production of buildings. Their early designs, such as the 1981 *A Delay in Glass, or, The Bride's Revenge*, consisted of performances and interventions that reorganized existing forms, as in their 1983 installation at Capp Street Projects in San

289. MVRDV, KM3, Beach City, 2005.

290. MVRDV, Hagen Island, Ypenburg, The Hague, 2000-2003.

291. Elizabeth Diller and Ricardo Scofio, Par(a)Site, Installation at The Museum of Modern Art, New York, 1989.

Francisco and their 1989 *Para-Site* exhibition at the Museum of Modern Art in New York. In *Delay* they reassembled the pieces of Marcel Duchamp's 1915–1923 *The Bride Stripped Bare by Her Bachelors, Even*, to show the sexism and system-thinking in that artwork, by literally reversing them in the course of the act. At Capp Street, a dining room table attached to the ceiling and chairs split down the middle defied not just gravity but social expectations as well. In the Museum of Modern Art exhibition, Diller and Scofidio added security cameras that filmed visitors as they circulated through the museum, making the institution's hidden control structure visible and celebrating it with exposed viewing devices located in what was supposed to be a gallery for looking at art, not at one's self being watched.

In the work that summed up much of their early work before they began concentrating on the production of buildings, Diller and Scofidio produced a kind of anti-architecture. The 2004 *Blur*, an installation on a lake in Switzerland, was supposedly a pavilion exhibiting the essential properties of that country. In reality, it did not represent at all, but frustrated viewing and interpretation. Consisting of ten thousand steam jets emanating from a steel grid floating over the water, *Blur* was a cloud. You could ascertain its contours, explore its misty spaces on walkways, and even use it (to drink bottled water in a bar perched near the structure's top), but it deliberately never cohered into a building. It always remained an uncertain and, above all else, shrouded and shrouding presence. Blurring the information that surrounds us and the information that is being collected about us was to Diller and Scofidio perhaps the most radical act of design possible.

The work of these and other designers verges not only on a merger with technology, or even disappearance, but also on a cynical display of those instruments' negative power. This is not altogether unexpected, as computer and communication technologies go beyond merely opening up new spaces and possibilities to also restrict existing ones. Rather than allowing the production of the kind of expressive structures of which some designers dream, these technologies have rationalized the design process in a manner that limits possibilities. Objects are now designed as much by consumer research and engineering as they are designed to express or represent any of their functions. They must appeal to as many people as possible, they must fit seamlessly into the hand or on the head, they must not have any aspects (such as spikes or steps) that can intrude into the flow of daily life and thus endanger it, and, in the case of most manufactured objects, they have to be designed not just to minimize the use of material but also to fit as efficiently as possible into a standard-size shipping container.

In architecture, this is called "value engineering"; in industrial design, it is just part of the way of doing business. Nowhere are the results of such extreme rationalization as evident as in graphic design, where the liberty promised by the appearance of the Web as a site for communication in 1995 has given way to such pressure on the available

292. Diller and Scofidio + Renfro, Blur Building, Swiss Expo, Yverdon-les Bains, 2002.

293

screen space that everything from type to colors has become completely standardized. The space of the website, once so full of promise, has turned from the exuberance of the Ringstrasse or the Paris Opera to the banality of sprawl. Only limited variations are possible. The only way to escape this situation appears to be to create "bad" design, as in the retro-postmodernism of the firm FAT or the willful manipulation of standard graphic design tools to create compositions that are off-kilter and disturbing. With his magazines *Re* and *Butt*, Joop van Bennekom has become a master at this approach, as have Meire and Meire in Berlin.

The easiest thing to do, however, is to go with the flow of data and the circulation of goods, people, and information it facilitates. To make this art might mean to make form, image, and space out of all this movement of information, people, and things. The state of the art in that sense is defined by Jonathan Ive's designs for Apple computer, and particularly for the iPod, iPhone, and iPad. These objects combine a concern for ergonomics with a recall of the iconic color and form of modernism: white and geometric. The combination leads to rounded edges, while the reality of how these objects are used reduces them to as thin and small a presence as the designers can make them. They are streamlined and disappearing into a Miesian "almost nothing," or into Dieter Rams's notion that we should have "as little design as possible." Yet, at the same time, they are emblems of something that remains between our body and the world, between technology and us: it is form as efficient and minimal as possible, and that reduction gives the Apple products their power.

The equivalent of the iPod aesthetic in architecture is a revived minimalism. Spearheaded by David Chipperfield and John Pawson in England and Tadao Ando in Japan, it consists of architectural frames that are as minimal and yet as insistent as feasible. In the hands of these dense minimalists, as much of the building's systems and components as possible disappears into shells that are usually concrete and are made slightly larger than they need to be. The result is a concentration on an insistently present geometry, as well as the appearance of spaces (whether real or implied through window frames) that are also slightly larger than they need to be. These designers see their objects as clear forms that provide shelter while resisting the acidic streamlining of functionality and security inherent in modernity, but in most cases the buildings convey a sense of being defensive bulwarks. Moreover, the resources necessary to construct nonfunctional concentrations of both space and material make such designs most suited to the expression of luxury, whether in expensive stores, the homes of wealthy clients, or those institutions meant to display collective wealth, such as museums.

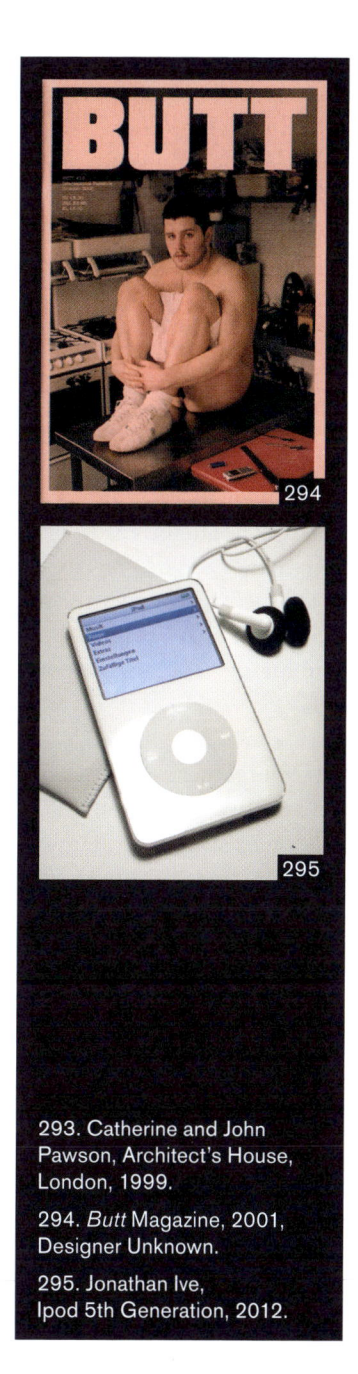

The irony is that space, the greatest discovery and raison d'etre of modernism, has become a luxury good now reserved for the most refined part of the middle class that once needed, created, and inhabited that space. Space is one of the most valuable things in contemporary culture, as evidenced by everything from real estate prices to the amount you are willing to pay for a few extra inches of space on an airplane. "Personal space" has become the definition of what you want to achieve, replacing a desire to be an actor in the wider space of the world. The architecture and design that makes you feel you have the largest and most exclusive space possible, or that lets you imagine such a space as endless, answers most directly to the modern call for isolation. Some might argue that this dissolution of social ties is the logical outcome of a modernism bent on dissolving all physical as well as social and economic reality, and that we are thus experiencing a realized utopia that lets us float through a world of continual change and movement within our own bubble. Philosopher Peter Sloterdijk has elevated the bubble as the very model of what human beings want to achieve, the externalization of the womb through a process of modernization that leads to the controlled world we all inhabit.

293. Catherine and John Pawson, Architect's House, London, 1999.

294. *Butt* Magazine, 2001, Designer Unknown.

295. Jonathan Ive, Ipod 5th Generation, 2012.

To live in the bubble, however, you must first submit to systems out of your control. These range from air conditioning and security devices that control your space to the technology that keeps cars and airplanes running. You might even have to give up your body to live in the virtual world, or let your body be completely filled with chemicals and foreign additions that replace the frail flesh with a more perfect bubble for whatever the human essence might be. You must thus also give up the real world as much as possible. You must live online and in a glow of security, artificial light, and air, as well as with forms reduced for both ease of use and ease of production.

To a few members of the socioeconomic elite, as well as perhaps to the most enlightened souls, this might be possible. Most of us, however, still inhabit a real world that is becoming ever more confusing and seemingly out of control. Modernization has now reached into the furthest corners of the globe and into every aspect of our lives. It is almost impossible to escape. The modern world is neither perfectly rational nor perfectly just, however. It is messy and quite often destructive of human and natural life. It is also awesome in its appearance and impossible to comprehend. This new reality rears itself all around us and seems to be designing itself almost automatically.

In his 1989 book *Postmodern Geographies*, Edward Soja described Los Angeles as "the alpha and the omega" of Western civilization: it is both the beginning of a future modernism and the summation, or maybe implosion, of all past cultures. The city is a collage of so many different cultures coming together in one place that it is a microcosm of the world. That combination of the largest Nicaraguan and Honduran populations outside of their countries with similar concentrations of Israelis, Iranians, Koreans, and other nationalities is, in turn, only possible because L.A. is an open city, one less constrained by laws of immigration and self-expression than any other place in the world has ever been—despite any attempt to restrict those movements of peoples and ideas. The physical reality of this global collage does not resemble a city so much as an endless assembly of human dwellings mixed with all the other bits and pieces, from factories to shopping malls to roads, that shelter human activities. Most of these forms appear not in pure shapes but in fragments. Houses are assemblies of references to everything from Spanish haciendas to English cottages. The shopping mall has become an L-shaped group of stores around a parking area. The factory has fallen apart into workshops hidden in lofts where things are made or stored for just-in-time delivery and giant blocks of warehouses where these objects are kept and moved around. Over half the city's space is given over to roads and other circulation areas.

Los Angeles, in other words, represents and spreads out the victory of free space. Goods and people move freely around its endless boulevards from one far-flung concentration of activities to another. This space seems independent of nature, as it crosses mountains and spreads ever further through the hinterlands. It also has no frame, no fixed points, and few places of concentration. Los Angeles is one giant collage that changes continually, and where space is completely miasmic. The systems that control the city are continually under threat of breaking down, as traffic stalls, crime soars, and planning becomes impossible. Free space occurs close to the chaos that Venturi thought gives force, but it does not seem to cause architects or designers to create any of the shapes that might allow for avoidance. All that can stop the city is nature itself, in the form of cataclysmic events such as earthquakes or through the sheer absence of water, for human beings have created a monster that feeds on itself, near chaos and filled with waste and injustice, but still growing in ever more unpredictable forms.

There are versions of Los Angeles all across the United States—from Phoenix and Las Vegas to Houston and Orlando—as well as throughout the world. The fast-ing metropolises are sprawling and almost out of control. Mexico City and São Paulo, Tokyo and Guangzhou, Lagos and Cairo, are all much larger than any traditional city has ever been. They have virtually no controls on their growth, and their forms are becoming increasingly more difficult to understand. Though they are all more concentrated than the Los Angeles model common in the Western world, these new cities are no longer growing around one center, with radiating avenues or parks, or any of the other spaces that might both control and represent their character. Nor have they developed the kinds of objects or monuments that might fix their new spaces in place. What monuments you do find there are versions of Western objects, often designed by architects from Europe or the United States, decreed by state officials and sitting in alien splendor in "development zones" or other new parts of these urban dynamos.

Somehow a new space is emerging in these cities, one that we must understand and, if we cannot shape it, we must guide if we are going to continue to believe in the modernist dream of giving form to the modern world and, through design, transforming new space into the place of human dwelling. We must address a reality that is cellular, mass-produced, subject to continual change, and thus made to last for as short a period as possible; it is fragmentary, layered, and above all else intense and compressed, even as it extends ever further out into the surrounding landscape. It is also gray or putty-colored, and formless. It is difficult to even see, let alone grasp.

The city of Hong Kong is one of the places where this space has appeared most clearly. Because of an accident of geopolitics, the island after the Second World War became the site for one of the most concentrated spates of development in human history. On either side of the Hong Kong harbor, tall apartment blocks, office towers, and hotels rose up next to each other. The government, which owned and controlled all the land, limited future expansion to very small portions of what was an English enclave. As a result, architects perfected a few basic forms for high-rise buildings, of which the most common became a forty-two-story block. The spaces in such buildings were sold, as elsewhere in Asia, as completely bare containers. The result was a realization of Le Corbusier's dream of a city of towers in a sylvan setting, though here the vision became standardized and monotonous: the towers sprung up next to each other, and the green landscape remained largely untouched. Within each of the blocks, the space resembled the open loft that modernist architects had seen as the basic building block of all inhabitation. Inside these shells, inhabitants then built the modern equivalent of the Frankfurt kitchen and filled it completely with consumer goods.

The dense forest of towers that seemed to merge into one structure, whose contours and components changed as you moved around and through the central island and Kowloon, contrasted sharply with the subtropical vegetation on the steep slopes around these concentrated moments of architectural technology. The contrast was further heightened by the fact that the laws of economics removed almost all detailing from the buildings, while not allowing the designers to turn them into the open, steel-framed glass blocks that would deny their own existence. Instead, you encountered a spread of similar materials, from stucco to mass-produced windows to the same air-conditioning units and drying balconies, across a three-dimensional object of urban scale and made up of interchangeable bits and pieces.

When the Hong Kong model began spreading to urban growth areas from Taipei in Taiwan to Seoul in South Korea and to Bangkok in Thailand, few of the other sites could match the concentration, both natural and political, that turned Hong Kong into such a coherent mass. These other cities married the intensity and the modular and cellular qualities of Hong Kong's towers with the lateral

296. Jordi Bernado, View of Hong Kong.

297. View of Seoul, Photographer Unknown.

spread more common to American cities. Clumps of identical residential towers began springing up on their outskirts and around infrastructural nodes, such as major railroad or mass transit stations. In cities such as Seoul and Taipei, the overall urban pattern rose up into multiple stories, turning the city into not so much a collage of towers as a solid mass of blocks that petered out around its edges before reassembling itself further into the countryside where developers or the government decreed satellite cities. The buildings were almost without an exception featureless, but their bases soon became hollowed out into dense warrens of activity. Vertically stacked retail stores and restaurants not only rose up as much as six stories in many office and residential blocks, but also spread down several stories underground, a model first developed in Tokyo. Around railroad stations and major urban intersections, such stacks turned into giant malls that spread out along the avenues and then underground. In Bangkok, one area consists of almost ten square blocks of nothing but multistory shopping malls connected by elevated transit systems, while in Osaka, the mall around the central train station spreads out across four levels under six square blocks of the city.

What is the urban space of such cities? One of the most remarkable aspects of these cities is the bleeding of public into retail, both in type and in space. The space you inhabit—a new kind of limbo space—when you are out of your bubble moves continually between spaces intended for movement, which is nominally publicly controlled, and the space devoted to shopping or to such functions as banking. The real demarcation between zones with different functions and ownership is usually the invisible change in temperature created by the presence of air conditioning. These ambiguous spaces also have no focal point, and in fact are designed to encourage one to wander from store to store, or to bypass the traffic up above. The only way you know your place is through the presence of signs. These carriers of information can either tell you what to buy or where you are, but they are disassociated from the built structure. It is as if the facade has finally come peeling off the building, leaving only neutral and fragmented frames behind. Neither the material of which these frames are made nor their contents give any clues to tell you of what they consist. Instead, they attempt to be as smooth and anonymous as possible to concentrate your attention on the goods or the work at hand and to let the signs stand out more clearly.

At its best, as in a city such as Singapore, this limbo space has the kind of fluidity of which modernist architects dreamed, while at the same time it creates an artificial environment that offers you a social bubble to replace the private one—at least when you are shopping, working, or otherwise making yourself a productive member of the modern economy. Because Singapore has a forgiving climate, the retail malls underneath the buildings are able to be open to the air, erasing the boundaries between public and private space, at least in appearance. The embedding of technology in everything from road tollbooths to parking garages also promotes the sense of an effortless flow. At the same time, the city-island's overall planning, devised by Dutch urban designers after the Second World War, creates more or less logical rhythms between the clumps of development and protected open space. Historical patterns have also broken down some of the larger residential blocks into slivers that rise to seemingly impossible heights from very small plots. As a result, the kind of fragmentation and concentrated cellular growth developed in Hong Kong is combined with a sense of flow that makes the whole island seem like one collective, middle-class bubble. Singapore is also a city of immigrants, and thus presents a smaller-scale and more coherent version of Los Angeles's global collage. The city is well aware of its best characteristics and, like an increasing number of fast-growing metropolises, is using tools of spatial as well as statistical analysis to guide its future growth to make the best use of these characteristics.

298. Jimmy McIntyre, Marina Bay Sands, Singapore, 2012.

If Singapore represents an attempt to create a smoothly functioning "bubble city," cushioned by isolation and the presence of a great deal of money derived from trade and shipping, themed environments such as those created by the Disney Corporation are the attempt to produce a completely artificial bubble removed altogether from urbanity and even everyday life. Disneyland, opened in 1954 amid the Los Angeles sprawl, was a place of escape around a "Magic Mountain" where you could imagine you were inside a movie for a few hours. By the time the company opened Disney World in Orlando, Florida, in 1971, however, their spatial control and ambitions had grown. Disneyland was escape, but Disney World wanted to be a concrete alternative to the confusion and less than ideal conditions of daily life. The fantasy area was built on top of an almost primeval swamp, and vied for the visitor's attention with EPCOT, the Experimental Prototype City of Tomorrow. This collection of science and science fiction displays initially turned out to be a failure and had to be extensively reprogrammed and redesigned, probably because it was constructed just at the time when its intended audience had lost faith in both progress and the spheres, towers, and abstract geometries that architects (and Disney) thought represented their future.

What saved Disney World was postmodernism: the addition of hotels by Michael Graves and his colleagues reminded visitors that they were in a resort environment, a place of hedonism and escape. The buildings looked familiar, while the technology remained out of sight in hidden service roads and trash collection corridors buried underground. Disney World edited out reality and replaced it with a controlled version of what the modern world could look like. They also began to employ architects who believed that it was possible to resurrect another age of urban coherence. Calling themselves New Urbanists, these architects began designing suburban housing developments that look like old villages, complete with homes that resemble neo-Colonial cottages and grids of streets that warp to focus on central shopping and transit areas. As in other residential communities, the presence of invisible technology, such as electricity, water, and sewage lines, allows these environments to exist. In addition, these communities depend on sprawl, for all work and shopping opportunities, as well as all the other amenities of daily life, are located elsewhere. The communities enclosed themselves in secure, sometimes even gated, boundaries in which residents could live out the fantasy that Disney World only let them visit.

In the Las Vegas strip, such developments and Disney-like "theming" came together. Each of the large casinos developed themed environments as condensations of the urban cores of historic cities, ranging from Paris to New York to Venice. Each of these spaces has gambling as its principal function, but you can carry out that otherwise ritualistic activity in a cavern with invisible boundaries, artificial light and air, and security vouchsafed by countless cameras, while imagining you are in a perfected version of any of these cities. Some of the spectacle spills over to the outside in the form of miniature versions of the Eiffel Tower or the New York skyline, as well as in battles between pirates and English soldiers carried out six times a day in a fake lagoon on the street. Las Vegas thus has the air of itself being a collage of all of the world's cities and of modernism's repressed fantasies. The themed environments exert such an attraction, moreover, that people spill out into the street, creating one of the world's densest and most vibrant public spaces. Here it is impossible to inhabit your bubble, and you have to give yourself over to the fragmented spectacle of urbanism. Las Vegas has a core that presents a successful spectacle of urbanity.

299. Michael Graves, Swan and Dolphin Resort, Disneyworld, 1988-1990.

300. Lars Lerup, Diagram of Zoohemic/Aerial Fields. *Stim and Dross*, 1995.

That it is all an artifice and can only exist due to the engine of gambling did not prevent Las Vegas from becoming, together with Orlando, the fastest-growing city between 1990 and 2010 in the United States. This growth came not only from the casinos, but also from such activities as shipping and warehousing and, most importantly, from Las Vegas's development into the ultimate suburb. Collecting people from all around the country and soon the world, it became more than anything else a place where the middle class could afford to live in their own secure, air-conditioned bubble in a subdivision that spread throughout the landscape without any seeming rhyme or reason. Las Vegas and other Southwestern cities became the epitomes of sprawl, existing not because of a central core, but despite the lack of such urban form. They were reproductions of human-made space, barely contained by the thinnest and cheapest construction formed into structures that gave just a hint of being home. Most of the actual space was given over to empty lawns and, above all else, space for circulation. Pockets of technological intensity, both at the level of the individual in homes and at the urban level in themed focal points, designed to look familiar, and collaged across the landscape, became the norm for American cities. Critic Lars Lerup, in his 2001 book *After the City*, distinguished between these "stims," or points of stimulation—whether they were casinos or museums, churches or shopping malls, living rooms or dens—and the "dross" that makes up all the formless structure—from housing, to places to work and shop, to roads—that allows these moments to occur.

The recession of the late naughts paused the spread of sprawl, as well as the construction of stims, but had a severe impact only in the most highly stretched locations, such as Phoenix, Las Vegas, and Dubai. Calls for more concentrated and human-scaled development, as well as for construction that respects the environment, will no doubt lead to novel forms of construction. Yet, the dissipating nature of computer and communication technologies, which facilitate the movement of goods, people, and ideas without borders, as well as the corrosive effects of a capitalist global economy that forces such movement and the breakdown of social structures of cohesion from the family to the state, continue to generate the logic for ever more sprawl.

This model for urban sprawl has arisen in the United States most fully in cities such as Las Vegas, Orlando, Phoenix, and Houston, in which there was not much of a center to begin with. Now the model is consciously being adopted by cities in other countries. This is most evident in the Arabian Peninsula and most particularly in the United Arab Emirates, where cities such as Abu Dhabi, Dubai, and Doha are growing up as instant sprawl across the abstract expanse of the desert. These cities take artificiality to their logical extreme, as there is no visible means to support their growth beyond the presence of oil and gas hidden under those same sands. Their governments are converting those funds into attractors such as airports, shopping malls, and trading floors, but above all else they are turning these cities into places where you might live safely in a bubble far removed from the rest of the world. In the most extreme example of such a development, the city of Dubai has constructed a land development consisting of islands in the Arabian Gulf that, when you look at them from above, resemble a map of the whole world, thus allowing you to own and build a perfected and safe version of global reality. Even if some of these extreme examples might not be viable, both Dubai and its Emirates neighbors continue to develop enclosed compounds for living, attracting buyers and visitors from Russia, Europe, and the United States.

To be sure, the cities of the Emirates also realize that they need "stims" to bring people to them. They are investing not only in economic attractors but also in cultural facilities and tall buildings that will, they hope, give what were recently small villages a sense of place at a scale appropriate to their governments' ambitions. These projects, such as the combination of museums and performance spaces being planned in Abu Dhabi and Doha, are being designed by some of the world's best

301. Las Vegas.

302. Ramon Prat, View of The Palm, Dubai, 2008.

303

and most famous architects, including Frank Gehry, Zaha Hadid, Jean Nouvel, and Arata Isozaki. This is not architecture that grows out of the native conditions of the place, however, nor is it an attempt to frame and give meaning to contemporary developments in those places. Instead, these buildings are like jewels the rulers have collected to crown the city, and their designs have more to do with the designers' abstract ideas about how to shape constructions than they are objects that have any relation to their sites or their functions. The recession only made their presence all the more vital to the region's continued growth.

One of the most magnificent pieces of recent architecture I have seen is the Burj Khalifa in Dubai, which opened in January 2010, in the teeth of the recession. Currently the tallest building in the world, it is a living rebuke to F. Scott Fitzgerald's sense of limits. Rising up to the height of almost three Empire State Buildings stacked on top of each other, it looks out over clusters of suburban development leading to a desert that is nothing but land waiting to be developed. It represents the height of composition as well as technology, and is the best-designed skyscraper I have ever seen. But it is only the iconic marker in a much larger development that consists of a large shopping mall and several suburban compounds, each one divorced from its setting and promising a bit of utopia within its confines.

The sites where construction is taking place at a scale and pace unparalleled in human history emphasize how irrelevant architecture in the traditional sense has become. If there is still something that remains a form you can recognize as having been designed for that particular place and time, it is there to perform exactly that function: to make a spectacle of a place for a time. Architecture, when it survives in buildings, survives

303. Adrian Smith and Skidmore, Owings, and Merrill, Burj Khalifa, Dubai, 2007-2009.

304

305

306

as a sign of itself, a representation of the act of forming space in a place so that it can be a condenser of social and economic power. It is a work of art about such an act. Its effects are like those you can find in theme parks or, increasingly, in virtual reality: spectacular, fluid, and amorphous. Great architecture seems destined to be an icon of itself and a container of special effects.

This disappearance of design into signing empty space with icons is also evident in the other design fields. In industrial design and furniture, forms are disappearing either into collages that are reassemblies of existing materials and forms or into minimal objects that have as few distinguishing characteristics as possible. Soon they will dissolve either into their environment or into the body itself, becoming ergonomic prosthetics integrated into the human being and his or her projection into the world. In graphic design, the composition of messages is dissolving into the message itself as messages continually recombine themselves automatically on the screen of the computer or television. Where it still exists in the "real" world, graphic design exists as the composition of markers in "way-finding" devices that help one find one's way through sprawl. Even on the printed page (insofar as it still survives), design either disappears or messes up the way you read.

Messing up the system has, ironically, become perhaps the last refuge of modernism. If modernism first appeared as an attempt to represent modernity, it has become a way of showing and experiencing the contradictions inherent in the modern world. Architects and designers can create enigmatic icons, contingent collages, and purposefully unusable or indecipherable moments that above all make you aware of the fact that you are still aware.

In a concrete manner, this messing up rather than solv-

304. 2012 Architects, Superuse Bar Expresso, Delft, 2012.

305. Theaster Gates, Dorchester Project, Chicago, 2009-2013.

306. Alfredo Brillembourg and Hubert Klumpner, Torre David, Caracas, 2011-2012.

ing means that the work of design is increasingly one of reuse. When asked to make a building, architects have to first ask themselves if it is necessary. Do we really need another new structure that will use up irreplaceable natural resources and empty land, or can we reuse what we already have? Second, if you do build, can you renovate and reuse? Finally, why not scavenge and source detritus, as the Dutch architects Superuse Studios, Rural Studio in Alabama, or Amateur Architects in China do? Can we think of buildings as a way of making us aware of what there is, was, and potentially could be, as the artist Theaster Gates does? Can we think of the work of design in general as the act of gathering what already exists into new assemblies, and even the reuse of existing forms and ideas? Can design be an agent of social change that works on the level of infrastructure, as Urban Think Tank of São Paolo has proposed? Can modernism ultimately be an act of reflecting, rethinking, and reusing? Can it even be an act of unmaking, of making us aware by showing us what is not there, as the Belgian collective Rotor or the artist Pierre Huyghe have done in several exhibitions?

In all this, what remains when everything is less and less, or nothing, or contingent, or just a gathering together, is the maker, the user, and the perceiver. For, that is the one hidden point of modernism: in that new space opened up by modernity, in the conception of technology, and in the picturing of this new world, there is still one point. That point is the person who is experiencing that space, however fluid it might be. That point is also the conception or assembly of the object. That point is, finally, the addresser and the addressee, the reason for representation itself.

Perhaps such a fixed point, something one might call a human being, is a fiction. It is entirely possible that there is no such thing as a coherent person defined by a human body and who has something we think of as a consciousness. Speculations on this subject have

307. Rural Studio, Corrugated Cardboard Pod, Newbern, 2001.

been a favorite pastime of scientists, science fiction writers, and philosophers alike. Yet, those very musings point to the task of what you might think of as modernist design: to figure it out. To fix a point in time and place that we might call human at the very center of a world of modernity: that is the task of that peculiar conceit, now almost two centuries old, that we might still call modernism.

SELECTED READINGS

Chapter 1

Beecher, Jonathan, and Charles Fourier. *The Visionary and His World*. Berkeley: University of California Press, 1986, pp. 241–258.

Benjamin, Walter. "The Work of Art in the Age of Mechanical Reproduction." 1936. In *Illuminations*, ed. Hannah Arendt, trans. Harry Zohn, pp. 217–262. New York: Schocken Books, 1969.

Bergdol, Barry, et al. *Bauhaus 1919–1933*. New York: The Museum of Modern Art, 2009.

Brickerhoff Jackson, John. *Landscape in Sight: Looking at America*. New Haven: Yale University Press, 1997.

Carey, John. *The Faber Book of Utopias*. London: Faber and Faber, 1999, pp. 184–230.

Etlin, Richard E. *Symbolic Space: French Enlightenment Architecture and Its Legacy*. Chicago: Chicago University Press, 1994.

Faber, Monika, et al. *Vienna's Ringstrasse*. Cologne: Hatje Cantz, 2014.

Ginzburg, Moisei. *Style and Epoch*. 1924. Trans. Anatole Senkevitch, Jr. Cambridge, MA: MIT Press, 1982.

Hall, Thomas. *Planning Aspects of Europe's Nineteenth-Century Capital Cities: Urban Development*. London: Taylor & Francis, 1997.

Hayden, Dolores. *Seven American Utopias: Architecture of Communitarian Socialism, 1790–1975*. Cambridge, MA: MIT Press, 1976.

Jones, Peter. *The 1848 Revolutions*. 1991. London: Routledge Publishers, 2003.

Lemagny, Jean-Claude. *Visionary Architects: Boulee, Ledoux, Lequeu*. Santa Monica, CA: Hennessey & Ingalls, 2002.

Leslie, Thomas. *Chicago Skyscrapers, 1871–1934*. Champaign-Urbana: University of Illinois Press, 2013.

Loos, Adolf. "Men's Fashion." *Neue Freie Press*, May 22, 1898, n.p.

Margolin, Victor. *The Struggle for Utopia: Rodchenko, Lissitzky, Moholy-Nagy, 1917–1946*. Chicago: University of Chicago Press, 1997.

Marx, Karl, and Friedrich Engels. *The Communist Manifesto*. 1848. https://www.marxists.org/archive/marx/works/1848/communist-manifesto/.

Molenaar, Joris, et al. *Van Nelle: Monument in Progress*. Rotterdam: Van Hef Publishers, 2005.

Olsen, Donald J. *The City as Work of Art: London, Paris, Vienna*. New Haven: Yale University Press, 1988.

Reichardt, Rolf, and Hubertus Kohle. *Visualizing the Revolution: Politics and Pictorial Arts in Late Eighteenth-Century France*. London: Reaktion Books, 2008.

Reps, John W. *The Making of Urban America: A History of City Planning in the United States*. Princeton: Princeton University Press, 1992.

Ruedi Ray, Katherina. *Bauhaus Dream-house: Modernity and Globalization*. London: Routledge Publishers, 2011.

Schorske, Carl E. *Fin-de-Siècle Vienna: Politics and Culture*. 1961. New York: Vintage Books, 1981, pp. 24–115.

Stern, Robert A. M., David Fishman, and Jacob Tilove. *Paradise Planned: The Garden Suburb and the Modern City*. New York: Rizzoli International Publications, 2013.

Sullivan, Louis. "The Tall Office Building Considered." In *Kindergarten Chats*, pp. 202–213. 1917. New York: Dover Publications, 1979.

Taverne, Ed. *In 't Land van Belofte, in de Nieue Stadt: Ideal en Werkelijkheid van de Stadsuitleg in de Republiek, 1580–1680*. Diss., Universiteit Groningen, 1978.

Tschichold, Jan. *The New Typography*. 1928. Berkeley: University of California Press, 2006.

Vidler, Anthony. "The Scenes of the Street: Transformations in Ideal and Reality, 1750–1871." In *On Streets*, ed. Stanford Anderson, pp. 29–112. Cambridge, MA: MIT Press, 1986.

---. *The Writings of the Walls*. New York: Princeton Architectural Press, 1987.

Waissenberger, Robert. *Vienna in the Biedermeier Era, 1815–1848*. New York: Rizzoli International Publications, 1986.

Warfield Simpson, John. *Visions of Paradise: Glimpses of Our Landscape's Legacy*. Berkeley: University of California Press, 1999, pp. 43–64.

Wright, Frank Lloyd. "The Art and Craft of the Machine." 1904. In *Writings and Buildings*, pp. 54–73. New York: Penguin Press, 1974.

Chapter 2

Adams, Henry. *The Education of Henry Adams*. 1918. New York: Modern Library, 1931.

---. *Esther, Mont Saint Michel and Chartres, The Education of Henry Adams*. New York: Library of America, 1983.

Banham, Reyner. *The Architecture of the Well-tempered Environment*. London: Architectural Press, 1969.

---. *Theory and Design in the First Machine Age*. London: Architectural Press, 1960.

Beaumont, Matthew, and Michael Freeman, ed. *The Railway and Modernity: Time, Space and the Machine Assemblage*. Bern: Peter Lang International Academic Publishers, 2007.

Belanger Grafton, Carol. *Victorian Design from the Crystal Palace Exhibition*. 1851. New York: Dover Publications, 2010.

Berlyn, Peter, and Charles Fowler. *The Crystal Palace*. 1851. Books on Demand, 2014.

Bolotin, Norman, and Christine Laing. *The World's Columbian Exposition: The Chicago World's Fair of 1893*. New York: Preservation Press, 1992.

Clark, T. J. *The Paintings of Modern Life: Paris in the Art of Manet and His Followers*. Princeton: Princeton University Press, 1999.

da Costa Meyer, Esther. *The Work of Antonio Sant'Elia: Retreat into the Future*. New Haven: Yale University Press, 1995.

Dierkens-Aubry, Francoise, et al. *Horta: Art Nouveau to Modernism*. New York: Harry N. Abrams, 1997.

Emmerson, Charles. *1913: In Search of the World before the Great War*. New York: PublicAffairs, 2013.

Fogelson, Robert M. *Downtown: Its Rise and Fall, 1880–1950*. New Haven: Yale University Press, 2001.

Geist, Johann V. *Arcades: The History of a Building Type*. Cambridge, MA: MIT Press, 1985.

Giberti, Bruno. *Designing the Centennial: A History of the 1876 International Exhibition in Philadelphia*. Lexington: University of Kentucky Press, 2002.

Huxtable, Ada Louise. *Frank Lloyd Wright: A Life*. New York: Viking Penguin Press, 2004.

Illies, Florian. *1913: The Year before the Storm*. New York: Melville House, 2013.

Jonnes, Jill. *Eiffel's Tower and the World's Fair Where Buffalo Bill Beguiled Paris, the Artists Quarreled, and Thomas Edison Became a Count*. New York: Viking Press, 2009.

Kirkland, Stephane. *Paris Reborn: Napoleon III, Baron Haussmann, and the Quest to Build a Modern City*. London: St. Martin's Griffin Press, 2013.

Kruty, Paul. *Midway Gardens*. Champaign/Urbana: Illinois University Press, 1998.

Lancaster, William. *The Department Store: A Social History*. Leicester: University of Leicester Press, 1995.

Le Corbusier. *Towards a New Architecture*. 1923. Trans. Frederick Etchell. New York: Dover, 1995.

Lissitzky, El. *Russia: An Architecture for World Revolution*. 1930. Cambridge: MIT Press, 1986.

Manieri-Elia, Mario. "Toward an 'Imperial City': Daniel H.

Burnham and the City Beautiful Movement." In *The American City: From the Civil War to the New Deal*, ed. Giorgio Ciucci et al., pp. 1–142. London: Granada Publishing, 1980.

Margolin, Victor. *The Struggle for Utopia: Rodchenko, Lissitzky, Moholy-Nagy, 1917–1946*. Chicago: University of Chicago Press, 1997.

Marinetti, Filippo Tommaso. "Manifeste du Futurisme." *Le Figaro*, February 20, 1909, p. 1.

Meeks, Carol V. *The Railroad Station: An Architectural History*. 1956. New York: Dover Publications, 2012.

Quinan, Jack. *Frank Lloyd Wright's Larkin Building: Myth and Fact*. Chicago: University of Chicago Press, 2006.

Sant'Elia, Antonio, "Manifesto of Futurist Architecture." 1914. http://www.unknown.nu/futurism/architecture.html.

Scheerbart, Paul. *Glass Architecture*. 1914. New York: Praeger Publishers, 1972.

Schivelbusch, Wolfgang. *The Railway Journey: The Industrialization of Time in the Nineteenth Century*. Berkeley: University of California Press, 1977.

Schwartz, Frederic. *The Werkbund: Design Theory and Mass Culture before the First World War*. New Haven: Yale University Press, 1996.

Taut, Bruno. *Alpine Architecture*. 1917. Munich: Prestel Verlag, 2004.

Visitors Guide to the Centennial Exhibition and Philadelphia 1876. Philadelphia: J. B. Lippincott, 1876.

van Wesemael, Pieter. *Architecture of Instruction and Delight: A Socio-historical Analysis of World Exhibitions as a Didactic Phenomenon (1798–1851–1970)*. Rotterdam: 010 Publishers, 2001.

Chapter 3

Aldrich, Megan. *Gothic Revival*. London: Phaidon Press, 1994.

Bolger Burke, Dennis, et al. *In Pursuit of Beauty: Americans and the Aesthetic Movement*. New York: Rizzoli International, 1986.

Brandstatter, Christian, and Wiener Werkstatte. *Design in Vienna 1903–1932*. New York: Harry N. Abrams, 2003.

Davies, Colin. *Arts and Crafts Architecture*. London: Phaidon Press, 1997.

DeJean, Joan. *The Age of Comfort: When Paris Discovered Casual and the Modern Home Began*. New York: Bloomsbury USA, 2009.

Gere, Charlotte. *Nineteenth-Century Decoration: The Art of the Interior*. New York: Harry S. Abrams, 1989.

Giedion, Sigfried. *Mechanization Takes Command: A Contribution to Anonymous History*. 1948. New York: Oxford University Press, 1977, pp. 329–510.

Girouard, Mark. *Sweetness and Light: The "Queen Anne" Movement, 1860–1900*. New Haven: Yale University Press, 1977.

Greene, Harvey. *The Light of the Home: An Intimate View of the Lives of Women in Victorian America*. New York: Pantheon Books, 1983.

Kaplan, Wendy, ed. *The Arts and Crafts Movement in Europe and America: Design for the Modern World, 1880–1920*. London: Thames & Hudson, 2005.

Kent, Conrad, and Dennis Prindle. *Parc Guell*. New York: Princeton Architectural Press, 1993.

Loos, Adolf. "The Poor Little Rich Man." 1900. In *Spoken into the Void: Collected Essays, 1897–1900*, pp. 124-129. Trans. Jane O. Newman and John H. Smith. Cambridge, MA: MIT Press.

MacCarthy, Fiona. *William Morris: A Life for Our Time*. New York: Knopf, 1995.

McIntosh, Christopher. *The Swan King: Ludwig II of Bavaria*. New York: Viking, 1982.

Miller, Norbert. *Fonthill Abbey: Die Dunkle Welt des William Beckford*. Munich: Carl Hanser Verlag, 2012.

Moravanszky, Akos. *Competing Visions: Aesthetic*

Invention and Social Imagination in Central European Architecture. Cambridge, MA: MIT Press, 1998.

Peterson, William S. *The Kelmscott Press: A History of William Morris's Typographical Invention*. Berkeley: University of California Press, 1991.

Rabate, Jean-Michel. *1913: The Cradle of Modernism*. Oxford: Blackwell, 2007.

Rosner, Victoria. *Modernism and the Architecture of Private Life*. New York: Columbia University Press, 2005.

Ruskin, John. *The Two Paths*. 1862. London: Kessinger, 2010.

Scully, Vincent. *The Shingle Style and the Stick Style: Architectural Theory and Design from Downing to the Origins of Wright*. New Haven: Yale University Press, 1971.

Semper, Gottfried. *The Four Elements of Architecture and Other Writings*. Trans. Harry Francis Mallgrave. 1989. Cambridge: Cambridge University Press, 2011.

Silverman, Deborah. *Art Nouveau in Fin-de-Siècle France*. Berkeley: University of California Press, 1989.

Thornton, Peter. *Authentic Décor: The Domestic Interior, 1620–1920*. New York: Viking Press, 1984.

Viollet-le-Duc, Eugene-Emmanuel. *The Architectural Theory of Viollet-le-Duc: Readings and Commentaries*, ed. M. F. Hearn. Cambridge, MA: MIT Press, 1990.

Wagner, Richard. *The Art-Work of the Future and Other Works*. 1895. New York: Bison Books, 1993.

Chapter 4

Behne, Adolf. *The Modern Functional Building*. 1926. Los Angeles: Getty Research Institute for the History Art and the Humanities, 1996.

Benton, Tim. *The Villas of Le Corbusier and Pierre Jeanneret, 1920–1930*. Basel: Birkhauser, 2007.

Blagojevic, Ljiljana. *Modernism in Serbia: The Elusive Margins of Belgrade Architecture 1919–1941*. Cambridge, MA: MIT Press, 2003.

Blau, Eve. *The Architecture of Red Vienna, 1919–1934*. Cambridge, MA: MIT Press, 1999.

Doesburg, Theo van. "Towards a Plastic Architecture." 1924. Modernist Architecture: A Database of Modernist Architectural Theory. http://modernistarchitecture.wordpress.com/2010/10/19/theo-van-doesburg%E2%80%99s-%E2%80%9Ctowards-a-plastic-architecture%E2%80%9D-1924/.

van Duzer, Leon. *Villa Muller: A Work of Adolf Loos*. New York: Princeton Architectural Press, 1996.

Eliel, Carol S., and Francoise Ducros. *L'Esprit Nouveau: Purism in Paris, 1918–1925*. New York: Harry N. Abrams, 2001.

Fox Weber, Nicholas. *Le Corbusier: A Life*. New York: Alfred A. Knopf, 2008.

Hammer-Tugendhat, Daniela, Ivo Hammer, and Wolf Tegethoff. *The Tugendhat House: Ludwig Mies van der Rohe*. Berlin: Walter De Gruyter, 2014.

Hays, K. Michael. *Modernism and the Posthumanist Subject: The Architecture of Hannes Meyer and Ludwig Hilberseimer*. Cambridge, MA: MIT Press, 1995.

Henderson, Susan B. *Building Culture: Ernst May and the New Frankfurt am Main Initiative, 1926–1931*. Bern: Peter Lang International Academic Publishers, 2013.

Hitchcock, Henry-Russell, and Philip Johnson. *The International Style: Architecture since 1922*. New York: Museum of Modern Art, 1932.

Jackson, Neil, Jo Lintonbon, and Bryony Staples. *Saltaire: The Making of a Model Town*. London: Spire Books, 2010.

Le Corbusier. *Towards a New Architecture*. 1923. Trans. Frederick Etchell. New York: Dover, 1995.

---. *L'Esprit Nouveau Articles*. 1925. London: Architectural Publications, 1998.

---. *The City of Tomorrow and Its Planning*. Trans. Frederick Etchell. New York: Dover, 1987.

Lesnikowski, Wojciech. *East European Modernism: Architecture in Czechoslovakia, Hungary, and Poland between the Wars, 1919–1939*. New York: Rizzoli International, 1996.

Levin, Michael D. *White City: International Style Architecture in Israel; A Portrait of an Era*. Tel Aviv: Tel Aviv Museum 1984.

von Moos, Stanislaus. *Le Corbusier: Elements of a Synthesis*. Cambridge, MA: MIT Press, 1979.

Otto, Christian F., and Richard Pommer. *Weissenhof 1927 and the Modern Movement in Architecture*. Chicago: University of Chicago Press, 1991.

Overy, Paul. *The Rietveld Schroeder House*. Cambridge, MA: MIT Press, 1988.

Petersen, Ed, ed. *De Stijl*. Amsterdam: Atheneum, 1968.

Risselada, Max, and Beatriz Colomina, eds. *Raumplan versus Plan Libre: Adolf Loos and Le Corbusier, 1919–1930*. 1993. Rotterdam: NAI010 Publishers, 2013.

Sartoris, Alberto. *The Elements of Modernist Architecture*. 1931. New York: Rizzoli International, 1995.

Schulze, Franz. *Mies van der Rohe: A Critical Biography*. 1985. Chicago: University of Chicago Press, 2012.

Stiever, Nancy. *Housing Design and Society in Amsterdam: Reconfiguring Urban Order and Identity, 1900–1920*. Chicago: University of Chicago Press, 1998.

Sweeney, Robert, et al. *Schindler, Kings Road, and Southern California Modernism*. Berkeley: University of California Press, 2012.

Taverne, Ed, ed. *J.J.P. Oud: A Poetic Functionalist, 1890–1963*. Rotterdam: NAI Publishers, 2001.

Troy, Nancy J. *The de Stijl Environment*. Cambridge, MA: MIT Press, 1983.

Wit, Wim de. *The Amsterdam School: Dutch Expressionist Architecture*. Cambridge, MA: MIT Press, 1983.

Chapter 5

Albrecht, Donald. *Designing Dreams: Modern Architecture in the Movies*. New York: Harper & Row, 1986.

Buddensieg, Tilmann, and Henning Rogge. *Industriekultur: Peter Behrens and the AEG, 1907–1914*. Cambridge, MA: MIT Press, 1984.

Cheney, Sheldon, and Martha Cheney. *Art and the Machine: An Account of Industrial Design in Twentieth-century America*. 1936. New York: Acanthus Press, 1992.

Ferriss, Hugh. *The Metropolis of Tomorrow*. 1929. New York: Dover, 2005.

Fitzgerald, F. Scott. "My Lost City." 1932. In *The Crack-up*, ed. Edmund Wilson, pp. 23–33. New York: New Direction Books, 1993.

Hildebrand, Grant. *Designing for Industry: The Architecture of Albert Kahn*. Cambridge, MA: MIT Press, 1974.

James, Kathleen. *Erich Mendelsohn and the Architecture of German Modernism*. Cambridge: Cambridge University Press, 1997.

Loewy, Raymond. *Industrial Design*. Woodstock, NY: Overlook Press, 1979.

Lupton, Ellen, and J. Abbott Miller. *The ABCs of the Bauhaus and Design Theory*. New York: Princeton Architectural Press, 2000.

Meikle, Jeffrey L. *American Plastic: A Cultural History*. Trenton, NJ: Rutgers University Press, 1995.

---. *Twentieth Century Limited: Industrial Design in America*. Philadelphia: Temple University Press, 1979.

Nye, David E. *Electrifying America: Social Meanings of a New Technology*. Cambridge, MA: MIT Press, 1990.

Okrent, Daniel. *Great Fortune: The Epic of Rockefeller Center*. New York: Viking Books, 2003.

Pallasmaa, Juhani, ed. *Alvar Aalto: Furniture*. Cambridge, MA: MIT Press, 1985.

Remington, R. Roger. *American Modernism: Graphic Design 1920 to 1960*. London: Laurence King Publishing, 2003.

Robinson, Cervin, and Rosemarie Haag Bletter. *Skyscraper Style: Art Deco New York*. New York: Oxford University Press, 1975.

Scarlett, Frank, and Marjorie Townley. *Arts Decoratifs, 1925: Personal Recollections of the Paris Exhibition*. New York: John Wiley & Sons, 1975.

Smith, Terry. *Making the Modern: Industry, Art, and Design in America*. Chicago: University of Chicago Press, 1993.

Spencer, Herbert. *The Pioneers of Modern Typography*. 1969. Cambridge, MA: MIT Press, 2004.

Voge, Peter, et al. *The Complete Rietveld Furniture*. Rotterdam: 010 Publishers, 1993.

Ward, Janet. *Weimar Surfaces: Urban Visual Culture in 1920s Germany*. Berkeley: University of California Press, 2001.

Wilk, Christopher. *Thonet: 150 Years of Furniture*. New York: Barron's, 1980.

Wilson, Christina. "Cedric Gibbons: Architect of Hollywood." In *Architecture and Film*, ed. Mark Lamster, n.p. New York: Princeton Architectural Press, 2000.

Wilson, Richard Guy, Dianne H. Pilgrim, and Dickran Tashjian. *The Machine Age in America, 1918–1941*. New York: Harry N. Abrams, 1986.

Windower, Michael. *Art Deco: A Mode of Mobility*. Quebec: The University of Quebec Press, 2012.

Chapter 6

Baker Munro, Sarah. *Timberline Lodge: The History, Art, and Craft of an American Icon*. Portland, OR: Timber Press, 2009.

Betsky, Aaron. *The U.N. Building*. London: Thames & Hudson, 2005.

Caro, Robert A. *Power Broker: Robert Moses and the Fall of New York*. New York: Alfred A. Knopf, 1974.

Cohen, Jean-Louis. *Design in Uniform: Designing and Building for the Second World War*. Paris: Editions Hazan, 2011.

Culvahouse, Tim, ed. *The Tennessee Valley Authority: Design and Persuasion*. New York: Princeton Architectural Press, 2007.

Ghirardo, Diane. *Building New Communities: New Deal America and Fascist Italy*. Princeton: Princeton University Press, 1989.

Heidegger, Martin. "The Question Concerning Technology." 1954. In *The Question Concerning Technology and Other Essays*, pp. 3–35. New York: Harper & Row Publishers, 1977.

Holston, James. *The Modernist City: An Anthropological Critique of Brasilia*. Chicago: University of Chicago Press, 1989.

Ibelings, Hans. *Twentieth-Century Urban Design in the Netherlands*. Rotterdam: NAI Publishers, 1999.

Krier, Leon. *Albert Speer Architecture, 1932–1945*. New York: Monacelli Press, 2013.

Lindinger, Herbert, ed. *Ulm Design: The Morality of Objects*. Cambridge, MA: MIT Press, 1991.

Marinetti, Filippo Tommaso. "Manifeste du Futurisme." *Le Figaro*, February 20, 1909, p. 1.

Martins, Reinhold. *The Organizational Complex: Architecture, Media, and Corporate Space*. Cambridge, MA: MIT Press, 2003.

Mertins, Detlef, ed. *The Presence of Mies*. New York: Princeton Architectural Press, 1994.

Painter, Borden. *Mussolini's Rome: Rebuilding the Eternal City*. New York: Palgrave Macmillan, 2005.

Pugh, Emily. *Architecture, Politics, and Identity in Divided Berlin*. Pittsburgh: University of Pittsburgh Press, 2014.

Ryklin, Mikhail. "'The Best in the World': The Discourse of the Moscow Metro in the 1930s." In *The Landscape of Stalinism: The Art and Ideology of Soviet Space*, ed. Eugeny Dobrenko and Eric Naiman, pp. 261–276. Seattle: University of Washington Press, 2003.

Schulze, Franz, and Edward Windhorst. *Mies van der Rohe: A Critical Biography*. Chicago: University of Chicago Press, 1985.

Schumacher, Thomas. *Surface and Symbol: Giuseppe Terragni and the Architecture of Italian Rationalism*.

New York: Princeton Architectural Press, 1991.

Sierli, Martino, and Cees Nooteboom. *Brasilia–Chandigarh: Living with Modernity*. Basel: Lars Muller, 2010.

Somer, Kees. *The Functional City: The CIAM and the Legacy of Cornelis van Eesteren, 1928–1968*. Rotterdam: NAAI Publishers, 2007.

Speer, Albert. *Inside the Third Reich*. 1967. New York: Simon & Schuster, 1997.

Stevens, Joseph E. *Hoover Dam: An American Adventure*. Norman: University of Oklahoma Press, 1990.

Tarkhanov, Alexei, Sergei Kavtaradze, and Mikhail Anikst. *Soviet Architecture of the Stalin Era*. New York: Random House, 1992.

Vossoughian, Nader, and D'Laine Camp. *Otto Neurath: The Language of Global Polis*. Rotterdam: NAI Publishers, 2008.

Wharton, Annabel Jane. *Building the Cold War: Hilton International Hotels and Modern Architecture*. Chicago: University of Chicago Press, 2001.

Chapter 7

Adamson, Paul, and Marty Arbunich. *Eichler: Modernism Rebuilds the American Dream*. Layton, UT: Gibbs Smith, 2002.

Bakema, Jan, et al. *Team X Primer*. Cambridge, MA: MIT Press, 1968.

Bosman, Jos, et al. *Team X*. Rotterdam: NAI Publishers, 2006.

Cook, Peter, et al., eds. *Archigram*. London: Praeger, 1973.

Giedion, Sigfried, José Luis Sert, and Fernand Léger. "Nine Points on Monumentality." No publisher. 1943, http://www.ub.edu/escult/doctorat/html/lecturas/sert1.pdf.

Hall, Peter. "Opening Ceremonies: Typography and the Movies." In Lamster, *Architecture and Film*, n.p.

Heller, Steven. *Paul Rand*. London: Phaidon Press, 2000.

Heller, Steven, and Elaine Lustig Cohen. *Born Modern: The Life and Design of Alvin Lustig*. San Francisco: Chronicle Books, 2010.

Kahn, Louis I. *Writings*. New York: Rizzoli International, 1991.

Lamster, Mark, ed. *Architecture and Film*. New York: Princeton Architectural Press, 2000. Kindle Edition.

Le Corbusier. *The Modulor*. 1954. Basel: Birkhauser Publishers, 2000.

Le Corbusier et al. "The Charter of Athens." 1933. *Getty Conservation Institute*. http://www.getty.edu/conservation/publications_resources/research_resources/charters/charter04.html.

Marling, Karal Ann. *As Seen on TV: The Visual Culture of Everyday Life in the 1950s*. Cambridge, MA: Harvard University Press, 1994.

McCoy, Esther. *Case Study Houses 1945–1962*. Santa Monica, CA: Hennessey & Ingalls, 1977.

Mumford, Eric. *The CIAM Discourse on Urbanism, 1928–1960*. Cambridge, MA: MIT Press, 2000.

Mumford, Lewis. *Technics and Civilization*. 1934. Chicago: University of Chicago Press, 2010.

---. *The Lewis Mumford Reader*. New York: Pantheon, 1986.

Neutra, Richard. *Survival through Design*. New York: Oxford University Press, 1954.

Ockman, Joan. "Architecture in a Mode of Distraction: Eight Takes on Jacques Tati's Playtime." In Lamster, *Architecture and Film*, n.p.

Olsberg, Nicholas, and Jocelyn Gibbs. *Carefree California: Cliff May and the Romance of the Ranch House*. New York: Rizzoli International, 2012.

Pelkonen, Eeva-Liisa. *Alvar Aalto: Architecture, Modernity, and Geopolitics*. New Haven: Yale University Press, 2009.

Rosa, Joe. "Tearing Down the House: Modern Homes in the Movies." In Lamster, *Architecture and Film*, n.p.

Rowe, Colin, and Fred Koetter. *Collage City.* Cambridge, MA: MIT Press, 1979.

Scheidegger, Ernst, Stanislaus von Moos, and Maristella Casciato, *Chandigarh 1956: Le Corbusier, Pierre Jeanneret, Jane B. Drew, E. Maxwell Frye.* Zurich: Scheidegger und Spies Verlag, 2010.

Summerson, Sir John. *Heavenly Mansions and Other Essays.* 1949. New York: W. W. Norton, 1998.

Thompson, Janet, and Alexandra Lange. *Design Research: The Store that Brought Modern Living to American Homes.* San Francisco: Chronicle Books, 2010.

Travers, David, ed. *Arts & Architecture: The Complete Reprint.* Los Angeles: Taschen America, 2008.

Wagenaar, Cor, ed. *Happy: Cities and Public Happiness in Post-War Europe.* Rotterdam: NAI Publishers, 2004.

Williams Goldhagen, Sarah. *Louis Kahn's Situated Modernism.* New Haven: Yale University Press, 2001.

Williams Goldhagen, Sarah, and Rejean Legault, eds. *Anxious Modernisms: Experimentation in Postwar Architectural Culture.* Cambridge, MA: MIT Press, 2001.

Wiseman, Carter. *Louis I. Kahn: Beyond Time and Style; A Life in Architecture.* New York: W. W. Norton, 2009.

Chapter 8

Auther, Elissa, and Adam Lerner, eds. *West of Center: Art and the Counterculture Experiment in America, 1965–1977.* Minneapolis: University of Minnesota Press, 2012.

Brand, Stewart. *The Last Whole Earth Catalog.* New York: Random House, 1971.

DeKoven, Margaret. *The Sixties and the Emergence of Postmodernism.* Raleigh, NC: Duke University Press, 2004.

Dickstein, Morris. *Gates of Eden: American Culture in the Sixties.* New York: Basic Books, 1977.

Eisenman, Peter, et.al. *Five Architects: Eisenman, Graves, Gwathmey, Hejduk, Meier.* New York: Oxford University Press, 1975.

Gurshkin, Paul, ed. *The Art of Rock Posters from Presley to Punk.* New York: Abbeville Press, 1993.

Halberstam, David. *The Best and the Brightest.* New York: Random House, 1970.

Haney, Robert, and David Ballantine. *Woodstock Handmade Houses.* New York: Ballantine Books, 1976.

Jacobs, Jane. *The Death and Life of Great American Cities.* New York: Random House, 1961.

Jacopetti, Alexandra. *Native Funk and Flash: An Emerging Folk Art.* San Francisco: Scrimshaw Press, 1974.

Jencks, Charles. *The Language of Post-Modern Architecture.* New York: Rizzoli International, 1977.

Keim, Kevin, ed. *You Have to Pay for the Public Life: Selected Essays of Charles W. Moore.* Cambridge, MA: MIT Press, 2001.

Lindner, Mark. *Nothing Less than Literal: Architecture after Minimalism.* Cambridge: MIT Press, 2004.

Lyndon, Donlyn, and Jim Alinder. *The Sea Ranch: Fifty Years of Architecture, Landscape, Place, and Community on the Northern California Coast.* New York: Princeton Architectural Press, 2004.

McDonough, Tom. *Guy Debord and the Situationist International: Texts and Documents.* Cambridge, MA: MIT Press, 2002.

Meadows, Donella H., et al. *The Limits to Growth: A Report for the Club of Rome's Project on the Predicament of Mankind.* New York: Universe Publishing, 1972.

Moore, Charles, Gerald Allen, and Donlyn Lyndon. *The Place of Houses: Three Architects Suggest Ways to Build and Inhabit Houses.* New York: Holt, Rinehart and Winston, 1974.

Petit, Emmanuel. *Irony; or, The Self-Critical Opacity of Postmodern Architecture.* New Haven: Yale University Press, 2013.

Portoghesi, Paolo. *After Modern Architecture.* 1980. New York: Rizzoli International, 1982.

---. *Architecture 1980: The Presence of the Past; Venice Biennale.* New York: Rizzoli International, 1980.

Rudofsky, Bernard. *Architecture without Architects: A Short Introduction to Non-Pedigreed Architecture.* New York: Museum of Modern Art, 1964.

Sadler, Simon. *The Situationist City.* Cambridge, MA: MIT Press, 1999.

Scott, Felicity D. *Architecture or Techno-Utopia: Politics after Modernism.* Cambridge, MA: MIT Press, 2007.

Summerson, Sir John. "Heavenly Mansions." 1948. In *Heavenly Mansions and Other Essays.* 1949. New York: W. W. Norton, 1998.

Tafuri, Manfredo. *Architecture and Utopia: Design and Capitalist Development.* Cambridge, MA: MIT Press, 1976.

Venturi, Robert. *Complexity and Contradiction in Architecture.* New York: Museum of Modern Art, 1966.

Woods, Anthony C. *Preserving New York: Winning the Right to Protect a City's Landmarks.* New York: Routledge, 2008.

Chapter 9

Arnell, Peter, and Ted Bickford, eds. *Frank Gehry: Buildings and Projects.* New York: Rizzoli International, 1985.

van Berkel, Ben, and Caroline Bos. *Move.* Amsterdam: Goose Press, 1999.

Betsky, Aaron. *False Flat; or, Why Dutch Design Is So Good.* New York: Phaidon Press, 2003.

---. *Icons: Magnets of Meaning.* San Francisco: San Francisco Museum of Modern Art, 1997.

---. *Violated Perfection: Architecture and the Fragmentation of the Modern.* New York: Rizzoli International, 1990.

Blackwell, Lewis, and David Carson. *The End of Print: The Grafik Design of David Carson.* San Francisco: Chronicle Books, 1995.

Davies, Colin. *High Tech Architecture.* New York: Rizzoli International, 1988.

Davis, Mike. *City of Quartz: Excavating the Future in Los Angeles.* London: Verso, 1990.

Derrida, Jacques. *Dissemination.* Chicago: University of Chicago Press, 1991.

Eisenman, Peter. "Conceptual Architecture II: Double Deep Structure 1." *A+U* 39 (1974): 83–88.

---. *Diagram Diaries.* New York: Universe Publishing, 1999.

---. *House X.* New York: Rizzoli International, 1992.

Foster, Hal. The Anti-Aesthetic: Essays on Postmodern Culture. Port Townsend, WA: Bay Press, 1983.

Foucault, Michel. *Discipline and Punish: The Birth of the Prison.* New York: Random House, 1977.

Hays, K. Michael, ed. *Oppositions Reader: Selected Readings from a Journal for Ideas and Criticism in Architecture, 1973–1984.* New York: Princeton Architectural Press, 1998.

Ibelings, Hans. *Artificial Landscape: Contemporary Architecture, Urbanism, and Landscape Architecture in the Netherlands.* Rotterdam: NAI Publishers, 2000.

---. *Twentieth-Century Urban Design in the Netherlands.* Rotterdam: NAI Publishers, 1999.

Koolhaas, Rem. *Delirious New York: A Retroactive Manifesto for Manhattan.* London: Thames & Hudson, 1978.

---. *S, M, L, XL: OMA, Rem Koolhaas, and Bruce Mau.* New York: Monacelli Press, 1998.

Leach, Neil. *Rethinking Architecture: A Reader in Cultural Theory.* London: Routledge, 1997.

Lefebvre, Henri. *The Production of Space.* 1974. London: Blackwell Publishers, 1991.

Libeskind, Daniel. *Line of Fire.* Milan: Electa, 1988.

Savage, John. *Punk: An Aesthetic.* New York: Rizzoli International, 2012.

Soja, Edward. *Postmodern Geographies: The Reassertion of Space in Critical Social Theory.* London: Verso, 1989.

Tschumi, Bernard. *Cinegram Folie: Le Parc de la Villette.* New York: Princeton Architectural Press, 1987.

---. *Event Cities.* Cambridge, MA: MIT Press, 1994.

---. *Manhattan Transcripts.* New York: Wiley & Sons, 1994.

Turcotte, Bryan Ray, and Christopher T. Miller. *Fucked Up + Photocopied: Instant Art of the Punk Rock Movement.* San Francisco: Gingko Press, 1999.

Vanderlans, Rudy, and Zuzana Licko. *Émigré: Graphic Design into the Digital Realm.* New York: Wiley & Sons, 1994.

Wigley, Mark. *The Architecture of Deconstruction: Derrida's Haunt.* Cambridge, MA: MIT Press, 1995.

Chapter 10

Betsky, Aaron, et al. *Experimental Architecture in Los Angeles.* New York: Rizzoli International, 1992.

Bruegmann, Robert. *Sprawl: A Compact History.* Chicago: University of Chicago Press, 2005.

Gareau, Joel. *Edge City: Life on the New Frontier.* New York: Doubleday, 1991.

Gates, Theaster. *Twelve Ballads for Huguenot House.* Cologne: Walter Koening, 2012.

Kanna, Ahmed. *Dubai: The City as Corporation.* Minneapolis: University of Minnesota Press, 2011.

Kotkin, Joel. *The New Geography: How the Digital Revolution Is Reshaping the American Landscape.* New York: Random House, 2000.

Kwinter, Sanford. *Far from Equilibrium: Essays in Technology and Culture.* Barcelona: Actar, 2008.

Landa, Manuel de. *War in the Age of Intelligent Machines.* New York: Zone Books, 1991.

Lepik, Andres. *Small Scale, Big Change: New Architectures of Social Engagement.* New York: Museum of Modern Art, 2010.

Lerup, Lars. *After the City.* Cambridge, MA: MIT Press, 2001.

Marling, Karal Ann, ed. *Designing Disney's Theme Parks: The Architecture of Reassurance.* New York: Flammation, 1998.

Mau, Bruce. *Massive Change.* New York: Phaidon, 2004.

Mitchell, William J. *City of Bits: Space, Place, and the Infobahn.* Cambridge, MA: MIT Press, 1995.

MVRDV. *Meta City / Data Town.* Rotterdam: 010 Publishers, 2000.

Ramaker, Renny, et al. *Simply Droog: 10+1 Years of Innovation and Discussion.* Rotterdam: 010 Publishers, 2004.

Rotor. *Ex Limbo.* Milan: Fondazione Prada, 2011.

Schumacher, Patrick. *The Autopoiesis of Architecture.* Vol. 1, *A New Framework for Architecture.* New York: Wiley & Sons, 2011.

---. *The Autopiesis of Architecture.* Vol. 2, *A New Agenda for Architecture.* New York: Wiley & Sons, 2012.

Schwarzer, Mitchell. *Zoomscape: Architecture in Motion and Media.* New York: Princeton Architectural Press, 2004.

Shelton, Barry, Justyna Karakiewicz, and Thomas Kvan. *The Making of Hong Kong: From Vertical to Volumetric.* London: Taylor & Francis, 2010.

Sloterdijk, Peter. *Bubbles: Microspherology.* New York: Semiotexte, 2011.

---. *In the World Interior of Capitalism: Towards a Philosophical Theory of Capitalism.* New York: Polity, 2013.

Soja, Edward. *Postmodern Geographies: The Reassertion of Space in Critical Social Theory.* London: Verso, 1989.

Spuybroek, Lars. *NOX: Machining Architecture.* London: Thames & Hudson, 2004.

Sudjic, Deyan. *The 100 Mile City.* New York: Harcourt Brace, 1992.

Thomsen, Nato, ed. *Living as Form: Socially Engaged Art from 1991–2011.* Cambridge, MA: MIT Press, 2012.

Waldheim, Charles, ed. *The Landscape Urbanism Reader.* New York: Princeton Architectural Press, 2006.

INDEX OF NAMES

A. M. Cassandre (Adolphe Jean-Marie Mouron): 171, 197.
Aalto, Alvar: 159, 161, 223, 224, 225, 231, 233, 262, 338, 340.
Adams, Henry: 66, 67, 68, 69, 70, 71, 73, 335.
Adigard, Erik: 291, 293.
Albers, Anni: 160, 161, 169.
Alva Edison, Thomas: 158, 159, 335.
Arnell: 278, 342.
Ashbee, Charles Robert: 107, 108.
Bakema, Jaap: 211, 225, 340.
Bakema, Jacob B.: 211, 225.
Bakker, Riek: 301.
Baptiste, Jean: 33.
Barnack, Oskar: 159.
Baron Haussmann, Georges-Eugène: 78, 79, 82, 191, 247, 335.
Baumeister, Willi: 56.
Bayer, Herbert: 212.
Beall, Lester: 197.
Beardsley, Aubrey: 116, 252.
Beck, Harry: 164, 165.
Beckford, William: 103, 336.
Beeke, Anthon: 257, 258.
Behrens, Peter: 134, 157, 158, 202, 212, 338.
Bel Geddes, Norman: 162, 234.
Benjamin, Walter: 49, 50, 279, 334.
Berg, Max: 86, 87.
Berkeley, Busby: 168, 169, 334, 335, 336, 337, 338, 339.
Bernadó, Jordi: 321.
Bernhard, Lucian: 55, 56.
Bertoni, Flaminio: 257.
Bickford: 278, 342.
Bohr, Niels: 93.
Bos, Caroline: 297, 342.
Boullée, Étienne-Louis: 33.
Boyarsky. Alvin: 283.
Brand, Steward: 251, 253, 341.
Brandt, Marianne: 54, 160.
Breuer, Marcel: 54, 160, 161, 204, 205.
Brinkman, Johannes: 56, 57, 147.
Burchartz, Max: 56.
Burle Marx, Roberto: 212, 215.
Burnham, Daniel: 71, 336.

Cattermole, George: 103.
Chareau, Pierre: 138, 167.
Charles, Jules: 63.
Chermayeff, Ivan: 212.
Chipperfield, David: 316.
Cieślewicz, Roman: 257.
Comfort, Louis: 116, 117.
Conklin, Lee: 252.
Cook, Peter: 227, 340.
Costa, Lucio: 212, 213, 215, 219.
Cret, Paul Philippe: 172, 173.
Crosby, David: 246, 247.
Cubitt, Lewis: 77.
Cuypers, Pierre: 109, 111, 114.
David, Jacques-Louis: 33.
Davis, Mike: 280, 281, 342.
De Carlo, Giancarlo: 263.
De Klerk, Michel: 144, 145.
De Meuron, Pierre: 297, 299, 300, 301.
De Saussure, Ferdinand: 282.
De Vries, Natalie: 311, 312, 313, 343
Derrida, Jacques: 282, 342.
Deskey, Donald: 181.
Diller and Scofidio: 313, 314, 315.
Donald D. Parkinson, Frank: 173.
Dorwin, Walter: 234.
Dreyfuss, Henry: 162, 163.
Droog: 308, 309, 310, 343.
Duchamp, Marcel: 314.
Dutert, Ferdinand: 75.
Dylan, Bob: 258.
Eames, Charles and Ray: 229, 231.
Ehn, Karl: 148, 149.
Eiffel, Gustave: 74, 75, 325, 335.
Eisenman, Peter: 269, 282, 283, 284, 303, 341, 342.
El Lissitzky: 50, 51, 55, 280, 334, 335, 336.
Eleanor: 173.
Engels, Friedrich: 32, 64, 92, 141, 334.
Entenza, John: 228.
Fellheimer, Alfred T.: 173.
Ferdinand I, Emperor of the Austrio-Hungarian Empire: 34, 35.
Ferris Ferstel, Heinrich: 37.
Ford, Henry: 93, 159.
Foster, Norman: 227, 289, 310.

Fourier, Joseph: 33, 334.
Freud, Sigmund: 93.
Friedman, Dan: 258.
Fuller, Buckminster: 163.
Gallé, Émile: 115.
Gaudí, Antoni: 115.
Geddes, Patrick: 140, 141.
Gehry, Frank: 275, 278, 279, 280, 281, 282, 284, 290, 297, 300, 311, 327, 342.
Geuze, Adriaan: 302.
Gibbons, Cedric: 168, 169, 339.
Giedion, Sigfried: 236, 336, 340.
Ginzburg, Moisei: 151, 152, 334.
Girard, Alexander: 232.
Graumans, Rody: 308, 308.
Graves, Michael: 269, 270, 271, 324, 341.
Greiman, April: 290, 291.
Gropius, Walter: 53, 54, 55, 149, 232.
Güell, Eusebi: 114.
Guevara, Che: 253.
Gwathmey, Charles: 269, 341.
Hadid, Zaha: 284, 286, 287, 289, 303, 329.
Halprin, Lawrence: 248, 249.
Hamilton, Richard: 312.
Hans: 117.
Hansen, Theophil: 37.
Hargreaves, George: 302, 303.
Haring, Hugo: 149, 151.
Harrison, Wallace: 181, 202, 210.
Heckscher, August: 260.
Hein Eek, Piet: 308.
Hejduk, John: 269, 341.
Herwegen, Peter: 103.
Herzog, Jacques: 297, 299, 300, 301.
Hessels, Paul: 308.
Hirshberg, Jerry: 297.
Hoffmann, Hoffmann, Josef: 118, 167.
Hood, Raymond: 179, 181.
Horta, Victor: 83, 313.
Howe Bancroft, Hubert: 67.
Hugh: 177, 338.
Hunt, Richard: 68, 71, 73.
Hutten, Richard: 308.
Igarashi, Takenobu: 257.
Irving Turner, William: 196, 197.
Isozaki, Arata: 329.
Ive, Jonathan: 316, 317.
Jackson, Dakota: 256.

Jacobs, Jane: 254, 341.
Jacobsen, Arne: 210, 211, 233, 234.
Jastrzębowski, Wojciech: 256.
Jefferson, Thomas: 40, 41, 261.
Jencks, Charles: 272, 273, 341.
Johannes Pieter Oud, Jacobus: 147, 149, 151, 338.
Johnson, Philip: 206, 271, 272, 337.
Johnston, Edward: 164, 165, 212.
Jones, Owen: 33.
Jongerius, Hella: 308, 309.
Joseph II (Emperor of the Austrio-Hungarian Empire): 35.
Jourdain, Frantz: 81.
Juhl, Finn: 233.
Jujol, Josep Maria: 115.
Kahn, Albert: 173, 175, 338.
Kahn, Louis: 225, 237, 238, 239, 240, 241, 242, 243, 249, 262, 266, 299, 300, 340, 341.
Kalashnikov, Michael: 202, 203.
Kantner, Paul: 247.
Kaufmann, Gordon: 198, 199.
Kaufmann, Richard: 140.
Khrushchev, Nikita: 234, 235.
Klimt, Gustav: 116, 118.
Klutsis, Gustav: 55.
Koenig, Pierre: 229.
Koolhaas, Rem: 303, 304, 305, 312, 342.
Kubitschek, Juscelino: 213, 215.
Kós, Károly: 109.
László, Paul: 173.
Latz, Peter: 302, 303.
Le Corbusier (Jeanneret-Gris, Pierre-Edouard): 58, 59, 65, 131, 132, 133, 134, 138, 140, 151, 152, 153, 161, 166, 202, 203, 205, 210, 213, 218, 219, 220, 221, 222, 225, 242, 253, 260, 261, 269, 270, 300, 304, 321, 335, 337, 338, 340, 341.
Le Quément, Patrick: 296.
Lechner, Ödön: 109.
Ledoux, Claude Nicolas: 33, 334.
Lefebvre, Henri: 281, 342.
Legault, Rejean: 238, 341.
Léger, Fernand: 236, 340.
Lemaire, Lenica, Jan: 257.
Leonidov, Ivan: 51.
Lequeu, Jean Jacques: 33, 334.
Lerup, Lars: 325, 326, 343.
Libera, Adalberto: 192, 193, 195.
Libeskind, Daniel: 283, 284, 285, 287, 342.

Loewy, Raymond: 162, 163, 164, 170, 234, 338.
Löffler, Berthold: 116.
Loos, Adolf: 39, 40, 41, 117, 119, 121, 124, 136, 137, 138, 140, 334, 336, 337, 338
Lustig, Alvin: 212, 340.
Lutyens, Edward: 111.
Lyndon, Donlyn: 248, 249, 251, 341.
Maas, Winy: 311, 312, 313, 343.
Majorelle, Louis: 115, 117.
Malevich, Kazimir: 51, 55.
Mallet-Stevens, Robert: 138, 166, 167.
Manship, Paul: 180.
Marinetti, Filippo Tommaso: 91, 92, 194, 195, 336, 339.
Marinus Dudok, Willem: 145, 146, 147.
Marx, Karl: 32, 64, 92, 141, 148, 149, 211, 334.
Matano, Tom: 296, 297.
Mavignier, Almir: 213.
May, Ernst: 149, 151, 337.
Mayer, Albert: 218.
Mayne, Thom: 310, 311.
McCoy, Esther: 228, 340.
McNeill Whistler, James: 105.
Medgyaszay, István: 109.
Meier, Richard: 269, 341.
Melnikov, Konstantin: 51, 166, 263.
Mendelssohn, Erich: 165.
Mies van der Rohe, Ludwig: 134, 135, 136, 137, 138, 150, 160, 161, 166, 206, 207, 209, 210, 259, 271, 304, 337, 338, 339.
Miller, Herman: 231, 232, 235.
Mockbee, Samuel: 311.
Moholy-Nagy, László: 55, 334, 336.
Mok, Clement: 292, 293.
Molnàr, Fritz: 139.
Mondriaan, Piet: 125.
Moore, Charles: 248, 249, 251, 259, 261, 275, 341.
Morris, William: 107, 108, 116, 117, 256, 336, 337, 341.
Moser, Koloman: 116, 117.
Moses, Robert: 200, 201, 339.
Mososco, Victor: 252.
Mucha, Alphonse: 116, 117.
Mumford, Lewis: 222, 340.
Murray Dixon, Lawrence: 169.
Musil, Robert: 119.
Nakashima, George: 236.
Napoleon III: 78, 335.
Nash, John: 101, 103, 247.
Nelson, George: 12, 231, 232, 233, 234, 235.

Neurath, Otto: 189, 197, 301, 340.
Neutra, Richard: 228, 340.
Newenham Deane, Thomas: 105
Niemeyer, Oscar: 212, 213, 215, 219.
Nixon, Richard: 234, 235.
Noguchi, Isamu: 181, 235, 237.
Nouvel, Jean: 329.
Nowicki, Matthew: 218.
Olbrich, Josef: 118, 119.
Otis, Elisha: 45.
Palmboom, Frits: 301, 302.
Panton, Verner: 233.
Parkinson, John: 173.
Pawson, John: 316, 317.
Paxton, Joseph: 63.
Perret, Auguste: 210, 211.
Perriand, Charlotte: 132, 162.
Petrus Berlage, Hendrik: 111, 113, 143, 144, 147.
Pettit, Henry: 65.
Piano, Renzo: 289, 291.
Piciatentini, Marcello: 195.
Plakken, Wild: 258.
Plecnik, Josef: 109, 111.
Porsche, Ferdinand: 202.
Portoghesi, Paolo: 273, 341.
Prat, Ramon: 327.
Rand, Paul: 212, 340.
Remy, Tejo: 308.
Rennie Mackintosh, Charles: 167.
Riefenstahl, Leni: 186, 187.
Rietveld, Gerrit: 127, 128, 129, 130, 159.
Ringstrasse: 35, 36, 37, 39, 42, 48, 121, 187, 191, 305, 316, 334.
Rivera, Diego: 181.
Rockefeller, John D.: 179, 180, 181, 182, 191, 202, 206, 209, 210, 304, 338.
Rogers, Richard: 227, 289, 291, 310.
Rossi, Aldo: 266, 267, 269, 297, 299.
Roth, Emery and Sons: 210, 211.
Rotondi, Michael: 311.
Rudofsky, Bernard: 251, 342.
Ruhlmann, Émile-Jacques: 167.
Ruskin, John: 106, 107, 337
Saarinen, Eliel: 111.
Saito, Makoto: 293.
Salt, Titus: 141.
Sant'Elia, Antonio: 91, 92, 313, 335, 336.
Sartoris, Alberto: 139, 338.

Sauvage, Henri: 81.
Saville, Peter: 292.
Scharoun, Hans: 149, 150.
Scheerbart, Paul: 89, 336.
Schindler, Rudolf: 130, 131, 138, 228, 338.
Schmidt, Friedrich: 37.
Schroeder-Schraeder, Truus: 125, 126, 128, 129, 130.
Schuitema, Paul: 56.
Schütte-Lihotzky, Margarete: 149.
Scott Key Fitzgerald, Francis: 182, 183, 329, 338.
Scully, Vincent: 261, 337.
Semper, Gottfried: 35, 37, 106, 107, 118, 337.
Sert, José Luis: 236, 340.
Shulman, Julius: 229.
Sijmons, Dirk: 302.
Skidmore, Owings and Merrill: 205, 207, 209, 210.
Sloterdijk, Peter: 317, 343.
Smithson, Alison and Peter: 225.
Soja, Edward: 280, 281, 318, 342, 343.
Sottsass, Ettore: 270, 271.
Speer, Albert: 187, 189, 191, 339, 340.
Stalin, Jospeh: 191, 193, 339, 340.
Stam, Mart: 160, 231.
Starck, Philippe: 294, 295.
Stenberg, Vladimir: 55.
Sternberg, Georgii: 55.
Stickley, Gustav: 108, 109, 256.
Stills, Stephen: 246, 247.
Stirling, James: 263, 264, 265, 266, 269, 300.
Strauss, Joseph: 199.
Stumpf, William: 257.
Stutchbury, Peter: 311.
Sullivan, Louis: 45, 46, 182, 334.
Summerson, John: 222, 251, 271, 341, 342.
Sussman, Deborah: 273.
Sutnar, Ladislav: 212.
Tafuri, Manfredo: 253, 254, 278, 281, 342.
Tanaka, Ikko: 257.
Tati, Jacques: 234, 235, 340.
Taut, Bruno: 87, 89, 157, 336.
Terragni, Giuseppe: 192, 193, 194, 195, 339.
Thonet, Michael: 158, 159, 160, 231, 339.
Tschichold, Jan: 55, 334.
Tschumi, Bernard: 284, 285, 287, 343.
Turnbull, William: 248, 249, 251.
Van Alen, William: 178, 179.
Van Berkel, Ben: 297, 303, 342.
Van Brunt, Henry: 69, 71.

Van de Velde, Henry: 111, 118, 119, 121, 124.
Van den Broek, Jo: 211, 225.
Van der Jagt, Peter: 308.
Van Doesburg, Theo: 124, 125, 128, 301, 337.
Van Eesteren, Cornelis: 189, 197, 301, 340.
Van Eyck, Aldo: 227, 263.
Van Rijs, Jacob: 311, 312, 313, 343
Vanderlans, Rudy: 290, 291, 343.
Venturi, Robert: 258, 259, 260, 261, 262, 264, 271, 319, 342.
Viemeister, Tucker: 295.
Violet-le-Duc, Eugene Emmanuel: 107.
Wagenfeldt, Wilhelm: 160, 161, 162.
Wagner, Richard: 35, 111, 172, 337.
Wagner, Steward: 173.
Wank, Roland: 173.
Ware, Samuel: 79.
Webb, Michael: 227.
Webb, Philip: 107.
Weber, Jens: 317.
Wegner, Hans: 233, 234.
Werken, Hard: 258.
Whitaker, Richard: 248, 249, 251.
Wiene, Robert: 166.
Wild, Lorraine: 292, 293.
Williams Goldhagen, Sarah: 238, 341.
Wilson, Joseph: 65.
Wilson, Wes: 252.
Woods, Lebbeus: 287, 289.
Woodward's, Benjamin: 105.
Wright, Frank Lloyd: 46, 48, 84, 85, 86, 92, 113, 115, 116, 130, 146, 175, 177, 180, 232, 335, 336.
Wright, Russel: 235, 237.
Wyatt, James: 103.
Yokoo, Tadanori: 257.
Zeisel, Eva: 235.
Zwart, Piet: 55, 56.

ILLUSTRATION CREDITS

Figures 003, 005, 006, 007 © Mollik, Kurt; Reining, Hermann, and Wurzer, Rudolf. *Planung und Verwirklichung der Wiener Ringstraßenzone.* Ed. F. Steiner, 1980. ISBN 3515024816, 9783515024815

Figure 013 © *Jefferson.* Plan of Jefferson, Ohio, from Titus, Simmons & Titus, Atlas of Ashland County, Ohio, Philadelphia, 1874.

Figure 014 © *A Plan of the City of Cleveland.* Redrawing in 1855 by L.M. Pillsbury of the original plan of Cleveland, Ohio, by Seth Pease in 1796, from *Journal of the Association of Engineering Societies, Transactions,* Vol. 3, No. 10, 1884.

Figure 015 © *Map of the City of San Francisco and Surrounding Country.* View of San Francisco, California, drawn by George H. Goddard, published by Snow and Roos, San Francisco, 1868.

Figure 016 © *The City of Chicago,* View of Chicago, Illinois, published by Currier and Ives, New York, 1892.

Figure 017 © El Lissitzky, *Beat the Whites with the Red Wedge,* 1919.

Figure 034 © *Bird's Eye View, World's Columbian Exposition at Chicago,* 1893. View of the Chicago Fair of 1893, from Humert Howe Bancroft, *The Book of the Fair.* Chicago, 1893.

Figure 047 © Photographic collection. FPS Employment, Labour and Social Dialogue. Brussels.

Figures 070, 071 © Prelovšek, Damjan. *Jože Plečnik: 1872-1957.* Yale University Press, 1997.

Figure 074 © *Sketches of "Kragsyde", Summer Residence of G. Nixon Black, [Manchester-by-the-Sea, MA],* Peabody and Stearns, *American Architect and Building News,* Vol. 17, No. 480, March 7, 1885. (AIA Archives)

Figures 101, 102 © Streekarchief Gooi en Vechtstreek, Hilversum. Wagenaar, Gor. *Town Planning in the Netherlands since 1800. Responses to Enlightenment Ideas and Geopolitical Realities.* 010 Publishers, Rotterdam, 2011.

Figure 103 © Netherlands Architecture Institute (NAi), Rotterdam. Wagenaar, Gor. *Town Planning in the Netherlands since 1800. Responses to Enlightenment Ideas and Geopolitical Realities.* 010 Publishers, Rotterdam, 2011.

Figures 110, 111 © Deutsche Verlags-Anstalt GmbH, Stuttgart. Kirsch, Karin. *The Weissenhofsiedlung. Experimental Housing Built for the Deutsche Werkbund, Stuttgart, 1927.* Ed. Rizzoli New york.

Figure 121 © BY-SA 2.5, Vicens, Creative Commons, 2009.

Figure 131 © Zevi, Bruno. *Erich Mendelsohn Opera Completa. Architetture e Immagini Architettoniche.*

Figure 134 © *Pavillon des renseignements et du tourisme,* 1925, Photograph *L'Illustration,* original size 20X16 cm, coll. J. L Cohen.

Figure 147 © *Ford Plan, Highland Park; Model T body-to-chassis mock-up.* Photograph courtesy of Albert Kahn Associates.

Figure 148 © *Geo. N. Pierce Plant, interior of the Assembly Building.* Photograph by Joseph Klima, courtesy of Mrs. Barnett Malbin.

Figure 149 © *Ford Motor Company Engineering Laboratory, Dearborn, Michigan, 1922;* interior. Photograph courtesy of Ford Archives, Henry Ford Museum.

Figure 298 © Jimmy McIntyre.

Figure 306 © Urban Think-Tank.

Notes

The remaining images are taken from the Internet, copyright unknown.

Making It Modern. The History of Modernism
in Architecture and Design.

Author
Aaron Betsky

Editorial Coordination
Ricardo Devesa

Editorial Assistant
Marta Ariza Béixer
Xisca Florit Sans

Graphic Design
Ramon Prat
Lucía López Casanegra

Copyediting
Paula Woolley

Search of illustrations
Pau Pedragosa

Publisher
Actar Publishers, New York, Barcelona, 2016
www.actarpublishers.com

Printing and binding
Tiger Printing

Distributed by
Actar D Inc.
New York
355 Lexington Avenue, 8th Floor
New York, NY 10017
T +1 212 966 2207
F +1 212 966 2214
salesnewyork@actar-d.com

Barcelona
Roca i Batlle 2
08023 Barcelona
T +34 933 282 183
eurosales@actar-d.com

The author and Actar Publishers are especially grateful to theses image providers. Every reasonable attempt has been made to identify owners of copyright. Should unintentional mistakes or omissions have occurred, we sincerely apologize and ask for notice. Such mistakes will be corrected in the next edition of this publication.

Copyrights
© 2016 Actar Publishers
© Text and Images by the authors

This work is subject to copyright. All rights are reserved, whether the whole or part of the material is concerned, specifically the rights of translation, reprinting, re-use of illustrations, recitation, broadcasting, reproduction on microfilms or in other ways, and storage in data banks. For any kind of use, permission of the copyright owner must be obtained.

ISBN 978-1-940291-15-4
Library of Congress Control Number: 2015946203
A CIP catalogue record for this book is available from the Library of Congress, Washington D.C., USA.

Printed and bounded in China.